Shiksa

Shiksa

The Gentile Woman in the Jewish World

CHRISTINE BENVENUTO

St. Martin's Press ❧ New York

www.stmartins.com

Library of Congress Cataloging-in-Publication Data

Benvenuto, Christine.
    Shiksa : the gentile woman in the Jewish world / Christine Benvenuto.
        p. cm.
Includes bibliographical references (page 275).
    ISBN 0-312-31146-X
    1. Gentile women. 2. Women in Judaism. 3. Jews—Identity. 4. Jewish con-
verts. 5. Judaism—Relations. 6. Benvenuto, Christine—Religion. I. Title.
    BM720.N6B48 2004
    296'.082—dc22

                                                        2003015946

First Edition: March 2004

10 9 8 7 6 5 4 3 2 1

For Jay

Contents

Acknowledgments

For encouragement, support, introductions, and ideas, I wish to thank the Five College Women's Studies Research Center and the many people who gave of their time during the writing and production of this book, including Nichole Argyres, Rachel Cowan, Deborah Eisenbach-Budner, Larry Fine, Nan Fink Gefen, Susannah Heschel, Diane Higgins, Pamela Malpas, Egon Mayer, Susan Niditch, Esther Perel, Letty Cottin Pogrebin, and Jody Rosenbloom. I am indebted to the women, mostly quoted anonymously in these pages, who generously opened up their lives to me: without them, this book would not exist. For making all things not only possible but worth doing, my deepest love and gratitude belong to Jay, Gabriel, Yael, and Nasia.

Some material in this book originally appeared, in different form, in *Tikkun* and *Moment* magazines.

Introduction

For 1,000 years, Eastern European Jews and their descendants have used the term shiksa *to refer to a non-Jewish woman who lures Jewish men away from religion and family. This attractive will-o'-the-wisp, as folk imagination would have it, is seductive, immoral, ignorant, and insensitive to Jewish values. It is not just that she is unsuitable to the warmth of traditional Jewish family life—she will destroy it!*

— *EDWIN FRIEDMAN, "THE MYTH OF THE SHIKSA"*

WITHIN THE Jewish people, the gentile woman has long been a magnet for intense feelings, from male yearning to communal hatred. She is simultaneously an erotic trophy and a parent's worst nightmare, the butt of crude jokes and a force credited with the power to bring down a people. Her almost mythic status has tangled historical roots in the culture's most potent fears and fantasies, and wide-ranging repercussions in the Jewish community today.

Yet, surprisingly, very little has been written about the actual non-Jewish women who make their way into the Jewish community, some through intermarriage and other liaisons, others entirely outside of relationships with Jews. Fleeting references and belittling caricatures aside, the gentile woman within Judaism remains a nebulous figure, veiled by layers of unexamined assumptions.

Let's begin with the S word.

While few people are familiar with the term *shaygetz* for a non-Jewish male, everyone knows the word *shiksa*. And though shiksa—meaning simply "gentile woman," but trailing a stream of complex connotations—is often tossed off casually and with humor, it's about as noxious an insult as any racial epithet could hope to be.

Shiksa is derived from the Hebrew verb *shakaytz*, meaning "to abominate or loathe an unclean thing." The Torah, the Hebrew Bible, constantly warns Jews not to let the *shikutzim,* the hated things, into their houses. But people generally don't need to be reminded not to open their doors to something loathsome. Biblical commentators assume that the shikutzim couldn't all have been quite as nasty as they were made out to be. In fact, some must have been almost irresistible.

The forbidden fruits that shiksa's ancient etymological forebear referred to were not the women of non-Jewish cultures but the religious idols and the food. Creatures of the sea, air, and land considered detestable, and not permitted by Jewish dietary laws, range from such taste treats as locusts, a delicacy for some Israelite neighbors, to shellfish and pork. The local graven images seem to have been even more seductive. Against them, the Torah is especially vociferous in cautioning Jews. These homemade gods were abominations, and to bring them into a Jewish dwelling was to curse and defile it.

But how do we get from animals and icons to gentile women?

In its present form, the word was coined by the Yiddish-speaking Jews of Eastern Europe. According to scholars of Yiddish, precisely where, when, and how *shakaytz* became *shiksa* may be impossible to trace. But since at least the eighteenth century, and probably much earlier, the word has been variously used to mean "young gentile girl," "gentile female servant," trollop or "gay lady," and finally, any gentile female at all. Contempt for gentiles as well as envy of the freedoms they enjoy are reflected in the less familiar shaygetz, identifying a gentile male or, sometimes, a Jewish man or boy caught misbehaving—that is, *acting* like a gentile. Is it significant that a Jewish male can, in uncomplimentary terms, be a shaygetz, while a Jewish woman or girl is never a shiksa?

Prohibitions against food, fetishes, and females all share a concern over creating impenetrable domestic borders: this it's okay to take home, this it isn't. Jewish law entails a series of separations—pure from polluted, everyday from sacred, kosher from nonkosher, Jew from gentile—designed to foster group cohesion. And it would seem that group cohesion and the suppression of forbidden desires are intimately intertwined.

Whether the prohibitions are more successful at controlling desire or inspiring it, the Eastern European invention of shiksa serves as a reminder that the mingling of Jews and gentiles is not an exclusively New World threat to Jewish homogeneity. In fact, gentile women have been part of Jewish communities since long before there were Jewish enclaves in Europe, since long before there was a Europe. From the very beginning, the Torah assigns non-Jewish women significant roles in the drama of Jewish peoplehood.

In Bereshit, or Genesis, an elderly Mesopotamian couple named Abram and Sarai receive God's summons to leave their home and everything they know, to journey to a strange land and enter into a special relationship, a covenant, with God. They become Abraham and Sarah, Judaism's first converts, mother and father to the Jewish people.

But the establishment of Jewish identity doesn't end with Abraham and Sarah. The entire Torah is a record of the creation of a people and the forging of Jewish identity out of otherness. Again and again it portrays individual Jews and entire generations grappling with, attempting to escape, and ultimately embracing, Jewish identity. If the conversion narrative is a literary genre, the Torah can arguably be read as the greatest novel of conversion ever written.

The non-Jewish woman plays pivotal, sometimes central roles in this epic of identity, in some cases while remaining an outsider, at other times becoming one of the family in ways we might now recognize as equivalent to conversion. She is the deceptive, honey-lipped angel of death, the submissive bearer of Jewish children, the courageous ally, the prostitute with a heart of gold, the wife and mother who brings her family closer to their Jewish roots. She is Jezebel, Potiphar's wife, Ruth, Hagar, Tamar, Rahab, Zipporah, and many others.

According to the sages, what happens in the earliest Jewish families represents the pattern of the entire Jewish future. So perhaps it's no surprise that, dressed in twenty-first-century garb, each of these archetypes is alive and well in the American Jewish community today. But as the widespread use of the term *shiksa* implies, the gentile woman's long residence within the Jewish people has done little to mitigate the strong feelings she arouses. Ze'ev Chafets, an American-born Israeli journalist, offered unintentional support for the continuing social acceptability of the designation *shiksa* when he was quoted in the *Washington Report on Middle East Affairs* in April 1998. "She is a shiksa," Chafets said of his wife, adding that, "Jews who would rather cut off their tongues than say 'nigger' or 'spic' . . . talk about . . . 'shiksas' with blithe indifference. . . . But terms like 'shiksa' no longer sound like charming yiddishisms to me; they seem like slurs. . . ." It would be difficult to imagine a white man, Jewish or gentile, referring to his African-American wife as a "nigger" before decrying others' use of the term. But when it comes to non-Jewish women, everyone seems to have something to say.

Louis Berman finds gentile women coveted by Jewish men for their "sex appeal and sexual acquiescence" in *Jews and In-*

termarriage. "Seductive, immoral, ignorant, and insensitive to Jewish values" is the stereotype Edwin Friedman reports in his essay "The Myth of the Shiksa." Surveying American Jewish fiction in an essay called "The Quest for the Ultimate *Shiksa*," Frederic Cople Jaher argues that "A blend of arrogance and defensiveness prompts many Jews to claim that *shiksas* are more carnal and promiscuous than women of their own faith because Christians are less intelligent, refined, and clean than themselves." In *Intermarriage: The Challenge of Living with Differences Between Christians and Jews*, Susan Weidman Schneider remarks that "A non-Jewish woman who does not convert to Judaism is more likely to be considered 'selfish' by her husband's family, whereas a non-Jewish man in the same situation is judged to be acting out of his own strong religious convictions." In *Embracing the Stranger: Intermarriage and the Future of the American Jewish Community*, Ellen Jaffe McClain points out that a gentile woman is expected to be a tall, blond, and sexy status symbol, appreciative of and submissive to Jewish men. Of the Jewish man who acquires such a prize, the assumption is that "If he can't find a Jewish woman to feed his fantasies . . . he can find a non-Jewish woman who will." Popular culture takes a slightly different view. In his essay, "The Mouse that Never Roars: Jewish Masculinity on American Television," Maurice Berger finds "shiksas" put to frequent use propping up the wimpy Jewish man of the box. "His love interest is most often cool and critical; she demands respect and often makes her partner beg for her affection." The popular HBO series *Sex and the City*, believed by many to walk the cutting edge of contemporary dating concerns, put its own spin on this TV-eye view during its 2003 season. When Jewish attorney Harry tells arch-WASP girlfriend Charlotte that he could never marry a non-Jew, he justifies their sexual relationship with the self-deprecating excuse that he never expected a shiksa goddess to fall in love with him. When Charlotte decides to convert to Judaism, the show recasts her as another stock character of

Jewish humor: the too-Jewish convert, pressuring Harry to celebrate Shabbat with her when all he wants to do is watch baseball.

It's no mystery why Jewish views of gentile women are unavoidably bound up with sex and intermarriage. Currently roughly half of all American Jews choose non-Jewish partners, forming unions that bring large numbers of gentiles, who may or may not ultimately convert, into the Jewish community. A Jewish Outreach Institute study recently found that intermarried households will soon outnumber all-Jewish homes, though this finding is disputed by some opponents of outreach to interfaith families. Whatever the current statistics, intermarriage in the Jewish family is nothing new. Recent genetic evidence suggests that Jewish communities all over the world were founded by Jewish men and gentile women.

The results of a University of London study published in 2002 reveal that in Europe, North Africa, and the Middle East, the men and women in Jewish populations have radically different genetic histories. While Jewish men in far-flung communities tend to share distinctive genetic traits, indicating common Middle Eastern ancestors who lived some four thousand years ago, the genetic signatures of the Jewish women in these communities do not resemble one another, nor do they resemble the genetic signatures of the men. Commenting on his findings, one of the researchers involved in the study, Dr. David Goldstein, said, "The men came from the Near East, perhaps as traders. They established local populations, probably with local women."

The implications of these discoveries are profound. For several thousand years, Jewish identity has been transmitted matrilineally, from a mother to her children; within the Orthodox and Conservative movements, it still is. Yet it now appears that Jewish cultures, including the Central and Eastern European Ashkenazi communities from which the majority of American Jews trace their descent, were created by a handful of Jewish fathers and "local," that is, gentile mothers—the very women some believe Jewish survival depends upon keeping out.

Just as in these communities, intermarriage among American Jews for generations has meant, almost invariably, Jewish men marrying gentile women. Even now, when Jewish women have begun "marrying out" in numbers comparable to their brothers, popular belief has it that their change of heart owes as much to pragmatism as preference: there simply aren't enough Jewish men to go around.

In the current climate of panic over Jewish continuity, gentile wives and mothers are particularly threatening. Not only is Jewish identity traditionally traced matrilineally but as long as women are charged with raising children and instilling ethnic and religious fealty, there will be the sense that a home can only be as Jewish as the woman who runs it. Jewish attitudes toward gentile women have also been fed by sexism, reflected in the stale presumption that what non-Jewish women have to offer is not their minds; racism, particularly when a woman's ethnic origins are other than white Anglo-Saxon Protestant; and classism, as, for decades, Jewish men were supposedly willing to "marry down" economically in order to obtain the trophy of a gentile wife.

But the animosity directed at gentile women goes beyond rational concerns and even ingrained prejudices to offer a glimpse into the subconscious of the American Jewish community. In the guise of spiritual seductress, enticing Jewish men away from their heritage, the gentile woman is a scapegoat for the fear that, by their own neglect, American Jews will bring about the destruction of Judaism. Contradictorily, when she actively pursues conversion, she is equally effective at touching off Jews' ambivalence about their own religious identity.

We live in a time when Jewish identity is once again in a process of transition and turmoil, when questions about who is Jewish, even what it means to be Jewish, are subjects of fervent debate. Jews have achieved full integration, indeed assimilation, into American culture. With each generation, alienation from Judaism seems to grow, and with it, the gap between the secular, American values of diversity and inclusiveness on the one hand and the deeply conflicting Jewish values of continuity and strong ethnic boundaries on the other. To many American Jews, their religion is antiquated and remote, their traditions isolating, their history a crushing burden.

In such circumstances, it might logically be assumed that few gentiles are attracted to Judaism. Just the opposite is true. An estimated ten to fifteen thousand converts are entering Judaism each year, most of them women. Conversion is on the rise, as is a new kind of convert: a woman motivated by conviction, not convenience. One who isn't trying to placate disapproving in-laws, who may, in fact, come to Judaism entirely outside the context of a relationship with a Jew, or after years of intermarriage and child rearing. One who eagerly embraces Jewish identity and wishes to assert herself as an active member of the Jewish people.

Yet according to Jewish demographers, the gentile partner in an intermarriage is still statistically unlikely to convert, the family she and her partner create unlikely to identify as Jewish. And there is intense disagreement within the Jewish community about whether and to what extent conversion should be promoted among the non-Jewish members of interfaith couples, with sharply divergent opinions of whether such outreach is a means of strengthening the community or further diluting it. The low conversion rate among intermarried gentiles and Jewish ambivalence toward proselytizing are situations with many causes. Are Jewish attitudes toward gentile women one of them?

Will a woman received with fear and distaste—in short, as a shiksa—feel motivated to observe Jewish holidays? Will she raise her children as Jews, encourage Jewish involvement for her partner? She may experience pressure to convert, but is unlikely to be *invited* to do so, with warmth and respect—or to be genuinely welcomed if conversion does occur. Despite Jewish law's unambiguous position that a convert is to be regarded as indistinguishable from other Jews, unease over her presence is not necessarily resolved by conversion at all. Some Jews use the terms *non-Jewish* and *convert* as if they were interchangeable, and refer to unions between born Jews and converts as intermarriages. Once an Other, always an Other?

The reality is that non-Jewish and converted women have always been a part of Judaism, and they are here to stay. In a multicultural Jewish community composed of born and converted Jews as well as gentiles, fears and prejudices about gentile women have very real costs. Studies of intermarriage suggest that the children of Jewish-gentile unions in which such attitudes are allowed to fester grow up alienated from Judaism, while many Jewish demographers prophesize the demise of American Judaism if "mixed" families continue to find themselves marginalized in the Jewish community.

As someone who was once a reviled outsider—"worse than Hitler" in the words of one Jewish organization's mass-mailing campaign against intermarriage—and who is now a committed Jew, this is all familiar and fertile terrain. For me, shiksa is a word that is neither humorous nor benign. It is an instant red flag, one that I raise as a signal that this book will confront head-on controversial and complex issues that I have never seen addressed frankly and directly.

Tracing the evolving Jewish stance toward gentile women and women converts, we will look closely at the repercussions of that stance, both on individual lives and on Judaism. In their own words and from their own perspectives, we will hear the stories of gentile women and women converts—including an account of my own highly idiosyncratic path to Judaism—making their homes amid the sexual and racial tensions, the contradictions, the stereotypes, the riches, and the realities of American Jewish life today. We will examine the fallout from the tradition of matrilineal descent, which simultaneously places the entire burden of Jewish continuity on Jewish women while making pariahs of gentile women and their children within the Jewish community. And we will meet with the biblical figures who seem to anticipate the permutations of so many contemporary lives and reveal so much about the roles in which gentile women have been cast—roles that run the gamut from seductive agent of assimilation to "too-Jewish" convert, from the rival of Jewish women to dauntless heroine.

Throughout this exploration, my intention is not to harangue the Jewish community into improving its treatment of non-Jewish women or converts. Giving voice to stories long silenced yet inextricably woven into the texture of Jewish life, I hope to make clear what we have to gain: by letting go of attitudes that force a wedge between Jewish and gentile women, parents and children, different segments of our communities, we can stop hurting ourselves, our families, and Judaism itself. We can create a community strengthened by the tremendous gifts—including their children, who make up at least a quarter of the next generation of American Jews—that gentile women and converts have to give. These are gifts that Judaism can't afford to waste.

Running counter to Jewish disaffection, there is a spiritual and cultural renaissance taking place among some American Jews, a growing movement to reclaim an ancient tradition and to reinvest it with the hopes and passions of a new generation. A crucial catalyst for this renaissance has come from women. In the past three decades, Jewish women have begun laying claim to their mothers, approaching the Torah with fresh eyes and burning questions. Probing the roots of their Jewish personae, they are digging into midrash, rabbinic speculations and stories that elaborate on the Torah's spare narrative. Augmenting the sparse details of biblical women's lives, they are inventing their own midrash in the form of novels, poems, plays, visual arts, and dances.

In this vibrant and creative milieu, the time is ripe to clear away old clichés and to acknowledge and celebrate a long overlooked aspect of our heritage: some of our Jewish mothers were not born Jewish.

Shiksa

1

A Place Without Sidelines

O_N A bright, cold December morning, I sat in synagogue and listened as the rabbi announced that a brand-new Jew was about to enter God's covenant with the Jewish people.

With my husband and his mother, our son and daughter and a friend, I climbed the steps to the bimah, the raised platform from which the Torah is read. The congregation sang "*Mah tovu*," extolling the beauty of Israel's tents and dwelling places, and then I read a Psalm.

"*Brucha Haba-ah*," the rabbi said. "Blessed is she who enters."

The rabbi explained that Jewish tradition teaches that just as Abraham, patriarch of the Jewish people, brought men into the covenant through the ritual of *brit milah,* circumcision, so matriarch Sarah brought women into this relationship by having them take up residence in her tent. It was this ritual, *brit ohel,* or covenant of the tent, that we were symbolically enacting.

My husband, who had been holding our eighteen-day-old daughter, now handed her to his mother, and he and our friend unfurled my tallit, or prayer shawl, above the baby like a canopy.

The rabbi spoke again, in Hebrew and then in English: "As she has entered into the covenant, so may she enter into Torah, chuppah [a loving relationship], and a life of good deeds. Our

1

God and our ancestors' God, sustain this child who is to be known in Israel and the world as Yael."

Yael was wrapped in the tallit. I took my daughter in my arms, touched her tiny fist to the waiting Torah scroll and then brought it to her lips. We recited a *shehecheyanu*, a prayer blessing God for bringing us to this moment, and the congregation broke into *Simon Tov Umazel Tov*, the song for all joyous occasions.

The entire ceremony had taken only a few minutes. But for me it was an event I had been dreaming of, not just for the nine months of pregnancy but for years. It was a new beginning and the culmination of a long process of growth and struggle. Though I wasn't thinking of it then, even our daughter's name would come to symbolize the way the disparate strands of my own journey were coming powerfully together at this moment in time. My husband had asked, and I had agreed, to name our daughter Yael, after the Biblical woman warrior who slays an enemy of the Jewish people: a Jewish heroine who didn't happen to be Jewish.

Like many Jewish feminists, it was a given for me that our daughter would formally enter God's covenant with Israel, just as our son had on the day of his circumcision five and a half years before. It was a given for *us*, but not for Judaism. I had put this simple ritual together myself from different sources because Jewish tradition offers its daughters no counterpart to the circumcision ceremony that celebrates the birth of sons. In this way, we were expressing our joy and gratitude for the birth of our child. We were also making a public statement, with our Jewish community as witness, that we had every expectation that our daughter would one day embrace her tradition as a full and active participant, perhaps even as a warrior for her people.

Like many Jewish feminists, my own beginnings were very different. But in my case, neither family nor religion could be blamed. That my birth had not been celebrated with a Jewish initiation was a simple accident of fate. When I was born, I wasn't Jewish.

Glancing back over my history, there are so many moments at which it is difficult to connect the person I was with the person standing in synagogue that December morning.

First, there was the Catholic school girl, fascinated by the alien glimpses of life on her largely Jewish street.

I grew up in an apartment building where nearly all the tenants were over sixty and accents ranged from thick Russian-Yiddish to slightly Yiddish-inflected Brooklyn. At the far corner, men and boys in white prayer shawls over black suits filled the tiny Hasidic shul to its open doors, chanting and swaying improbably in the stark hot center of a summer day. In our building, observance was intermittent. My fading neighbors sat shivah, mourning with and for one another, the single young Jewish family held a circumcision to mark the birth of a son. And my friend's grandmother, a new widow with a clean white dish towel over her head, grieved over the Sabbath candles on endless Fridays at her kitchen table. As a child, I clung to the periphery of these mysteries, intrigued but invisible, an outsider.

Later, there was the ex-Catholic teenager and college student.

The Catholicism I inherited from my family was an uneasy fit for me as far back as I can remember. Like so many young people before and since, I was introduced to Christianity as a spectator sport for the mind; to engage with the teachings by asking questions and discussing ideas wasn't just discouraged, it was fundamentally at odds with the unthinking obedience upon which, we were taught, Catholicism depends. Also in conflict was my growing awareness of the Church as a social, political, economic entity and as a player in people's intimate lives—and any moral or spiritual mission that I could get behind. Within a year of leaving Catholic school, serious doubts had turned to permanent disaffection. At fourteen, armed with feminism and leftist convictions, I made a conscious decision to break with the Church. My Catholicism wasn't lapsed, like a magazine subscription. I was an atheist.

Having grown up in a Jewish neighborhood, and having, by the time I entered public high school, read *The Diary of Anne Frank* and the novels of Chaim Potok many times over—often at my desk at Catholic school, where the nuns had pointedly ignored them—it seems impossible that I could have reached the age of fifteen or sixteen unaware of the Holocaust. But I had read in isolation, with huge gaps in my understanding. When the subject was introduced in a history class I was devastated and shocked to discover that in the not-too-distant past, six million Jews had been systematically murdered—and no one around me ever spoke of it. The Holocaust became something of a preoccupation. I set about trying to correct my ignorance, reading books on my own, talking with Jewish friends and taking a class on the Nazi era.

This interest didn't translate into a warmth toward Jewish religion. I viewed religion only as a scourge visited upon the minds and bodies of the poor, the powerless, and especially, women, with as little patience for other traditions as for Christianity. It was during these high school years that I learned the misnomer "Judeo-Christian" and believed it. Judaism was just a variant of the Catholicism I'd been taught, another name for kowtowing to the fist-shaking, bearded old man in the sky who all thinking people already knew was only made of air. My Jewish friends shared my views on all this—if they thought about religion at all.

Finally, there was the young woman married to a Jew and treated with malice and derision by some Jews because of it.

I've heard that the gentile partner least likely to convert to Judaism is not the one who adheres to another faith but the one who is hostile to religion altogether. That sounds familiar: for me, the biggest leap was not to convert to Judaism but to embrace any religion at all.

After leaving Christianity behind, I didn't think about religion again until I fell in love with a Jewish boy in college who amazed me by seeing no contradiction between spirituality and a high IQ. We made a sport of knocking Karl Marx, God, and patriarchal religion back and forth between us. As far as I was concerned, I won every round. As far as he was concerned, he did.

What's certain is that we were both changed by these passionate, sometimes ferocious encounters. I played an aggressive role in raising his political and social consciousness. He developed a critical, questioning stance toward all schools of received wisdom, including that of the middle-class American Judaism in which he'd been raised. But when it came to his core Jewish beliefs, nothing I said ever seemed to shake him. We began living together while still in college, and married immediately after graduation. And from the very beginning we created ways to celebrate Judaism in our home.

We read the Book of Esther together on Purim, the Song of Songs on Passover. When he talked about his alienation from any larger religious community, confiding that he was turned off by what he knew of institutional Judaism, I urged him to forge his own path and search for a synagogue where he could feel at home. I accommodated his desire to eat only kosher food, and for each Rosh Hashanah, the Jewish New Year, made a special dinner and gave him a calendar for the New Year. Once, for our anniversary, I surprised him with the gift of a mezuzah, an ornamental case containing a prayer scroll that Jews affix to their doorposts.

If there was a contradiction between these gestures and my feelings about religion—and there was—it didn't trouble me. I understood that the person I loved was Jewish, that being Jewish was an essential part of who he was, and that abandoning that identity could never be a step in the right direction for him.

That doesn't mean that I was always comfortable accommodating Judaism in our lives: the dietary laws, or the sudden appearance of an odd and unexpected holiday, could be irritatingly inconvenient. Worse, I was prey to an occasional, anxious

5

realization that I had no idea where all this might end. Would my husband one day cross an invisible line in his spiritual journey, sprout a Hasid's forelocks and long black coat, and turn into a person I wouldn't even want to get near?

In retrospect, those fears weren't just illogical—they also held a certain insight. His practice of Judaism *was* a journey, not a fixed address. Like every journey, it was subject to disruption, chance, unplanned divergences, and even he couldn't know exactly where it might take him. What I didn't understand was that I was traveling on a parallel track of my own. I was only very slowly becoming aware that my life, too, would be undefinably diminished if Judaism, a tradition I was sure I would never find a place in, was not a part of it.

I enjoyed participation in Passover seders and the lighting of Hanukkah candles, rituals that were meaningful within the context of our relationship. When a pamphlet on Sabbath observance arrived in our mailbox I read it, and made my first independent connection with a concept central to Judaism. Here, in what I thought of as an irrational belief system, I discovered a beautiful and deeply sane vision of a day of rest, a still oasis inside the clutter and cacophony of daily life in which to devote oneself to—this is where I stumbled. An atheist couldn't dedicate a day to her relationship with God. I began to want that oasis even though I didn't acknowledge that life without it was a desert.

Learning of the Shekhinah, I was further intrigued. This female aspect of God described by Jewish mystics was a powerful challenge to the notion of the old man with the long white beard. I wasn't attracted to goddess worship. But a religion whose concept of the divine included a Sabbath Queen sheltering her people within the palace of her shimmering wings couldn't be entirely mired in a boys' club mentality—could it? Unfortunately, without exposure to flesh-and-blood women who were spiritual leaders, the idea of this mysterious lady remained magnificent yet partial, like taking the Venus de Milo or Winged Victory as a role model after a visit to the Louvre.

Gradually, very gradually, I was falling in love. But I continued to believe, not just for a little while but for years, that this love could never be reciprocated—there would be no place beneath those shimmering wings for me.

From time to time I talked about converting, but never seriously. No one else suggested it either. My husband, of course, knew better than to make a proposal he had every reason to assume would not be welcomed. We knew few Jews. Some didn't care that I wasn't Jewish. Those who did weren't thinking about how they could entice me into the fold. It was striking that, though my husband never once found himself on the receiving end of hostility for his choice of partner, my own experience was very different. I found that in some circles my non-Jewish identity could obliterate the need for common decency, let alone good manners.

There were occasions on which I attempted to welcome Jews into my home who did not return my greeting, then responded to my attempts to participate in conversation with either silence and condescending smiles, or by angrily dismissing whatever I had to say. There were insulting references to my Italian-American heritage that felt quite blatantly racist, and sneering reactions to my opinions—often from Jewish women—that were indistinguishable from garden-variety misogyny. As if, without Jewish lineage, a woman—or just a woman involved with a Jewish man?—was sure to be a bimbo.

Painful and maddening as they were, these incidents involved only a handful of people. But they kept us away from most Jewish institutions, and most Jews. Judaism was an exclusive club that certainly didn't want me for a member—or any other non-Jewish woman either. In the early days of our marriage, I heard two stories from my husband's family that served to conjure the invisible NO GENTILE WOMEN NEED APPLY sign hanging over the gateposts of the Jewish world.

An older cousin of my husband told us that, as a newly returned Vietnam War veteran, he went home to announce that he was going to marry a non-Jewish woman. For him, the battles weren't over: his mother's response was to reach out blindly for the first object she could put her hand on. Unfortunately for her son, this turned out to be a heavy table lamp with which she literally knocked him unconscious. While this (entirely factual) piece of family slapstick had no tragic results—the young man recovered and his gentile wife and two rosy-cheeked boys stood beside him while he told the tale—there was nothing amusing about the family's successful efforts to stop another marriage from taking place. When I met my husband's grandfather, he was a frail and lonely octogenarian, recently widowed. Stranded at what seemed to be literally the ends of the earth, in a vast institutional nursing home perched at the edge of the sea at Coney Island in Brooklyn, he found a lifeline in a fellow resident. The two wanted to marry and share a closer companionship for what turned out to be the very brief remainder of their lives. Unfortunately they weren't strong enough to withstand his family's disapproval: the woman wasn't Jewish.

If all this wasn't enough to convince anyone she wasn't welcome, I would sometimes receive reminders even in casual contacts with Jews I met on my own, men and women who were themselves the parents of young adults. We'd strike up a warm and open conversation and I'd eventually find myself invited to talk about my unpleasant experiences in the Jewish community. There'd be expressions of sympathy, exclamations of disapproval over the bad behavior of coreligionists. Then the moment would arrive. Without a trace of irony or self-conscious hesitation, always using the same words, the parent in question would bring out what I came to think of as the inevitable sentence: "Of course, I wouldn't want *my* son to marry one."

When, with my encouragement, my husband eventually joined a synagogue, we tentatively socialized with a few other Jews. On one memorable occasion, I mentioned to someone that, though I felt drawn to Judaism, as an atheist, there was nothing I could do about it. My confidant surprised me: he urged me to go and talk with the rabbi, and bring all my misgivings and confusion with me. This encounter was the first time anyone ever suggested that conversion was something I could actually do, that it would be a thing that at least some Jews might *like* me to do.

At the time, I didn't go to the rabbi. If atheism and the threat of rejection weren't absolute obstacles to conversion, a healthy sense of autonomy seemed to be. My fears were contradictory but never seemed to cancel each other out: if I worried that Judaism would spit me out, I also worried that I'd be swallowed whole. Conversion was a disappearing act into my husband's identity, into a tradition with a *mechitzah*, a ritual divider, growing out of the center of its heart, separating women and men and reserving Torah, learning, participation, personhood, for the men's side of the partition.

My sense that conversion equaled obliteration, at least for a woman, began to change when we moved to a new town and joined a new synagogue. After attending a smattering of Shabbat services, I decided to accompany my husband to synagogue on the eve of Yom Kippur, the Day of Atonement, for the first time. That night, the rabbi's words, the singing of the prayers and the unfamiliar melodies impressed me deeply, as did the rabbi and cantor themselves: two women standing before the packed sanctuary in white robes and flowing hair, the rabbi's threaded with gray, the cantor's sleek and dark. Together, they shattered my sense of Judaism as a religion in which women's marginal status was fundamental. Like two generations of a spiritual dynasty, they seemed to belong to the past or the future, or to the matriarchal fantasies I'd come across in my first brushes with feminism as a teenager.

For years my progress toward Judaism had been happening as continents drift, almost imperceptibly. On that Yom Kippur night I felt some definite movement. Not a very graceful movement—my heart jerked one step forward and left the rest of me off-balance, behind.

It took a while for the rest of me to catch up.

That same Yom Kippur my husband and I began making plans to start a family. Though thrilled at the thought of becoming a mother, I feared it might throw a wet baby blanket over the possibility of conversion. Conversion now, I reasoned, would look like a clumsy attempt to satisfy someone else's notion of proper Jewish motherhood. I had no patience with people who assumed I simply wanted to belong to the same religion as my husband and the children we would have, even if that was the only reason some Jews would welcome me. I wanted to want it for myself, and would have backed off, maybe perversely, if I suspected myself of just wanting to fit in.

These scruples slowed but couldn't stop what had been set in motion. For the first time, I entered into a period of active study. Unexpectedly, the experience didn't require the loss of autonomy I had feared. Rather than being subsumed into my husband's identity, I was expanding my own in a way that I had never imagined. I explored Judaism independently, took classes, read books my husband hadn't read, pursued my own questions. I found myself resonating with Jewish values and the rich tradition of oral and written stories often employed to teach them, with the holy days and festivals that mark the Jewish calendar. Suddenly it was me who was bringing new Jewish ideas and rituals into our home.

Which is not to suggest that becoming a Jew was ever, for a moment, simple for me.

I had been around Jews and Judaism all my life, but now that I was earnestly trying to get a handle on the spiritual core behind all the laws and customs, it seemed to keep slipping provocatively through my fingers. The same was true of my attraction: visceral, thriving, and always one step beyond rational understanding. On the one hand, I felt the impulse to stand during Shabbat services and yell, "Sign me up!" On the other, there were the moments when doubts and misgivings would convene like a *beit din*, a court of law, on the question of my conversion.

Warned about the convert's impulse to rewrite the past so that it leads inexorably to conversion, I didn't say I'd always wanted to be Jewish, even though I realized that this was in some way true. I didn't flirt with the idea of redeeming a Jewish soul somewhere in the nether reaches of my family history, squelched my excitement when reminded that my surname was frequently that of Italian Jews.

It lent a kind of legitimacy to my quest to speculate that my ancestry might have included *conversos*, Jews forced to opt for Christian baptism over the Inquisition's fires. That part of my history, if it had ever existed, was unrecoverable; but as a fantasy, its appeal pointed to a real and necessary aspect of the process of becoming a Jew. Trying to imagine a home in the Jewish world, consciously or unconsciously, I was looking for reflections of myself in that world. Had anyone like me been there before? Were there footsteps to follow, or was it up to me to clear the path? It was important that I knew women who had converted, and that I came across one or two contemporary conversion stories in my reading. Even more powerful was what I learned by going directly to the source. In the Torah, I saw that gentile women hadn't begun joining the Jewish people in recent generations—*we had always been there*. We'd been vilified as a group, demonized or lauded as individuals, and, most striking, represented as nuanced characters crucially involved in the formation of the Jewish people. The negative images of gentile women provided a framework for the worst of my experiences; the handful of heroic figures gave me something to live up to.

Nevertheless, my conversion jitters weren't at an end. As my Jewish involvement grew, I discovered another apprehension, fusty as an old shiksa joke but entirely new to me: How was my husband going to feel about having a Jewish wife? If anecdotal evidence, popular Jewish fiction, and demographic studies could be believed, Jewish men liked women who helped them forget where they came from. What if my husband had married a non-Jewish woman because that was exactly what he wanted?

The truth was that I had married a man secure enough in his own deeply spiritual Jewish identity to join his life to someone who didn't share it. Having a non-Jewish partner had never troubled him. But now my active explorations and increasing excitement about Judaism opened up new worlds of possibility in our relationship, our lives together. One night when I was all but committed to taking the final step, still hovering nervously on the brink, he brought up the subject himself. He told me how happy my conversion would make him, and also that he would never have said anything until he knew that it would happen whether he wanted it or not.

Even after I felt sure of Judaism, sure of my partner, I still continued to doubt myself. In classes designed for both Jews and gentiles in Jewish religion, history, and culture, I found stimulation and encouragement. But even in that context, some Jewish students insisted that Jews were born, not made: a convert could never *really* be Jewish. Could I argue, when they expressed yet another of my fears? How could I claim to be worthy of a place in this tradition?

I never answered those questions. But by this point I had learned that Judaism specialized in wrestling with questions, not resolving them, and that the ability to live with the unanswerable was as necessary a condition for Jewish inclusion as any other. Nothing but cowardice stood between me and the mikvah.

Immersion in the *mikvah*, the ritual bath required by Jewish law to contain a natural gathering of water, is the final step in the process of conversion. I had come to see the living water of the mikvah not as an agent of purification but as a medium of transition. A convert brings everything she is into the mikvah and emerges leaving none of it behind—and yet, she is changed.

It was time to take the plunge.

Beginning with the story of the first Jews, Abraham and Sarah, there's a recurring association between travel to a new land and becoming Jewish. This was an idea I found compelling, the sense that wherever it began, whatever the reasons it was undertaken, there was a journey in progress, a country ahead that, for all Jews, was entered finally by water. By crossing the Jordan. By being born. By immersion in a mikvah. By entering a sea that wouldn't part until I was over my head in it.

My conversion was a turning point in time. The process of becoming a Jew—the best Jew that I can be—continues.

Over time, I've discovered that making Judaism central to my life entails, in part, finding a place for myself at the center of Judaism. It means believing that, like every other Jew, I bear the responsibility and the right to care passionately about Judaism and its people and to do my part to ensure that both survive and flourish. That might mean speaking out on issues that concern me, within or on behalf of the Jewish community. It might mean being bold enough to believe that I have a Jewish identity worth imparting to my children. It might mean assuming a leadership role, not as a convert but as a Jew.

That feels like a very daring stance to take. Yet it's here that I believe the crux of so much of the struggle over Jewish identity lies: astoundingly for a religion so decentralized, based so much in the practices of families and small communities, so many Jews lack a basic feeling of entitlement toward Judaism.

Before my conversion, I envisioned Judaism as a place of engagement, without sidelines to stand on, a difficult place. I was right. Outside this place, the place where I live now, I was safe, not from anti-Semitic attack, since my allegiance was Jewish, but from the awesome challenge to re-create myself as a

Jew. Conversion meant crossing the borders of Judaism, the unknown country. Whether I would remain at the outskirts of that country or approach the active center would be a test of limits—my own, Judaism's.

2

Sexual Seduction = Religious Destruction: Gentile Women as Agents of Assimilation

We have broken faith with our God and have married foreign women from the peoples of the land. . . .

—*EZRA 10:2*

That Alice was so blatantly a shikse caused no end of grief. . . .

—*PHILIP ROTH,* PORTNOY'S COMPLAINT

JEWISH TRADITION is replete with images of gentile women.

From the archetypal stories inscribed on the parchment scrolls of the Torah to the Jewish press of early America, to contemporary novels and films, to timeless—and timeworn—Jewish jokes, the gentile woman is a constant presence in the narrative of the Jewish people. Taken as a whole, the catalogue of personae envisioned for her is multifaceted and contradictory. But there is one role in which she is so famously typecast that Jews and gentiles alike often believe she has played no other. That, of course, is the role of sexual seductress, the femme fatale who effortlessly lures the bedazzled Jewish male away from his own best interests, decimates his family line, and weakens the Jewish people by costing it so many of its reckless sons.

How did this specter arise, and why has she traveled so tenaciously across time and space from the ancient Middle East to twenty-first-century America? Is she based upon fact, with non-Jewish women doing their best to flesh out her contemporary manifestations today? If she is fantasy, how did and do the Jewish people serve themselves by keeping her stereotype alive? What impact does this image of gentile women have on the increasingly multicultural Jewish world of today? To answer these questions we need to go back to the start of Jewish time.

According to Jewish tradition, the Jews began life as a small and vulnerable band of nomads, a religious community at large in the desert. During their travels they became a nation, receiving from God the Torah, the divine charter that would define them—and that, through its laws, prohibitions, and stories, would also define their relationship to the non-Jewish women in their midst.

At this precarious beginning, the people's very existence depended upon their ability to establish group bonds sturdy enough to withstand the almost overwhelming odds of assimilating into their neighbors. When they looked at those neighbors, biblical Jews saw a powerful link between sexual and religious transgression. The spiritual practices of the Canaanite peoples who surrounded the fledgling Israelite nation often included both male and female ritual prostitution and orgiastic celebrations of their gods. If an Israelite man entered into a sexual relationship, including marriage, with a woman from one of these peoples, there was good reason to suspect that he might also join her in some form of idolatry.

So what's wrong with idolatry? For the Israelites, there was nothing worse. Monotheism is the crux of Judaism, a theology that posits a special relationship, a covenant, between the Jewish people and God: *one* God, *the* God, the God of all creation. In its essence it is a renunciation of the pagan beliefs and practices that had existed in the Middle East up to that time. It is also a distinct and in many ways progressive moral system that set itself apart from Canaanite cultures by introducing such innovations as the notion that, for example, even women and slaves had some rights, and by abolishing practices like human sacrifice.

At a time when Judaism was only just coming into being, struggling to distinguish itself as a religious identity, the danger of its men being absorbed into pagan cults is clear. What is amazing is that this tiny and embattled people did survive, all the way into the twenty-first century, while its idol-worshipping counterparts gradually disappeared. The Israelites didn't lose themselves in Canaan. Instead, as many scholars have suggested, the Canaanites may have lost themselves through intermarriage and conversion into the Israelites.

But like many of their contemporary counterparts, biblical Jews saw little reason to feel complacent that the future would include them. Today some American Jews dread assimilation into Christian society when they look at soaring intermarriage rates. Conservative rabbi Charles Simon is typical of many Jewish leaders in referring to intermarriage as "the major issue of the Jewish community." Mark I. Sirkin, a clinical psychologist specializing in intermarriage issues, says, "For many Jewish families facing intermarriage, it is the end of history." Similarly, the early Israelites feared complete annihilation when they watched one of their men vanish into the pagan mist. And what would tempt him into that mist if not the insidious charms of a gentile woman?

Foreign, Forbidden, Strange

Many books of the Torah (including Genesis, Exodus, Numbers, Deuteronomy, Judges, Ezekiel, Malachi, Ezra, and Nehemiah, among others) feature exemplary or cautionary tales of Jewish heroes who resist or succumb to the enticements of non-Jewish women, diatribes against these variously known foreign, forbidden, and strange women, and grave cautions to the Jewish sons of all generations who would consider associations with them. In these passages, a relationship with a non-Jewish woman is itself sometimes seen as a betrayal of a man's Judaism; at other times, it is considered the first step on the road to betrayal.

Addressing young Jewish men, these quintessential lines from Proverbs (5:3-10) don't mince words:

The lips of a strange woman drip honey;
Her mouth is smoother than oil;
But in the end she is as bitter as wormwood,
Sharp as a two-edged sword.
Her feet go down to Death;
Her steps take hold of Sheol [hell].
She does not chart a path of life;
Her course meanders for lack of knowledge.
So now, sons, pay heed to me,
And do not swerve from the words of my mouth.
Keep yourself far away from her;
Do not come near the doorway of her house
Lest you give up your vigor to others,
Your years to a ruthless one;
Lest strangers eat their fill of your strength,
And your toil be for the house of another. . . .

This dire warning has the ring of a 1950s antivenereal-disease campaign: as good as that foreign woman may look, as slick as her promises may sound, the path to her door is a shortcut to death. The Jewish man who entangles himself with her finds his vitality ruthlessly sapped, his life consumed by an ignorant, bitter, and hell-bent harridan, and nothing he produces will be his own. The writer of Proverbs may have a taste for exaggeration, but there is nothing unique in the notion that romance with a gentile woman is incompatible with a Jewish man's Jewish manhood. Perhaps it doesn't literally kill him (as we'll

SEXUAL SEDUCTION = RELIGIOUS DESTRUCTION

see, some sources suggest it does), but he risks death *as a Jewish man*. And his "house"—his family, the Jewish people—is sacrificed along with him.

The gentile woman described here is a kind of gold digger who works an unsuspecting Jewish man into an early grave to build up her coffers, or perhaps those of her family, or her gods. Like all gentile sirens, the means she uses to ensnare her man is sex. This is the dynamic deeply embedded in Jewish tradition's vision of relations between Jewish men and gentile women: aggressive female sexuality—that is, the sexuality of a gentile woman—is a destructive force that a Jewish man is all too easily persuaded to open himself up to. Once open, he is powerless to defend himself or his people. In the Jewish psyche this scenario, as unflattering to Jewish men as it is to gentile women, is as old as the human race itself, created along with the First Couple—not Adam and Eve but Adam and Lilith.

Lilith

In the mirror of traditional, male-centered Judaism, woman is Other, gentile woman is Extra-Other, and Lilith is the Otherest of them all.

In the creation story that opens Bereshit, or Genesis, God fashions man and woman—twice. The first time around, both sexes are created simultaneously, in God's image. In the second telling, God forms a man of earth and a woman later, from man's rib. Pondering the mystery of these dual versions of the story, the ancient rabbis reach the conclusion that while the second woman was clearly the Eve Adam knew and loved, the first was Lilith, an early model that proved even God could make mistakes.

Lilith leaps Jewish boundaries to haunt the mythologies of many cultures, tantalizing and terrorizing susceptible minds from ancient Sumer to the shtetls of Eastern Europe, inspiring innumerable incantations and practices to ward off her fatal charms. In Jewish lore she is a rebellious she-demon who preferred to flee paradise rather than subjugate herself to her husband, Adam. The antithesis of the virtuous Jewish wife, she is Jewish men's fatal attraction, a threat to their legitimate offspring, and a thief of their nocturnal emissions, which she uses to create demonic children of her own. She is sometimes known as the Northerner; it is also said that the Queen of the Sheba who sounded King Solomon's wisdom was actually Lilith in disguise.

A beautiful seductress enticing men to their doom and destroying Jewish families, Lilith is the Ultimate Shiksa, a stand-in for the gentile woman in the Jewish mind. That detail of her résumé is noted in passing by a few scholars and otherwise largely overlooked. It isn't, for example, usually mentioned by Jewish feminists who have laid claim to Lilith as a symbol of women's repression and resistance within a tradition that has been very much a man's world. On the other hand, it was obvious enough to Mike Resnick and Lawrence Schimel, authors of a justly obscure fantasy story, "The Shiksa." In their spin on the dysfunctional First Family, a shrewish Eve spends her time cooking inedible stuffed cabbage, while Adam's old flame, Lilith—a dark dominatrix who hangs out at S&M bars wearing five-inch heels—turns up to wreak erotic havoc with Cain.

Among traditional Jewish sources, Lilith receives the most attention in the Zohar, a thirteenth-century Spanish work of Jewish mysticism, or kabbala, written by Moses of Leon. The Zohar describes a Lilith classically un-Semitic and reminiscent of the foreign women Proverbs warns Jewish sons to avoid:

> Her hair is long and red like the rose, her cheeks are white and red . . . her mouth is set like a narrow door comely in its decor, her tongue is sharp like a sword, her words are smooth like oil, her lips are red like a rose and sweetened by all the sweetness of the world. . . . Yon fool goes astray after her and drinks from the cup of wine and commits with her fornica-

tions and strays after her. What does she thereupon do? . . .
She kills that fool and casts him into Gehenna [hell].

But the mystics don't stop at finding Lilith a threat to mortal
men; in their view, her powers of seduction extend to God.

The kabbalists envision a male God whose rightful mate is
the Shekhinah, the female aspect of the Divine, but who feels
the pull of Lilith. For them, Lilith is an enchantress who sends
her human victims laughing pleasurably to their deaths, while
the Shekhinah represents a perfect goodness that is a little
chilly, unsexy, hard to get near. In relation to God and the
Shekhinah, Lilith is sometimes called the Slave-Woman and is
likened to a handmaid who usurps her mistress's rightful place,
an idea that, as we'll see in chapter four, echoes the stories of
the patriarchs' liaisons with their wives' non-Jewish handmaids.

Just as the gentile woman isn't simply black in Jewish tradition but also white and gray, Lilith is not exclusively conceived
as a force of death and destruction. One mystic sees her not in
opposition to the Shekhinah but as an aspect of her. Rabbi Isaac
Hacohen, another thirteenth-century Spanish kabbalist, goes
further. Perhaps suggesting that forbidden sexual energies can
be channeled into spiritually productive practices, he declares
that "Lilith is a ladder on which one can ascend to the rungs of
prophecy."

But for most kabbalists, Lilith is clearly bad news.

For some, the worst result of the destruction of the Second
Temple in Jerusalem two thousand years ago, and the Jewish Diaspora, was that these events caused the Shekhinah to go into
exile with her people, leaving God to mate with Lilith; other
kabbalists describe the God-Lilith pairing as causing the destruction and Diaspora in the first place. Here the kabbalists
sound a little like those voices in the Jewish community today
who decry the disintegration of the Jewish people for giving rise
to intermarriage on the one hand, while blaming intermarriage
for the disintegration of the Jewish people on the other.

This chicken-and-egg routine aside, both the Lilith legends and contemporary fears demonstrate a profound inclination to understand the precarious fate of the Jewish people in terms of its relationship to the gentile women in its midst, and to link major disasters of Jewish history to this relationship. The gentile woman as an agent of Jewish destruction is an idea as seductive as Lilith herself, as meaningful to the creators of an ancient and esoteric philosophy as to some writers and thinkers today.

As an imaginative tool for projecting outside the community the dangers that threaten the Jewish people, including women's uncontrolled sexuality and reproduction, Lilith is a powerful strategy for safeguarding Jewish identity. But she is a strategy with complications. She pits the Jewish and gentile woman against each other, limiting each to being only what her nemesis is not. As a symbol of non-Jewish womanhood, she is problematic for the Jewish man who chooses a gentile partner, and, of course, for the gentile woman who enters—or, as in the case of Sharon Bascom, who tries to enter—that partnership herself.

Sharon Bascom

At thirty-three, Sharon Bascom° found herself in a brand-new job in a brand-new city. At the invitation of a friend, she had taken the leap from her native New England to Portland, Oregon, into a job managing one of the sites of a child-care company. "My immediate supervisor became one of my closest friends, at a time when I had very few friends," Sharon recalls now, some half dozen years later. "She invited me to go to synagogue with her. I went and I loved it. The songs, the ancient wisdom, the majesty and respect for the Torah—I loved all these things."

°The names of the women who share their stories, and some identifying details, have been changed, unless otherwise indicated. There are no composite portraits in this book.

As a nondenominational Christian, Sharon also found that the songs and prayers she was introduced to in synagogue resonated for her with the teachings of Jesus. It was a kind of resonance that didn't take her by surprise. Sharon had studied many world religions in a belief that all faiths are essentially one. Until her arrival in Portland, she had felt warmly welcomed by the friends she made at each stop on her spiritual sojourn. "Well," she says, "Judaism was different."

Initially it seemed very much the same. In the small, relatively open Conservative congregation, it was well known that Sharon wasn't Jewish, and no one seemed to care. Feeling that she'd been accepted into the fold, she attended Shabbat services nearly every Saturday morning, and sometimes on Friday nights as well. She still remembers the thrill she felt on one occasion when she was allowed to hold the Torah, the parchment scrolls containing the five books of Moses, an honor usually reserved for Jews.

While Sharon's loneliness at this point in her life made her especially appreciative of the family feeling that prevailed at the synagogue, she says it made her vulnerable to developments taking place at work as well. The same friend who had brought her to synagogue convinced Sharon to hire her son, Aaron, to work at the child-care site Sharon directed. From the first, Aaron showed a marked interest in Sharon that went far beyond the professional. In Sharon's account, his behavior—sexual innuendos, winks, touching—was downright unprofessional. Yet he convinced Sharon that he really cared about her, even attending Shabbat services, something he had rarely done before, to see her outside of work. They began to date. Then Aaron was promoted, and Sharon says his interest in her came to an abrupt end. She says she tried to rekindle the relationship, but soon realized she had to let it go. Aaron continued to attend services at the synagogue, with the difference that now he and his mother ignored Sharon. Then, Sharon recalls, came the crushing blow.

"One day an Orthodox woman stood up at synagogue, and

said, 'The goyish [non-Jewish] women are stealing good Jewish boys away from the faith, and it has to be stopped.'"

Sharon felt stunned, not only by the personal attack but by the silence of everyone else around her. "All my 'friends' that I had felt so close to for two years said nothing. For two years I sang with these people, cried with them, attended new moon celebrations with them, broke bread with them. They never respected me for who I really am."

Sharon left the synagogue in tears and never returned. Eventually she quit her job, and it was then that she learned that Aaron had complained both to his mother and to the company that Sharon had sexually harassed him. Though the company had not taken the complaint seriously, Sharon was outraged, particularly by one detail of Aaron's accusation. "He went so far as to say that I attended synagogue to be near him. That I would use a sacred space—which I attended far more often than Aaron did—to fulfill some other need was the ultimate disrespect of everything I had shared with these people for two years."

Sharon assumes that Aaron and his mother disclosed his accusations to the congregation, and that they were believed. She is aware of the demographic realities facing the Jewish people, and says she understands why any interfaith relationship might cause alarm. "I know it is a deep-seated fear that goyim are watering down the faith of their boys and girls. But in my case, my attending synagogue actually brought Aaron closer to his own faith, and caused him to attend more regularly." Her experience at the synagogue is still very much a source of bitterness and pain. Though Sharon says she loves the Torah and other aspects of Judaism, she plans to keep her distance from the Jewish community. "I know I will not be completely accepted no matter what I do. No other group I have entered has ever treated me that way, or anything close to it."

Jewish communal mores *can* be baffling to the non-Jew who attempts to operate within them—particularly to the non-Jewish woman who believes herself a benign, even welcome presence in a Jewish community only to run smack into the assumption that she is a kind of Lilith in disguise. Sharon had considered herself an accepted participant in synagogue life. What she discovered was that she was, in fact, an outsider. The congregation's inclusiveness didn't hold up against a rumor, and seemingly without hesitation, its members closed ranks against her.

When Sharon refers to non-Jews watering down the faith of Jewish sons and daughters, she is talking about two facts of statistical reality considered closely linked by the Jewish community: the prevalence of intermarriage, and the high percentage of intermarried Jews with no Jewish affiliation.

Results released by the National Jewish Population Survey for 2000–2001 say that the Jewish population in the United States is shrinking and aging. In 1990 there were 5.5 million Jews; in 2000, 5.2. In 1990, the median age of a Jewish community member was thirty-seven, as opposed to forty-two in 2000. It is in this context that the Jewish community considers the impact of intermarriage, which the survey places at 47 percent. According to demographer Egon Mayer, director of both the Center for Jewish Studies of the Graduate School of the City University of New York, and the Jewish Outreach Institute, during the years 1990 to 2001, approximately 505,000 Jewish adults got married, some 51 percent to someone who was not Jewish, another 9 percent to someone who had entered Judaism through conversion. A 1997 American Jewish Committee study found that only 14 percent of interfaith families identify primarily as Jewish, with one-third identifying as Christian and another third as both Jewish and Christian.

It isn't hard to understand why American Jews might see the demise of Judaism in these numbers, and why someone in Sharon's position might become a scapegoat for their fears. As already noted, some blame intermarriage on Jewish disconnection, others blame disconnection on intermarriage, but everyone seems to accept that there is a link between the two.

It must be said that what happened to Sharon flies in the

face of so many Jewish values that it would be difficult to name them all, values concerning hospitality and the sheltering of strangers, of concern for others' dignity and honor. But these are values that communities too easily forget, especially when feeling threatened. What Sharon found most galling was the charge that she was only in synagogue to snare a man. Let's imagine the congregation's perspective: having trusted in the sincerity of a stranger, having welcomed and embraced her, they are informed that they've been deceived, that her interest in Judaism is a pretence for another objective altogether. As Sharon laments, she worshipped weekly with this community for two years. Yet their confidence in her was so slight that not a single person rose to her defense. There was nothing in their experience of Sharon to dissuade the assembly from accepting a report that she was really a man-stealing Lilith. Or was there something that predisposed them to accept it?

Sexual suspicion of the gentile woman with an interest in Judaism is actually a tradition with a long history.

It has already been noted that pagan religious rituals were known to include an exchange of bodily fluids. Perhaps because of their origins in this milieu, Jews have long held to the belief that gentiles are more highly sexed than themselves, a belief that anecdotal sources from shiksa jokes to Woody Allen films to the conversations of Jewish college students would indicate some may be reluctant to let go of. "Uncivilized," "uninhibited," "promiscuous"—these are among the words Gary Porton uses to describe the way the postbiblical rabbis who codified Jewish law viewed gentiles. Some, he writes, were convinced that non-Jewish men would have sex with any female over the age of three years and one day, so a girl or woman who entered the Jewish people after this age "is *assumed* to have had intercourse." It is written into Jewish law that a gentile female is both highly libidinous and, from the age of three years and a day, sexually experienced.

The notion that a gentile woman might make use of the sacred in her quest for the profane is also a Jewish tradition. Genesis offers the story of Joseph, Jacob's favorite son, who is sold into slavery by his jealous brothers. Bought by an Egyptian named Potiphar, the talented and handsome Joseph attracts the attention of Potiphar's wife, who is nameless here, but who later tradition calls Zuleika. Zuleika makes an unsuccessful attempt to seduce Joseph. According to midrash, her come-on line with the upright slave is the claim that she is interested in conversion to Judaism for herself and her husband, and wants Joseph to instruct her.

Like Zuleika, Sharon Bascom was accused of feigning interest in Judaism in order to seduce a Jewish man. Received with this kind of suspicion, a gentile woman who is attracted to a Jewish man might well feel damned if she takes an interest in Judaism, damned if she doesn't. Keeping her distance from the community, she costs the Jewish people one of its sons; trying to get near, she may find herself accused of spurious motives. Not only is her interest in Judaism assumed to be a sham, her sexual conquest of a Jewish man is expected to turn his head toward her own religion. In Shemot, or Exodus, Jewish fathers are exhorted to avoid their non-Jewish neighbors when choosing daughters-in-law, because "when you take wives from among their daughters for your sons, their daughters will lust after their gods and will cause your sons to lust after their gods." As already noted, the use of the word "lust" can be taken literally.

The story of King Solomon told in I Kings would seem to illustrate the soundness of this advice. Solomon is credited with building the First Temple in Jerusalem, centralizing worship while fusing state and religion. He is also much vaunted for his knowledge and wisdom. Yet even this pillar of Judaism isn't immune to the temptation of foreign women. Lots of foreign women: seven hundred to be exact. Solomon is said to have taken some seven hundred non-Jewish women as wives and concubines. He allows them to worship their own pagan deities, "and his wives turn away his heart" from God. Solomon joins the women in their idol worship, initiating the dilution of Jewish spiritual practice that leads to the rampant—and bloody—paganism we'll encounter a little later in the story of Jezebel.

If foreign women lead to foreign gods, Jewish opinion in ancient times as well as our own holds that they also lead to non-Jewish children. In the Book of Nehemiah, the prophet tells us: "I saw the Jews who had married women of Ashdod, Ammon, and Moab; and half of their children spoke the language of Ashdod, and they could not speak their own language. And I contended with them and cursed them and beat some of them and pulled out their hair. . . . Shall we then listen to you and do all this great evil and act treacherously against our God by marrying foreign women?"

If Nehemiah's haranguing and hair pulling are impassioned responses to intermarriage, the Talmud goes coolly to the point in this condemnation of Jewish fathers of interfaith children: "This is one who marries an Aramean woman and raises sons out of her: he raises enemies for God."

The final chapter of the Book of Ezra offers a glimpse of this attitude played out in a community. Here we see Israelite men returning from exile in Babylon to build the Second Temple in Jerusalem, bringing with them Babylonian wives and the children who have been born to them. Upon their arrival, Ezra and other leaders decide that in order to appease God, and avert a terrible retribution, these women and children must be expelled from the community. A proclamation is issued calling for the men to "separate yourselves from the peoples of the land and from the foreign women," to which the entire congregation responds: "We must surely do just as you say."

The text is fascinating for what it tells us about these events, and even more so for what it leaves out. It records that every man with a foreign wife is seen individually by one of the elders, but omits all detail of what takes place during these interviews; we are left to assume that not a single man demurs when ordered to throw his wife and children out of their home. While the men are each listed by family name, the women and children are anonymous, their numbers unknown. We are told that these events take place during the season of heavy rains, when the men balk at assembling outdoors to discuss what is to be done. But we are offered no description of the women and children setting out in the deluge, suddenly homeless and without means of support. They are unseen and unheard throughout, and there is no information about where they are to go or how they are to fend for themselves. We hear the Israelites beat their breasts over the men's transgression in intermarrying, and bewail the expected divine retribution. But the shattering bonds between the returning exiles and their partners and children are passed over in silence. The writer of this story has no language for the grief of the families parting forever. This haunting scene is one we can only imagine for ourselves.

What we can be sure of is the depth of fear informing the actions of Ezra and the other elders, their certainty that brutally dividing "mixed" families is a better alternative to absorbing them. There is no mention of the men engaging in idolatrous practices, and their voluntary return is an expression of their desire to rejoin the Jewish people. Unlike Exodus' warning and Nehemiah's reportage, no complaints are lodged against the women's behavior or their children's religious identification. It is the *fact* of their foreignness that threatens to destroy the community, and that justifies their forced expulsion.

This objection to the inclusion of non-Jewish women in Jewish communities—that they are foreign in *essence*, regardless of behavior—has fought for survival in the Jewish community against the homogenizing influence of the multicultural American melting pot. Its case was made with clear, if hyperbolic, ferocity in an early twentieth-century work of fiction.

The Island Within

Eli looked concerned. "What's wrong?"

"Nothing," Arthur said. He felt a sudden sense of liberation. "Nothing except that she's a Gentile and I am a Jew. We're fond of each other and we understand each other intellectually, but at the emotional basis of life there is—no, no opposition—there's a divergence. You've heard of the parallel lines that can never meet?"

Much like the passage from Proverbs quoted earlier, Ludwig Lewisohn's *The Island Within* is a quintessential and cautionary tale of intermarriage, a glimpse into the cold heart and even colder hearth that awaits the out-marrying Jewish man. In this 1928 American novel, intermarriage is an intensely isolating experience for the Jewish partner, one in which protagonist Arthur Levy finds himself marooned with ill-defined tribal longings he can't comprehend, much less share.

In the scene above, Arthur frees himself from his marriage and his delusions when he comes to the conclusion that he and his non-Jewish wife are utterly incompatible. It takes him several years of marriage to admit this to himself, but the dullest reader could have saved him the time. From the moment Elizabeth and Arthur meet it is predetermined that they will never make each other happy. For Elizabeth has two failings, closely bound together, that render her an unfit mate for Arthur: she's not Jewish and she's a feminist.

Elizabeth is a New Woman of the 1920s, a writer more interested in career building than making a home or raising her child. She is cold, incapable of true empathy, not only with Arthur but, one suspects, with anyone. The novel contrasts her with Arthur's sister, who is married to a Jewish man, lives in a suburban Jewish ghetto, and has no life outside her home and the care of her child. She is miserable, yet despite every indication to the contrary, Arthur is convinced that her hellish marriage has a legitimacy that his lacks.

> All he knew was this, that, except in imitation of their Gentile sisters and more or less from the lips outward, Jewish women were not dissatisfied with their position and did not protest against the dominance of the male. He knew of none that did not rule unquestioned in her sphere nor of any that was not her husband's most valued councillor in his. . . .

Elizabeth is exceptionally out of sympathy with Arthur's Judaism, which is portrayed as a vague ethnic affiliation that he is unable to articulate even to himself, and which he chiefly remembers in response to anti-Semitism. In one scene, Elizabeth displays her insensitivity by reporting to Arthur that she protested against anti-Semitic remarks made at work, expecting that he will be pleased with her. "And Arthur, violently uncomfortable but unable to analyze his own discomfort at the moment, praised her in the expected sense." Later, Elizabeth and their baby are turned away from a hotel that doesn't welcome Jews when she attempts to register under Levy, her married name. Arthur hears about the incident from a third party. Does the fact that Elizabeth has not only weathered this experience but also learned not to share it with Arthur indicate a growing awareness of his feelings? Neither author nor protagonist dare to draw conclusions that might muddy the evidence gathered against Elizabeth. Not being Jewish, Elizabeth *can't* empathize with what it would mean to be the real target of anti-Semitic sentiments. In truth, she can't but harbor those sentiments herself.

> "Do you expect me to be satisfied with the society of the Goldmans and the Bergmanns and of some of your—ugh—colleagues and their wives?"
> "Jewish colleagues, you meant to say."

"No, I didn't, Arthur. I give you my word. At least it wasn't in any derogatory sense."

He bit his lips. There was no use going on with that question. It opened abysses unexplored, deliberately unexplored by himself.

Unexplored abysses. In *The Island Within*, an open exchange about cultural differences is beyond the pale of an interfaith marriage. Elizabeth and Arthur talk around their estrangement, when they talk at all. Since the novel is only concerned with depicting Arthur's perspective, we never discover how Elizabeth feels about the distance between herself and her husband. When Arthur faces it, he does so in conversation not with Elizabeth but with his brother-in-law, Eli, and the articulation is in itself a declaration that the marriage is over. What if instead Arthur had initiated that difficult conversation with Elizabeth? He might have been forced to hear and acknowledge a range of experiences and emotions as painful and complex as his own. He might have faced a torrent of questions about something even more frightening to him than the abysses of his marriage: his Judaism. Elizabeth hasn't coaxed Arthur into abandoning a religious commitment; no such commitment existed. To borrow Rabbi Harold Schulweis's wonderfully expressive term, Arthur and Elizabeth are an "interfaithless" couple, two people who bring to their marriage a mutual alienation from their disparate religious traditions and together create a spiritual void all their own.

The Island Within is unquestionably melodramatic and dated, yet it offers a take on interfaith relationships that persisted throughout the twentieth century and that some in the Jewish community hold to now. For updated variations on its theme, we turn first to a pair of romantic relationships, circa late 1960s and early 1970s, and then to the opinions of a young rabbi today.

Winnie Marks

In Winnie Marks's experience, Arthur's conclusion that Jewish men and gentile women are parallel lines that can never meet was still alive and kicking in the 1960s and 1970s, when she fell in love with not one but two Jewish men.

Winnie, fifty-five, teaches women's, African-American, and labor history at a small liberal arts college in Maine. Raised a Congregationalist on Boston's North Shore, she recalls that, growing up, "The real divisions were between Protestants and Catholics. Jews were there but they were almost invisible."

Her parents had come from middle- and upper-middle-class backgrounds, but their own household was relatively poor. The family moved constantly among the affluent towns north of Boston, where Winnie's father, a disabled World War II veteran with a passion for racial equality, taught in the public schools. Winnie's father died when she was twelve, but his values had a profound effect on the person she would become. For the six years after his death, Winnie watched her mother struggle to support her two children as a single wage earner. She died when Winnie was eighteen, leaving Winnie and her younger brother in the care of wealthy relatives, and very much alone.

Soon after her mother's death, Winnie entered the freshman class at a large Boston university. It was the mid-1960s, and political activism was heating up. Winnie studied with Jewish professors who had been "blackballed by the Ivy Leagues. All the Jews I knew had a strong commitment to social justice. The people that I admired on campus and off ended up being Jewish." One professor and his wife informally adopted Winnie, initiating what would become a lifelong experience for her of the kindness of Jewish strangers. As she met more Jews, she also discovered that these were people with whom she could share something important: thanks to World War II, many had lost family members.

"Everybody I knew who was not Jewish, except my brother and me, thought the world was a great place. We knew it was essentially unsafe."

Winnie got involved with the student senate, and it was there that she met Russ, the first love of her life. Russ was working-class, ambitious, industrious, and funny. Unlike most of the boys Winnie had known, he was able to talk about his feelings, a quality she later came to see as common among Jewish men. She recalls that he also had a kind of worldly wisdom that attracted her. "I had this kind of fatalism because of my parents' deaths that resonated with the Jewish world and with Jewish humor. When I met Russ, I thought, *Oh, people understand how I look at the world!*" Russ, Winnie says, taught her a lot about anti-Semitism. "He really educated me about what it meant for him to be Jewish."

Russ took Winnie's Jewish education to a new level when he brought her home with him.

His family lived in a small apartment in Boston that for Winnie was very reminiscent of the homes she had shared with her parents. But there the familiarity ended. "Normally I would have offered to help with the food. But here I didn't know the food at all." Not only were the dishes strange, but in Russ's secular home some, but not all, Jewish dietary laws were observed. "They wouldn't eat milk and meat together, but everyone ate shrimp!"

Russ's parents asked about her family and were sympathetic when they learned that both her parents had died. Russ's grandmother was also present, and it was she who inadvertently provided Winnie's most striking memory of the dinner. "At one point," Winnie recalls, "she reached to hand me a dish. Her sleeve moved up her arm, and I saw the numbers tattooed there. I froze. Everything clicked: the stories my father had told me, the book of photographs of concentration camp prisoners we'd had at home, Hitler, discrimination. It just kind of jolted me. It made everything real."

The gulf between Winnie and Russ's family was also real, at least in their minds. Winnie was fond of Russ's father, but with his mother there was never a point of contact. "She felt that I wasn't a Jewish daughter, that we didn't have much in common. Not that I was an enemy, but if Russ and I got married, there would be the children thing, the conversion thing."

For the year and a half they were together, Russ and Winnie did seem to be moving toward marriage. But for Russ as well as his mother, the differences between them were too great. "You're such a WASP [white Anglo-Saxon Protestant]," he would tell her whenever they disagreed. With her blue eyes and very long blond hair, Winnie looked the part. When Russ saw her in the context of her wealthy aunt's home, "He saw me as a classic WASP, even though I was so atypical, except physically." Though she didn't have money, Winnie had grown up surrounded by it, and by upper-crust etiquette. "Russ didn't understand a lot of subtleties of manners," Winnie recalls. Because he had political ambitions, she tried to smooth his rough edges. Not surprisingly, Russ didn't appreciate the help. "He'd say, 'This is such WASP shit.' He attributed it to ethnicity, but much later, I attributed it to class." While Winnie saw herself as trying to help Russ's career, he seems to have perceived her advice as an effort to whitewash his Jewishness. They broke up.

Eventually Winnie fell in love with another man. Avi was a professor thirteen years her senior, a prominent man on campus, active in the American Civil Liberties Union and in a variety of liberal political causes. He and Winnie saw each other from the middle of her junior year through her graduation from college, and lived together for a year after. "The Jewish education Russ started," Winnie says, "Avi finished."

Avi introduced Winnie to his native New York Jewish culture. Though she loved this milieu, her looks seemed to mark her an outsider. She recalls an archetypal encounter in a kosher restaurant. "The waiter approached the table and said something to Avi in Yiddish, and I caught the world 'shiksa.' Then I ordered a roast beef sandwich and milk," two things that could not both be served by a kosher establishment. "He told Avi something in Yiddish to the effect that, 'If you're going to hang out with a shiksa this is what you're going to get.'"

Avi's parents had emigrated from Russia as young people in the 1920s. While keeping religion at arm's length, they strongly identified culturally as Jews. As with Russ's family, Winnie was unable to form a relationship with them, and met with particular disapproval from Avi's mother, whom she recalls as a woman with an almost overwhelming, outsized capacity for love and a very important place in her son's emotional life. Eager to please his parents, Avi urged Winnie to convert to Judaism. "I talked with a rabbi and started classes, but I realized I just didn't believe in God." When she spoke to Avi about her problem, he responded, "Who believes in God? You're just supposed to convert!"

The relationship could go no further, and it soon ended. "I think he was really ambivalent," Winnie muses now. "He didn't want to marry a Jewish woman because it reminded him of his mother, of this total, engulfing passion. But there was a level at which he felt safer with that kind of love."

Winnie believes that ultimately neither Russ nor Avi could cope with their mothers' feelings about her. Having grown up within the close circle of their Jewish families, both men had already taken a step outside by becoming the first generation to be college educated. Winnie speculates that a second step was more than either cared to take. "I think when I showed up I was a symbol of them being taken away."

Unintentionally and unwittingly, Winnie played the gentile siren, threatening to lure a Jewish man—or two—to the precipice of his community. To maintain the relationship and reject that role, her only option was to go through the motions of a religious conversion that would not have been genuine for her. Such a conversion would have supported the suspicion we encountered in Sharon Bascom's story, that a gentile woman's interest in Judaism is bound to be a fraud, and that even one who wishes to convert will dilute a Jewish family. It's also possible that Winnie was caught in a double bind from which a sincere conversion couldn't free her. If either of these men were attracted to her because of her foreign, forbidden flavor, they may have needed her to *stay* foreign for the attraction to survive.

Despite her experiences, Winnie expresses no bitterness toward the Jewish world. She says she's grown comfortable with Jews seeing her as an outsider, and also assuming, as a Boston-area native, that she is Catholic—"All goyim are the same," she says with a laugh. Feeling like an outsider to her own culture, outsiderness itself is something she has made peace with. Nearly all the significant relationships she's had since Russ and Avi have been with Jews, but these days, her romantic partners are women. In the eyes of their Jewish families, she reports, "The lesbian issue supersedes my not being Jewish." Within the relationships, there have been "differences around food, holidays, around political sensibility in the most general way, of what is the social contract, how do you relate to your society." With one of her women lovers, the fact that she was not Jewish posed more of a problem, one reminiscent of her experience with Avi: Winnie felt that the love she offered could never measure up to the love of a Jewish mother. "She had the association that being loved by a Jewish woman— that was real love."

Winnie is now sharing her life with a woman who, though Jewish by birth, had no Jewish education and knew little about Jewish customs and holiday celebrations when they got together. In an ironic twist, it is Winnie, whose relationships with Russ and Avi couldn't withstand her indelible Otherness, who is now introducing Jewish observance into her and her partner's home. One way or another, Winnie says, "When you're with someone who's Jewish, it's always part of the conversation."

———

According to Jewish professionals, secular and religious, who work with intermarried couples, the conversation between many Jewish and gentile partners grapples richly and actively with questions of belief and faith, ethnic loyalty, personal and collective history. An interfaith couple can take nothing for granted, as many find to their chagrin. But at its best, the relationship may demand that both partners define amorphous identities, make up their minds about what they believe and the values they hold most dear—and commit to living by them.

That's a best-case scenario. What happens when the conversation is strained, freighted with half-spoken resentments and fears? What if there is no real conversation at all? Rather than a fruitful interchange, some Jewish leaders see nothing but deep disconnect in interfaith unions, an unalterable alienation between the two people involved that spreads outward, separating the Jewish partner from his Jewishness.

"Gentlemen, if you want to ensure Jewish kids and a Jewish life, if you want Judaism . . . to be a 'big part' of your lives, date Jewish women."

So writes Rabbi Toby Manewith, concluding an opinion piece penned in the spring of 2002 in response to White House Spokesman Ari Fleischer's engagement to a non-Jewish woman. The piece, "There Goes Another One: A Single Jewish Woman Laments the Loss of an Eligible Jewish Bachelor," appeared in *Washington Jewish Week* and was then syndicated in Jewish newspapers across the country, a clear sign that Manewith had touched a nerve.

Marrying out, Manewith says in conversation, may not be the result of a decision to "opt out" of the Jewish world, "but it's not opting in." Manewith, a Reform rabbi, is senior director of Jewish education for George Washington University's branch of Hillel, an organization for Jewish college students. When a Jew chooses to marry another Jew, it is a "subconscious or in many cases conscious way of opting in to the Jewish community," she maintains, though her view is contradicted by the lack of Jewish affiliation or involvement among a majority of American Jews, in-married or not. A person who marries out, Manewith adds, may think his Judaism isn't all that important to him. If he changes his mind later on, she believes it will be much harder to ask a non-Jewish partner to go along with a possible change in lifestyle.

In "There Goes Another One," Manewith laments Fleischer's marriage with a light touch that doesn't belie her seriousness. Conjuring an image reminiscent of Elizabeth and Arthur Levy, she anticipates a cultural disconnect between Fleischer and his bride, symbolized by their inability to share Jewish holiday recollections from childhood or to respond in kind to ethnic references. But Manewith makes no pretense of disinterest, either in print or conversation. Describing herself as a single woman in her midthirties, she is candid about feeling slighted by what she sees as a tendency for Jewish men to gravitate toward non-Jewish women. "It just saddens me a little bit to see yet another nice Jewish guy pick a non-Jewish mate," she writes. "What is a single Jewish woman to do?"

> I assume that Jewish mothers all over the country with single daughters in Washington shared my mother's disappointment. . . . [M]y father would reply, when given the opportunity, "A (insert pejorative Yiddish word for a non-Jewish woman here)?!?" And though it would never enter my lexicon, I understand the sentiment that such a word carries . . . that the woman is not Jewish is not a part of the story, to my father, to my parents, it is the story. The truth is, I share their, well, "disappointment" is not exactly the right word.

Disappointment may not be the right word for Manewith's reaction to Fleischer's intermarriage, but both she and her father understand that "shiksa," printed or not, *is* on target for their feelings toward his bride. Asked to describe "the sentiment that such a word carries," Manewith sums it up as frustration. "I don't agree with the word, I wouldn't use the word. But to me, being single, Jewish, educated, funny—I'm thinking, 'What, am I not good enough?' My father is thinking, 'What, my daughter is not good enough?'"

Manewith doesn't charge gentile women with kidnapping Jewish men. Nor does she blame Jewish men who choose to marry out, hypothesizing that the fault—there must be one—lies in an inadequate Jewish education. "Maybe I just don't want to be as cynical as to say Jewish men are attracted to Asian women—I pick Asian women at random—because of their feeling that Jewish women are any number of stereotypes."

Why do Jewish men marry out? Rabbi Edwin Friedman, a therapist whose work brought him into contact with thousands of interfaith couples, reported in 1982 that, "Over and over, I found that the Jewish partners who came from a family with a strong cultural tie felt intensely Jewish despite their decision to marry a non-Jew. *In their own minds, one seemed to have nothing to do with the other.*"

Ask the experts—Jewish counselors and demographers—today and they will probably say that intermarriage is a simple fact of modern life. Rabbi Steven Mason, a therapist who specializes in interfaith issues in the Hartford, Connecticut, area, says, "In the world we live in, intermarriage is going to happen. If you want to turn back the clock two hundred years, go back into the ghetto and lock the doors, okay. But you can't have it both ways."

New York cross-cultural psychologist Esther Perel seconds his view. "In the past you would have Jewish men and women not wanting to be with each other, but that's not as much the case anymore. More often it's just that Jews value the openness of American society. The American model is an individualistic model. The Jewish model is community, and these values clash."

While professionals speak of intermarriage as an equal-opportunity choice for Jewish men and women, popular wisdom continues to hold to the view that marrying out is first and foremost a Jewish man's game, and one in which he plays out his feelings toward Jewish and gentile women.

"Why do people keep on believing this?" muses Egon Mayer, the demographer. Mayer says Jews marry out because they can. "There isn't a lot that we can do to prevent it. The paterfamilias of today, of which I guess I'm one, are much more liberal. When I first got married, I was extremely careful to pick someone acceptable because I knew that otherwise there would be hell to pay." Mayer says that the effects of intermarriage on Jewish continuity concern him. "Am I concerned enough to try to block marriages, to prevent certain kinds of families? Absolutely not. When a lot of people say they are concerned, it's implicit that there's something that we should do about it. There's a lot that the Jewish community could do to be more welcoming, particularly to non Jewish women who have the experience of not being welcomed."

Like most Jewish population researchers, Mayer reports that intermarriage today is as apt to involve a Jewish woman as a Jewish man. The gender differences turn up when it comes to the likelihood that a non-Jewish spouse will choose some measure of Jewish affiliation. Among gentiles marrying Jews, some 5 percent of men and 12 to 15 percent of women will at some point convert to Judaism, while a Jewish Outreach Institute survey found non-Jewish women twice as likely as non-Jewish men to be interested in Jewish outreach programs.

But Mayer parts company from other demographers in doubting that Jewish men were *ever* more likely to marry out than Jewish women. According to Mayer, men are considered the prime instigators of intermarriage simply because outmarrying Jewish women once disappeared into their husband's Christian surnames, and weren't spotted by Jewish community census-takers. "I know the theories, that Jewish women were more controlled by their families, more influenced by them, that Jewish men have unresolved Oedipal complexes that lead them to choose non-Jewish women so as to avoid incest, the theory that they want to avoid the culture of the JAP [Jewish American princess]. The theory that Jewish women marry out because Jewish men have left them behind—that I think is a very peculiar theory. When one enters into courtship one doesn't consider demographics."

Unlike Mayer, Gary Tobin, president of the Institute for Jewish and Community Research in San Francisco, allows for a historical reality that Jewish men were much more likely to marry out than Jewish women until the present generation of marriageable adults. But asked to comment on the conventional belief that Jewish men *prefer* intermarriage, while their sisters are forced into it by default, Tobin explodes. "Bullshit! The men, beasts that they are, are chasing the blond shiksas, and don't appreciate good Jewish women? I think there are some *very* unpleasant stereotypes about Jewish women behind that."

Unpleasant stereotypes about Jewish women are certainly not on Rick Bowers's mind when he describes his own choice to marry outside the fold. When Rick talks about intermarriage, he talks about love.

Rick Bowers

"I married her because I loved her, I love her still," Rick says of Sally, his wife of twenty-eight years. "Maybe there are resentful Jewish women out there, I don't know."

Rick, fifty-two, was a corporate lawyer for many years before he made a career change to work for a non-profit Jewish organization. He is a past president of the thousand-member Reform synagogue in St. Louis, Missouri, where he and Sally attend Shabbat services weekly, and where Sally has also served on various committees. Though Sally was raised Episcopalian and has never converted to Judaism, Rick says that together, they live a Jewish life. His story is a counterargument to Manewith's claim that marrying out of the Jewish community means opting out of the Jewish community. But even Rick says he tried very hard not to marry Sally.

"I remember when I was thirteen years old, I wrote a letter to myself about how I wanted to have a Jewish life and a Jewish family," Rick recalls. His girlfriends had always been Jewish until the spring of his senior year in high school, when he started going out with a girl who had been his friend—Sally. "My parents had a fit," Rick says. "So I was mean to her, and went back to seeing Debbie, who was Jewish." Eventually Rick called Sally and asked her to go out with him again, to which she responded, "What about Debbie?"

The on-again, off-again romance persisted for six years. Rick and Sally would date until Rick gave in to parental pressure to break up with her. He'd comply for a while, then start seeing Sally secretly. Whenever he told his parents he and Sally were back together, they'd have another fit and he'd break off the relationship, only to begin the cycle again. "I asked my mother why I shouldn't keep seeing her while I was in college, and she said, 'You could end up getting married!'" When Rick told his parents that he did want to marry Sally, their response was to say that they wouldn't attend a wedding held in a church. Rick assured them that a church wedding wasn't part of the plan. Then they said they wouldn't attend a wedding on Saturday, the Jewish Sabbath. Again, Rick assured them. Finally they said they supposed they should congratulate him.

Rick says he didn't think about the family he and Sally would create, but that Sally never had any doubt that they would raise their children as Jews. Despite veiled objections from Sally's father, the couple moved to what was considered a Jewish neighborhood in the early years of their marriage; they also joined a Conservative synagogue. Sally wasn't comfortable there, but she began studying Hebrew nevertheless. "She figured that if she was going to be involved, she wanted to know what was going on."

Eventually they switched to the Reform synagogue, where Rick started an interfaith discussion group and spearheaded various campaigns for the greater inclusion of interfaith families and non-Jewish spouses. That these campaigns occasioned controversy in his congregation is something Rick feels he understands well.

"There's a part of being Jewish that is being connected to other Jews, it's a very deep-seated thing. But you can have a strong affinity with people in your own group without having to be negative about people in other groups," he says. "I think Jews have tribalistic attitudes, which partly means that they're very suspicious, they think about people differently if they're not Jewish, and that has a lot of negative consequences for trying to get intermarrieds involved in synagogue life. Jewish leaders may especially have concerns about non-Jewish women because of the roles often played by women in families."

The roles Sally plays in their family include Jewish mother. When their children, Naomi, twenty-four, and Barry, nineteen, were small, Rick and Sally jointly shared the responsibility for getting them to religious school, and attended family education events as a team. They worked together to create a Jewish home through Shabbat and holiday celebrations. Rick says both children have strong Jewish identities, though when he asked Naomi recently about her sense of herself as a Jew, her answer did cause some surprise. "It's not the first thing I think about when I think about myself," Naomi told him. "I think if it was, it would make me feel different from my mother and that's not the way I want to feel." Sally, who doesn't see her daughter's Jewish identification as a barrier between them, felt that she had made a mistake in not communicating this to Naomi more explicitly.

"Sally has always been involved and supportive," of the family's Jewish life, Rick says. "She says role modeling is important, and she has definitely been a role model of living a Jewish life."

Naomi's statement may indicate that there are limits, at least for her, to her mother's ability to model Jewish womanhood. But for Rick, a strong advocate for the full inclusion of non-Jews in Jewish ritual life, there is no contradiction involved in casting Sally as a Jewish role model. Still, subtle differences remain, and even in close families, some things just seem to go unsaid. While Rick handles much of the Jewish holiday cooking and leads Passover seders for his extended family, Sally always makes Shabbat dinner on Friday nights. "But she has never lit the Friday night candles," Rick admits, coming to this realization about an important Jewish women's ritual only as he says it. "First the kids did it, now I do it, or a guest. We've never even discussed it."

Rick is in good company. Assumptions about who does what when Judaism is practiced in an interfaith home are often unspoken within relationships and in the larger Jewish community. Instead, those most concerned about intermarriage predict dim prospects for Jewish practice in a marriage like Rick's, and stop there.

In eighteenth- and nineteenth-century America, the Jewish community discouraged conversion and was extremely unwelcoming to intermarried Jews. A Jew who married out was barred from synagogue membership, and if his wife attempted to convert, she was usually turned down. Yet even in this climate there were interfaith couples who created Jewish homes, raised their children as Jews, and attended religious services in congregations that were hostile to them. If Jewish men could stay committed to Judaism under these conditions, why is there so little expectation today that they will make the choice Rick has made, to take responsibility for the Jewishness of their homes?

Cross-cultural therapist Esther Perel would agree with Rabbi Toby Manewith that many Jewish men have been fed a meager Judaism that leaves them suffering a kind of spiritual scurvy. The difference is that she sees this not as a determining factor in why they enter an interfaith relationship but in how badly they may behave once they are there.

For fifteen years, Perel counseled intercultural and interracial couples in clinical practice and at Jewish centers such as the 92nd Street Y in New York City, also traveling throughout the United States, Canada, and her native Europe to train mental health professionals and lecture to communities. The Jewish men Perel encountered had a tendency to offer a kind of mission impossible to their non-Jewish partners. "The Jewish man has a passive attachment to his Jewish identity, which he experiences mainly as a vulnerability," Perel says. "His Jewish identity is mostly unexamined, and comes to the fore because of his interfaith love." Our hero, explains Perel, tells his non-Jewish partner: "I don't go to synagogue, I'm not religious, but I want you to raise my kids Jewish. You would do well to do away with anything that's yours and join me in mine, but I'm culturally illiterate, I have nothing to offer you except a spiritual desert, and I will not help you in any way." Such a man conveys to his partner that though she must be very careful to accommodate his hypersensitivity about anything touching on his cultural origins, he, threatened and repulsed by her Christianity, won't return the favor.

"This is a stereotypical, extreme version," Perel allows. "But it's also very common and true."

According to Perel, the factors that go into creating these attitudes in Jewish men are complex and varied. Aside from a religious educational system that for most Jews is mediocre at best, she points to the widespread attitude that the intergenerational transmission of Judaism is women's work. She also maintains that "American Jews haven't found a way to articulate their Jewish identities independently from anti-Semitism and the Holocaust. Basically, what these men offer these women is a graveyard Judaism. 'Join me at the Holocaust memorial.'"

The gentile woman involved with the man in Perel's profile looks very different from the self-serving and salacious predator of legend. Perel sees her as lonely, lacking guidance or support in her struggle to fit herself into a Jewish life. Carrying the whole burden for the couple's relationship, she is also the only one afraid that it will end.

Over the past two decades, Perel reports, it's become politically incorrect to demand that people change themselves, and she's watched the emphasis shift from an insistence that a woman convert to Judaism to pressure that she raise her children Jewishly. "When the kids are born, she might be unsure if she wants to go through with it. He'll say, 'But you promised!' Basically, she would always say yes to whatever it took for the relationship to exist."

When she counseled couples like these, Perel says, she considered it part of her job to tell the Jewish man that he should thank his partner for their relationship's existence. Raising his awareness of his arrogance and condescension toward his non-Jewish partner and her Christianity was also on her to-do list, Perel adds, as well as letting the man know that it isn't enough just to say that Judaism is important. "How does she know that you are Jewish?" Perel would ask her clients. "What do you do? If you say you like music, that you like to travel, I'll bet I can see it in your life. If you're asking her to live in Paris, you have to show her Paris."

Some Jewish men, of course, are not asking their gentile partners to live in Paris. Some want to run as far away from it as possible themselves. Others, having spent their lives in its colorless suburban outskirts, feel little impulse to venture any closer. In that situation, more than one gentile woman has been known to head off to Paris on her own.

What happens when a non-Jewish woman confounds expectations and tries to encourage Jewish exploration in her home? We've already noted that a gentile woman who shows an interest in Judaism may simply not be believed. But she can run into trouble even if her sincerity is clear, finding, like Elizabeth Levy with her protest against anti-Semitic slurs, that she has taken on a thankless task. With all the warnings about gentile women luring men away from the fold, it may be hard to believe that the one who causes strife by urging her man *toward* Judaism is also a Jewish staple. There's even a joke about her, one that turns up in many versions, but runs essentially like this:

> A man warns his son against marrying a non-Jewish woman. "A shiksa," the man says, "will cause trouble." The son marries a woman who converts to Judaism before their wedding. The Saturday after the wedding, the father calls the son to find out why he hasn't come to work at the family business. "It's Shabbos," the son explains. "My wife wants us to go to synagogue on Shabbos." To which the father replies, "I told you marrying a shiksa would cause trouble!"

Accused of biasing her husband against his assimilationist roots, Mary Rosenbaum is just that kind of troublemaker.

Mary Rosenbaum

A practicing Catholic, when Mary Rosenbaum married her husband, Ned, in 1963, she thought it was a shame that he knew so little about his Judaism. "I focused him," she says. "I poked at him."

Mary, who asked that she be identified by her real name, is the director of the Dovetail Institute, an on-line clearinghouse for resources supporting interfaith families. She says her husband's family had been secular Jews for six generations, and his parents had never belonged to a synagogue. Growing up, she adds, Ned's mother had been taught that the ideal was to be "a Jew in the house and a man on the street. She was told it was her duty as a Jew to assimilate." It was a big break with family tradition when, as a result of Mary's prodding, Ned began to explore

Jewish practice, and even more shocking when he broke off his graduate work in history to get a doctorate in Near Eastern and religious studies. Mary's influence on these decisions didn't win her any points with his parents. "I was seen, with some justification, as the cause of his Jewish involvement," Mary says with a laugh. "Because I belonged to the benighted religion"—Catholicism—"I had dragged him down."

While it was once the custom for some Jews to observe shivah, that is, ritually mourn a child who married out, it was Ned's embrace of Judaism that caused a rift between himself and his father. Early in his marriage, Ned's father wrote him a letter accusing him of betraying the family's values. "A Christmas tree was good enough for your grandfather," Ned's father told him.

Yet despite their high degree of assimilation, Ned's family still identified themselves as Jews, and Mary as an outsider—a possible source of anti-Semitic attack and at the same time an inferior. While Ned's grandmother warned him that Mary would hold his ethnic makeup against him in a fight, other family members expressed their distaste for Catholics. "I was referred to jokingly as the shiksa, especially if I was washing the dishes," Mary recalls.

None of this stopped Mary and Ned from choosing their own path. In the small Jewish community of Carlisle, Pennsylvania, where they lived for many years, Ned led services in the absence of a rabbi. While continuing to practice Catholicism, Mary initiated the Shabbat observances of lighting candles on Friday evenings in their home, and baking challah, the traditional braided loaves of bread. When she noticed that Ned had grown uncomfortable eating pork, she suggested that they keep a kosher kitchen, a commitment she's maintained for thirty years.

In the early days of their marriage, people thought that Ned might convert to Christianity, simply because of its cultural dominance. Later, when they lived in Israel for a time, Mary says she felt pressured to convert to Judaism, "that the woman should go along with the man." In fact, neither ever considered converting to the other's faith. They educated their three children in both Catholicism and Judaism, and now support their daughter's decision to be Jewish as well as their sons' choices not to affiliate with any organized religion. Ned occasionally accompanies Mary to church as a show of solidarity, she says, knowing he really isn't happy there. While considering herself "for better or worse a Catholic," Mary has always felt much more comfortable as an active participant in Ned's religious life, and continues to attend services with him at the Conservative synagogue he's joined near their new home in Austin, Kentucky.

"It's easier to be a Christian married to a Jew than a Jew married to a Christian," she says, "first and foremost for theological reasons. At a Jewish service I never hear a word I can't say amen to. I have a strong sense of the historical rootedness in Judaism of Christianity." Still, she doesn't say amen, or anything else, when prayers that evoke the people's special covenant with God are chanted. "I don't have a right to say that in a Jewish context."

Mary has learned, sometimes the hard way, not to assume that others will be as comfortable with her presence in a Jewish milieu as she is. In fact, she has often been made to feel entirely unwelcome. She recalls a party she and Ned attended soon after they moved to Carlisle, where all the other guests were Jewish. "We knew our hosts very slightly and no one else. When we came in, there was a discussion of intermarriage going on, and we joined in. Someone referred in outraged disbelief to a professor who had married a Catholic. I said, 'That's me.' Everyone was very upset."

More recently, Mary and Ned alternated teaching a class on Jewish literature at a nursing home. The class went well until Ned mentioned in one of his sessions that Mary wasn't Jewish. When it was her turn to teach, Mary found that her previously enthusiastic students had turned condescending, and insisted on explaining the material to her. One went so far as to lodge a complaint against her, saying she had come among them under false pretenses.

"After a couple of experiences like that I try to make it clear that I'm not Jewish, but it's a tricky point. I don't want to distance myself. Sometimes I'm not sure how much is in my head."

Demographer Egon Mayer might offer Mary a kind of cold comfort: the reasons to feel unwanted aren't all in her head. "Based on a lot of research over the past twenty-five years," Mayer says, "non-Jewish women usually feel very poorly received in the Jewish community, with some justification—they're not dreaming!"

Mayer points out that gentile women are much more likely than gentile men to put themselves on the line in the Jewish world, by having greater contact with in-laws and institutions such as Jewish schools and camps. Ironically, their willingness to enter a Jewish orbit, and bring their families into it, lays them open to a hostility that someone keeping the community at arm's length doesn't face.

In Mary's case, the fact that Judaism plays such a large role in her marriage is partly her own doing, and is not without cost to herself. She can't help but feel a little wistful sometimes, watching the large, happy Catholic families at her church, unified in their religious involvement. But she doesn't regret her choices. "I think the gifts outweigh the drawbacks," she comments.

There are many stories about non-Jewish women championing Judaism in their partners' lives. Dru Greenwood, Director of Outreach for the Reform movement actually makes the implausible claim that she has *never* heard any negative attitudes toward non-Jewish women expressed. Those attitudes may be out there, she says. "But there is also the attitude that non-Jewish women are bringing Jewish men in."

For someone like Mary, this is encouraging anecdotal evidence. But if the available statistics are to be believed, most intermarried couples are staying well away from Jewish involvement of any kind. Are gentile wives causing that disconnect, or simply doing nothing to repair it? Given Ned's ignorance of Judaism, if Mary had entered her marriage with a Catholic agenda, she would have found it fertile ground for a religious takeover. As a matter of course she could have set her Christian practices and beliefs in motion in their home, and Ned—with, or more likely without formal conversion—might simply have been swept along with them. And if she had done these things out of true religious fervor, coupled by an active enmity toward Judaism, she would only have been fulfilling Jewish expectations of several thousand years. In fact, she would have taken a place in a well-established lineage headed by one of the most notorious gentile women of all time.

Jezebel

While Lilith may be the prototype of the gentile woman who offers illicit sex and death in one tidy package, Jezebel represents the ultimate threat of assimilation through intermarriage.

Jezebel, whose story appears in I Kings, is the daughter of Ethbaal, king of Tyre and the Sidonians. In a strategic move meant to strengthen the Israelites' position in relation to their neighbors, she is married off to Ahab, king of Israel a few generations after Solomon.

By the time Ahab assumes the throne and marries Jezebel, the Israelites' ties to their faith have grown lax. Many have assimilated, adopting the pagan practices that had been gaining ground in the Jewish community ever since the days of Solomon and his seven hundred idolatrous wives. Ahab's kingdom is ripe for Jezebel, who brings with her a fanatical devotion to Baal and other Phoenician gods and goddesses, and a taste for such rites as infant sacrifice. Under her influence, Ahab builds a pagan temple and entertains the prophets of Baal at his table. Jewish prophets don't fare so well. Jezebel has them persecuted and slaughtered, earning herself the wrath of the prophet Elijah, who declares that his nemesis will one day be devoured by dogs. Elijah's prophecy is fulfilled eight years after Ahab's death, when Jezebel is thrown to the ground from an upper-story window of the palace, trampled to death by horses and makes a tasty snack for a pack of dogs who find only her skull, hands and feet un-palatable.

Whereas Lilith's extramarital enticements spell disaster for the men who succumb to them, and for their legitimate families, Jezebel poses another sort of menace altogether. By all appear-ances, she and Ahab make a fine team. Ahab isn't seduced by Jezebel; he marries her because it furthers his political interests to do so, and he seems happy enough to support her religious practices in ways that conflict—or should conflict—with his own. Jezebel, in turn, looks after her husband's concerns. In an incident that seems emblematic of their marriage, when Ahab lusts after another man's vineyard, Jezebel gets it for him by hav-ing the man stoned to death for a blasphemy he didn't commit.

In the end, Ahab and their eldest son are killed in battle, and Jezebel dies nastily. But much more is at stake here than the destruction of a single family. Already in the habit of neglecting their own tradition for the idol worship of their neighbors, the Israelites put up little resistance to religious incursion. Ahab's ambitious marriage to Jezebel places her in a position to annihi-late Judaism itself, along with those who cling to it.

Today, a lone gentile woman isn't likely to decimate the Jew-ish religion and its entire people, but the Judaism of her hus-band and his particular line, Jewish leaders say, is another story. Not long ago, it was understood that a Jewish man might en-hance his educational, professional and economic achievements with a gentile wife who offered social mobility. From the point of view of his family and community he might be acquiring the world at the cost of his Jewish soul, but he was more concerned about his standing in a wider sphere, where a Christian wife would be an asset. The early American Jewish population included many more single Jewish men than women, yet within the community it was believed that Jewish men married non-Jewish women more often out of preference than necessity. As the immigrant population increased, anti-Semitism rose with it, and the attractions of Old Country brides weren't obvious to career- and status-conscious young men.

The twin notions of Jewish women as guardians of the shtetl and gentile women as passports out of it persisted long past the era of Jewish immigration. Robert Gordis, in his 1978 book, *Love and Sex: A Modern Jewish Approach,* assumes that the desire to assimilate is a common motivator in choosing a spouse from outside the fold. "Jewish self-hatred," he writes, "exists in modern society as a reflex of age-old anti-Jewish prejudices in the non-Jewish majority. It supplies a powerful drive toward intermarriage."

According to cultural historian Sander Gilman, this self-hatred is a natural outgrowth of the way Jewish men were "feminized," characterized as weak and infirm in Western—particularly European—thought for centuries. But if they were unmanned by anti-Semitism and by the lifestyle of the pallid, ethereal scholar considered the masculine ideal among some Eastern European Jews and their descendants, Jewish men could assert their virility through the conquest of a gentile woman. In this American cliché, the helpless and none-too-savvy victim of Lilith and her sisters is transformed into a successful New World man. Oddly reminiscent of the mystic's view of Lilith as a spiritual ladder, the non-Jewish woman becomes one of the rungs on his climb to the (in this case, material) top, or, alternately, the trophy he awards himself for getting there. Traditionally described as sexy and devious, in this version, she is sexy and dumb. In both guises, she dilutes Judaism and weakens the Jewish people.

These days, Jews are solidly ensconced in mainstream culture, and it has to be assumed that few Jewish men feel a conscious necessity to use intermarriage for the purposes of assimilation. Yet if popular culture is to be believed, Jewish men still have gentile women on their minds, along with a host of ideas about their potential for sexual adventure and escape from ethnic ties. A little later we'll look at cinematic images of gentile women. Right now let's hear what Philip Roth and one of his dissenters have to say.

Philip Roth and The Shiksa

Non-Jewish women are central to Philip Roth's fiction. If they hadn't existed, he would have had to invent them.

The 1967 novel *Portnoy's Complaint* introduced Alexander Portnoy, prototype of the self-hating, sexually and emotionally dysfunctional Jewish man who spends much of the novel cataloging a chorus line of gentile conquests: stupid southerners, debutantes, WASP protohippies. Plagued by desire for non-Jewish women, he's convinced that they are equally enamored of him.

> Who knew that the secret to a *shikse's* heart (and box) was not to pretend to be some hook-nosed variety of *goy*, as boring and vacuous as her own brother, but to be what one's uncle was, to be what one's father was, to be whatever one was oneself . . . as far as a certain school of *shikse* is concerned . . . [her] knight turns out to be none other than a brainy, balding, beaky Jew. . . .

As this passage suggests, it isn't really women that Roth is obsessed with but men, and Roth's men are obsessed with themselves. No woman in a Roth novel could ever be confused with a three-dimensional figure who might walk off the page into real life. For Roth, women aren't women but the bats in his protagonists' belfries, the stimuli for their psychosexual twitches. For Alexander Portnoy, their bodies aren't even bodies. They're a battleground on which to play out rage and revenge against Protestant America. As he tells it, "I don't seem to stick my dick up these girls, as much as I stick it up their backgrounds—as though through fucking I will discover America. *Conquer* America—maybe that's more like it."

Later books refine this crude formulation, but Roth's men continue to romance and demean beautiful, vapid gentile women so insubstantial they may not really be there at all. In the narrative mosaic of *The Counterlife* (1986), brothers Nathan and Henry Zuckerman bleed into each other's lives from one chapter to the next, swapping a faulty heart, medically enforced abstinence, and a relationship of sorts with the sometimes Swiss, sometimes British, but always gentile Maria. Tall and beautiful, self-disparaging, pliant and accommodating to her men, Maria would seem to be the perfect gentile woman. But in most of their permutations, Nathan/Henry's brittle heart turns sex with Maria into a lethal proposition.

Like Elizabeth Levy in *The Island Within*, Maria displays Jewish solidarity, here by championing Israel at a gentile dinner party; once again, the act only serves to demonstrate the character's essential alienation from her Jewish lover. In her British incarnation, Maria tells Nathan she likes living in a "Jewish city," that is, New York, but complains of Jewish oversensitivity to perceived anti-Semitism. In her Swiss guise, she phones Henry after they've broken up to tell him that Christmas is helping her get over him, and asks if the season is cheering him as well: after a torrid affair in which he considered throwing over his life for her, Maria doesn't even know that Henry doesn't celebrate Christmas. In the end, Nathan, echoing Lewisohn's Arthur Levy, realizes that whether he and Maria are characters or real people, the gulf between them is simply too vast to bridge.

Jewish men and gentile women are still drawn together by a fatal attraction in *American Pastoral* (1997), a novel that makes the bizarrely retro—and, if taken seriously, deeply disturbing—

suggestion that the inescapable racial incompatibility of these couples will play out disastrously in the children they create.

Swede Levov is a well-to-do businessman for whom trophy bride Dawn is simply one of the dividends of talent and hard work. Dawn, erstwhile Miss New Jersey 1949, is the plastic bride atop Swede's cake, but unfortunately the cake is scorched by daughter Meredith, an anti-Vietnam war activist in hiding since she blew up a post office and general store, killing a doctor who was mailing a letter there.

Swede's brother refers to Dawn as "post-Catholic" and to Swede as "post-Jewish," and when their mother asks whether Dawn will convert before their child is born, he tells her that Swede is "a man to whom practicing Judaism means nothing, Mother, don't ask his wife to convert." But her postreligious lineage doesn't save Meredith from the scourge of "mixed" parentage. Like the demon offspring Lilith creates with unwitting Jewish men, Meredith is a monster, the product of an almost-perfect, loving Jewish father and a beautiful gentile mother who hates her ugly Jewish child. A coconspirator of Meredith's delights in tormenting the warm-hearted Swede:

> "She hated her because she's your daughter. It's all fine and well for Miss New Jersey to marry a Jew. But to raise a Jew? That's a whole other bag of tricks. You have a shiksa wife, Swede, but you didn't get a shiksa daughter. Miss New Jersey is a bitch, Swede. Merry would have been better off sucking the cows if she wanted a little milk and nurturance. At least the cows have maternal feelings."

The novel doesn't actually bear out this portrayal of Dawn, but so what? As with all Roth's gentile women, Dawn doesn't speak for herself. We see her through others' eyes, and she's whatever anyone else says she is. Here, she's the unnatural mother of a freakish child.

Roth's men can't find happiness with gentile women, and

can't seem to leave them alone. In 1987 Barbara Bartlett published a tongue-in-cheek potboiler suggesting that there were gentile women trapped by a similar lamentable addiction to Jewish men. *The Shiksa,* billed as the story of a "gently bred" Catholic woman "who can only love a Jewish man," claims that it "reveals the plight of the shiksa everywhere: alien in her own world, prey to an enchantment she'll never escape." Turning the tables on Jewish lore, it is the Jewish male in these interfaith liaisons who becomes a Lilith-like enigma, a "demon *meshuggah* lover."

In a prologue addressed to Alexander Portnoy, these women who love Jewish men too much are described as masochists whose painful pleasure is to personally make up for two thousand years of Jewish suffering. Protagonist Katherine Winterhaus does her best to bear out the claim that a non-Jewish woman would have to hate herself to love a Jewish man. In true pulp-novel style, Katherine spurns the advances of a "decent, attractive, virile young man who was absolutely right for her" to throw herself away on a series of inappropriate Jewish men who can't satisfy her in bed or out of it. Misogynists and sexual zeroes, Katherine's Jewish men are coldly critical and never shirk from hurting women. At the same time, they are supposedly interested in women's feelings in a way that gentile men would never be, and that gentile women find irresistible, to their doom.

The non-Jews in Katherine's life try to rescue her, to no avail. "The women will *never* accept you," cautions an ex-boyfriend, while from a friend who shares her disease Katherine learns that Jewish men make good husbands to Jewish wives, but don't treat gentile women well. Caught in the grip of her illness, Katherine can't heed these warnings, any more than she can stop including herself in what she refers to as Jewish men's "string of ultimately unsatisfying Gentile girlfriends."

There isn't much chance a man will be satisfied, Katherine tells herself, if he can't stop feeling like an outsider to his own success. "Was there enough money or fame or love in the world," she wonders about an eminent lover, "to compensate for the rejections of childhood? . . . By the age of thirty he'd gained enough celebrity to land him on the cover of *Time,* but not enough to make him forget the ghetto."

But if Katherine's lovers think of themselves as strangers in her Christian world, they aren't alone in that view. To Katherine they are shape-shifters, concealing their Jewishness to assume the guise of more or less normal—i.e., Christian—men, only to reveal their true selves at unexpected moments. On one occasion Katherine catches a Jewish boyfriend in the act of reading Psalms. Presumably the relentless stream of anti-Semitic one-liners that describe Katherine's reaction are intended to be comic. "It was as if she were seeing him for the first time; he appeared before her unmasked, unalterably Jewish. His nose grew larger as she stared at it." That Katherine's repulsion is in fact inspired not by genetics but religion is underscored when she goes home with this boy, and spots the mezuzah, the ornamental case containing a prayer scroll, on the doorpost of his house. "All that was alien, forbidden about Neil was exemplified at that moment by the religious symbol."

Intending to talk back to Philip Roth and for the long line of non-Jewish debs, babes and bimbos who make their mostly mute, hapless way through his fiction, *The Shiksa* ultimately confirms some of Roth's—and the Jewish community's—worst fears about gentile women. Following the promptings of an agenda all her own, such a woman pursues Jewish men she can't hope to satisfy. Emotionally deficient, a mental lightweight, she is unable to comprehend, much less offer support for, a Jewish man's struggle to come to terms with his historical and religious inheritance. She is a person to whom the very idea of the Jewish people is inimical, and the man she loves, or at any rate wants to possess, is secretly someone she finds just a little bit repulsive. Biblical wisdom, Ludwig Lewisohn, Ned Rosenbaum's grandmother, and *The Shiksa* are in accord: at heart, this woman is an anti-Semite.

Antiquated? Absurd? Sharon Bascom, Winnie Marks, Rick Bowers, and Mary Rosenbaum might well say so, and in light of their examples, this profile of non-Jewish women becomes a paranoid fantasy, deeply offensive to those it describes. But to paraphrase a cliché, just because you are paranoid doesn't mean no one's an anti-Semite. The people who have shared their experiences thus far are important parts of the story. Now we're going to complicate that story by hearing from Valerie Paulsen.

Valerie Paulsen

Valerie Paulsen, thirty-one, lives in a small town in Indiana where her life is organized around two central contradictions. She is an obstetrician who says she doesn't like children, and the wife of a Jewish man who says she doesn't like Jews.

The first contradiction is relatively simple. Valerie enjoys interacting with children in the circumscribed setting of a doctor's office, but doesn't want any of her own to come home to at night. The second is a bit more involved.

A nonpracticing Protestant, Valerie grew up in a family in which religion wasn't considered very important. But her father, a retired high school shop teacher whom she describes as a "spare the rod, spoil the child" kind of guy, seems to hold strong opinions on just about everything else—particularly Jews. "The school my father worked at was about thirty percent Jewish," Valerie recalls. "Most of the phone calls from parents that he received were from Jewish parents complaining that their son didn't get an A. The students who complained the most about getting their hands greasy in his auto mechanics class or stained in his woodworking classes were Jewish. The Jewish teachers at his building were allowed to take off work for High Holidays, but the Catholic teachers couldn't take off Good Friday unless they did it without pay. As a result, Dad believes the Jewish people are a greedy, arrogant, lazy group of people and has little use for them."

Having sent his daughter off to college with explicit instructions not to bring home "a Jew, a foreigner, or a black man," Valerie says his feelings about Jews are evident in his treatment of her husband. "He's offended that Jed is Jewish. I believe he feels as if the Jews have taken one more thing from him since my wedding day." The surprising thing about this is that Valerie doesn't hold it against him.

Valerie and Jed have been married for three years. They met while both were at medical school, before Jed dropped out to become a computer technician. As students, they were on the rifle team together and shared a preference for shopping at Wal-Mart and watching John Wayne and Clint Eastwood movies. "If you leave the religions out, Jed and I have a lot in common," Valerie comments. Valerie was happy to leave religion out, and for the first five years they were together, she knew nothing about Jed's Judaism except that it meant she had to keep their relationship a secret from her parents.

Lying about each other was another thing she and Jed had in common. But while it still pains Valerie to remember the years of deceiving her parents, she feels that it couldn't have been that hard for Jed to lie to his because he rarely saw them. "Jed's family's idea of a close relationship is not what I call a close family," Valerie says. Jed was raised in a kosher home with regular synagogue attendance and a policy of not attending interfaith weddings. For his parents, their son's wedding was no exception.

When Valerie and Jed told their parents that they were getting married, both sides reacted as expected. Valerie's mother cried, her father raged. But it's her in-laws' response that is burned into Valerie's memory. Jed's mother told her that she had nothing against her but the fact that she wasn't Jewish, implying that there was no way Valerie could understand her feelings. When Jed's parents asked how they would raise their children, and Jed told them they would be raised as Jews, his father called him an idiot and a fool, yelled that Jed was a disgrace to the family and threatened to cut him off financially.

"I was appalled that people would speak to their own flesh and blood in such a vicious manner," says Valerie. "I've heard my father describe my husband in words nearly identical to Jed's father, but Jed isn't my father's flesh and blood. That was the night that I realized that my in-laws were very different people, perhaps even mentally unstable people, and their opinion was not something I was going to need. I've tried very hard to examine my husband's mental state many times since. We've argued long and hard, but I've never seen him turn on me like a rabid dog. Sometimes I worry, though. After all, those are his parents and we often turn out like our parents."

With regard to her feelings about Judaism and Jews, Valerie has certainly turned out like hers. In one sense, Valerie's father couldn't have asked for a better Jewish family for his daughter to marry into; Jed's folks make it easy for Valerie to believe her father was right about Jews all along.

For their part, Jed's family views Valerie as part of a disturbing trend. Jed dropped out of medical school, then he married a non-Jewish woman, "throwing away his heritage, his religion, and his family," as one of his sisters told him. At Jed's mother's insistence, Valerie and Jed had one meeting with a rabbi before their wedding. For Valerie the chief benefit of this encounter was that the rabbi, who she thought was nice, offered explanations for Jed's parents' behavior. "He explained that they looked at me as a member of the KKK. He said that at the current rate of intermarriage and birth, in a relatively short time there would be no more Jews, and that this was probably at the root of my in-laws' behavior. When I look at his parents in this light, I can't excuse them, but I can understand them."

But in the three years that Jed and Valerie have been married, things haven't improved much. When they see his family, which is rare, Jed's mother makes social pleasantries, while his father and sisters ignore her. Almost as infuriating was the single overture made by Jed's brother-in-law, who told Valerie that it didn't bother him that she wasn't Jewish, but it bothered his wife and she was the one he had to live with. "I don't think he realizes that being Christian is a good thing, not something to be pitied." The only family member Valerie is on cordial terms with is Jed's grandfather, who, she says, treats her like a person. "He has never told me I was the ruination of his family. He is the only one of my in-laws to ever have told me I was doing anything right. I respect him."

In their life together, Jed's Judaism remains in flux. He goes to synagogue only on the High Holy Days, driving an hour to reach the nearest congregation, or three times as long to attend with his family. He keeps kosher during Passover but at no other time of year. Some days, Valerie says, he feels the need to buttonhole anyone he meets and talk about being Jewish. "He was raised to take great pride in his differentness from other people. I tease him that when we first met his standard greeting was to say, 'Hi, my name's Jed and I'm Jewish.'"

Valerie is happy to report that these days Jed is more relaxed. "He's a regular person. People don't realize he's Jewish until they've been around him a while. I realize that this sounds as if he's ashamed of his religion, and believe me that is not so. I think he has matured to the point that his identity is no longer based on how 'Jewish' he is." It's hard not to hear this statement as a textbook description of the effects of intermarriage on a Jewish man. The longer Jed is married to Valerie, the less publicly and socially Jewish he becomes, and the deeper underground his Jewish identity sinks.

Valerie's distaste for her husband's religion isn't based entirely upon ignorance. She has read a book about Judaism, and at one point tried posting her questions and concerns on the bulletin boards of interfaith Web sites. "The posts all seemed to say the same thing. 'If you're not converting, you are wrong and wasting our time, we don't want to talk to you.'" Surprisingly, she toyed briefly with the idea of converting, to please Jed's parents. But she didn't think anything would improve their opinion of her, and her heart really wasn't in it. She attended services a couple of times with Jed, and having always hated church services, found the synagogue experience even worse. "I was unimpressed," she says. "I am a Christian in my heart and soul. The feeble attempts to keep the ancient religion of Judaism alive in that Reform synagogue were incomplete Christian ceremonies to me."

Valerie is similarly unenthusiastic about nonreligious Jewish culture. Despite Jed's midwestern origins, she believes that "The Jewish culture is not so much a culture as a part of the country you are raised in. The Jewish culture is very similar, as best I can tell, to the New York–East Coast culture."

Valerie and Jed have no plans to have children, but they don't rule out the possibility that it may happen. If it does, Valerie says she won't stop Jed from passing on his Judaism, but neither will she participate herself. "I have no desire to live in a Jewish household and support Jewish rituals and customs," Valerie says. "I don't want to raise children who take no joy in Christmas, and I would feel like a hypocrite trying to raise children to be something I am not."

Valerie says that Jed loves her despite, not because of, her Christianity, and she returns the compliment. She likens her husband's Judaism to his inability to toss his own dirty laundry into the hamper: something she has to live with, but not love. Her encounters with the Jewish community, which she believes are typical of those of other non-Jewish spouses, range from the innocuous to the downright unpleasant, and serve to convince her that her father is right about Jews. "My in-laws for the most part appear to me as shallow, narrow-minded individuals who are in this world for themselves," she says. She paints a rather chilling portrait of her marriage when she describes keeping a watchful eye on Jed, hoping and praying that the moment will never come when, like Katherine Winterhaus's Psalm-reading boyfriend, he reveals his true colors, and turns out to be a Jew just like his parents.

"So far he hasn't proved to be like that, and I have little reason to expect him to develop into such an insect."

Valerie could serve as a poster child for a campaign against intermarriage. Instead of rejecting her father's virulent anti-Semitism through her relationship with Jed, she describes herself as increasingly embracing it. When Rabbi Toby Manewith insists that there'll be trouble for the Jewish spouse in an intermarriage who decides he wants to live a more Jewish life, one suspects she couldn't find a better test case than Valerie and Jed.

In my experience, Valerie's antipathy for Jews and Judaism is unusual, if not unique, among gentile women involved with Jewish men. Extreme, but not unusual, is her experience of feeling violently rejected by the Jewish world, her sense that nothing she could do would win her approval in Jewish eyes, and that she might as well save herself the pain of trying.

Attitudes toward non-Jewish women, usually muddied by fears about intermarriage and Jewish continuity, can sometimes be thrown into relief by a proposed conversion. When a non-Jewish daughter-in-law attempts to join the Jewish people and to raise Jewish children, a family's antipathy toward her becomes harder to explain away with the excuse that she represents a loss to the community. When she speaks of her reception in her husband's family, Grace Lewis, a thirty-two-year-old accountant who lives in an Upstate New York town, expresses anger and frustration quite similar to Valerie's but without the racist overtones. "It was horrendous," she says. "I was pressured into converting. We went to Reform classes and did a Reform conversion, but it wasn't acceptable to my in-laws. They insisted I do an Orthodox conversion." Having come to love many aspects of Judaism, Grace thought she would take that further step to appease her in-laws, who are not Orthodox themselves. Eventually, she gave up. Convinced by her in-laws that her Reform conversion is not valid, it is as if she has never converted at all. Of her husband she says, "The threat is that I'm taking him away from his roots, but I actually brought him closer through my classes, spending more time with his family, and a trip we took to Israel."

We'll take a closer look at the issues raised by conversion when we examine the experiences of converts in chapter seven. What it's important to clarify here is the deep gulf, unbridgeable by marriage or conversion, that exists for some Jews between themselves and the non-Jewish world. It is the perspective of a small outpost in a hostile wilderness, vulnerable to enemies, and if breached, easily destroyed. Valerie touches on this sense of a people targeted and under siege when she recalls being told by a rabbi that to her in-laws, she was little better than a Ku Klux Klansman.

If Valerie's anti-Semitism must be understood in the light of her upbringing and her encounters with Jed's family, the extremely unwelcoming stance taken by Jews like Grace's and her in-laws must also be viewed in context. The fear of gentile women as a genocidal threat is deeply imbedded in Judaism. In the examples we've looked at up to now, a woman is essentially seen as pursuing her own agenda when she goes after a Jewish man, however avaricious (our seductress of Proverbs), fatal (Lilith), erotic (Sharon Bascom and Zuleika), religious (Jezebel), neurotic (Katherine Winterhaus), or quite normally romantic (Winnie Marks) that agenda might be. The biblical story of Cozbi and Zimri goes a step further, depicting non-Jewish women in the service of another's cause. Literally in service: in this story, they are soldiers in an enemy army on a covert mission to destroy the Jewish religion.

Cozbi and Zimri

Following their miraculous escape from Egypt, the Israelites travel for forty years through the desert, stopping at many way stations and entering into endless skirmishes on their journey to the promised land. Numerous and well favored by God, they begin to inspire dread in the peoples around them. In one famous episode, Balaam, a prophet for hire, is paid by the king of Moab to curse the Israelites, then is unable to complete the job when his mule refuses to cooperate.

But where curses fail, seduction may succeed; Balaam sends women to lead the Israelites astray. At Shittim, the last place they stop, the men become sexually involved with the local women; since, as we've seen, the two activities were often linked in the ancient Middle East, they enter into their pagan religious rites as well. God retaliates by sending a plague that decimates the Israelites, advising Moses, their leader, that if they want to avert total destruction, they must execute the men who have transgressed. Taking the initiative, Phinehas, a priest, follows an Israelite named Zimri and his Midianite lover, Cozbi (which means "voluptuous"), into their tent, where he gores both of them with a single spear as they embrace. While the text in Bemidbar, or Numbers, is a little vague about exactly where Phinehas stabs them, later, Talmudic writers delight in specifying that the lovers were run through the genitals.

Something the text does specify is that both Zimri and Cozbi are the children of important leaders in their respective communities, a detail which underscores the idea that Cozbi's presence in Zimri's tent is an act of war, designed to destroy the Jewish people at the highest level, and that makes Phinehas's act a political, and not exclusively religious, gesture. Their execution instantly checks the plague, and Phinehas is hailed as a hero by God.

Needless to say, even those most vociferously opposed to intermarriage today don't call for such extreme measures to arrest it. And few Jewish leaders would cite Jewish-gentile coupling as the direct cause of a plague or other disaster. But some rabbis wishing to dramatize the dangers of interfaith relationships do resort to images of militarism and war to make their point. "The first step in our battle in the fight for Jewish continuity is the fight against intermarriage," declares Rabbi Alan Silverstein in his 1995 book, *It All Begins with a Date: Jewish Concerns About*

Intermarriage. Others go further, employing the language of ultimate devastation by comparing intermarriage with Nazi Germany's destruction of European Jewry. In 1987 Rabbi Ephraim Z. Buchwald launched his successful National Jewish Outreach Program, an organization that aims to engage unaffiliated Jews, with a flyer that spoke of "The Silent Holocaust," and read, in part, "Concentration camps and gas chambers aren't the only ways to exterminate the Jewish people . . . intermarriage . . . can accomplish the same evil end."

Who are the Nazis in this scenario?

Evangelical Christians and other anti-Semites might be sending emissaries to marry the Jewish people into oblivion— but it's not likely. Most gentiles who marry into Jewish families don't see themselves as pillagers of the Jewish community. Does that matter if the community is pillaged nonetheless? If a gentile woman doesn't intend to separate her partner from his faith, she also isn't going to lose much sleep over it if it happens.

In fact, that isn't always so. The antithesis of Rabbi Harold Schulweis's "interfaithless" couple, Zachary and Catherine Dresher, don't take their religions lightly. But while each respects the other's different path, Cathy worries that she is harming Zach, by being who she is and loving him.

Zachary and Catherine Dresher

Zach and Cathy Dresher, both thirty, met as college seniors in Arizona, became engaged soon after, and have been married for eight years. Cathy had a strongly religious upbringing in the Community of Christ, a Protestant church in which both her parents are ministers. Zach describes his father as "Conservative-Orthodox" and his mother as not much interested in her Judaism. The home he was raised in was observant, with a kosher kitchen and regular attendance at religious services, until his parents divorced when he was thirteen. "After that, it changed,"

Zach says. "There was no pressure to date Jewish people, which might have made a difference." Zach says he didn't want to avoid Jewish women, but on the other hand, "I guess I looked at my parents and thought, marrying someone Jewish is not necessarily going to make a successful marriage." In college, Zach looked at himself as well, and what he saw was that his friends weren't Jewish. He tried dropping in on his school's Hillel a couple of times, but says, "I don't remember there being anyone there to date." Here, as elsewhere in the conversation, Zach laughs at himself, as if to undercut how serious he is about everything he says. "At a certain point I sort of realized that I probably wasn't going to marry someone Jewish because I wasn't dating anyone Jewish."

In their reactions to Cathy and Zach's relationship, their families couldn't have been more unlike Valerie and Jed's. Cathy's folks, who have Jewish friends and an interest in other religions, were enthusiastic. Zach's mother, who had herself remarried a non-Jewish man, and even his observant father, who had remarried a converted woman, were warm and welcoming. "It's been amazingly easy as far as family," Cathy says. "I enjoy celebrating Passover and Hanukkah with his grandparents. His grandfather is from Poland and tells funny stories. When we did Passover alone it wasn't so great. Only Zach knew the songs and prayers."

Without the opposition of family to contend with, Cathy and Zach are focused on how to bring two very different religions together in one home, and on how to raise their two-year-old daughter, Ella. This, they're finding, isn't easy at all.

Their situation is complicated by Zach's work. A career navy man, he serves in the Civil Engineer Corps, and the family is forced to move every two years. The places they've lived so far haven't had much in the way of a Jewish community. In the Mississippi town where they are currently stationed, Zach says the Magen David, or "Jewish star," has been outlawed in public schools as a possible gang symbol, and the nearest synagogue is an hour's drive away. If the town is not the best place to be Jewish, Zach says, the navy isn't much better. "In eight years in the navy, I've only met two Jewish chaplains. There are always Christian services. It would be nice one time to have a Jewish service. I really like the navy, but I wish there were more Jewish chaplains."

Zach and Cathy have tried accompanying each other to religious services, without much success. Zach is acutely ill at ease in a Christian church, and with any mention of Jesus. For her part, Cathy found the Conservative services she attended with Zach "neat, a little odd, and mostly in Hebrew." At this point, they have a tentative plan to attend church and synagogue once a month each as a family, and if either wants more than that, they'll go on their own. They celebrate both sets of holidays with Ella, and try to emphasize, Cathy says, "God and strong moral values," things that both Christianity and Judaism have in common. But the dual-religion lifestyle that works in some homes isn't really a comfortable fit in theirs.

Zachary maintains that what is most important to him is belief in God and ethical living. "I've seen too many people who are religious who don't meet the standards of what God thinks people should be," he comments. At the same time, he can't give up hoping for a spiritually unified family. Growing up, he knew nothing about the relatively liberal Reform movement in Judaism, and has never attended a Reform service. But lately he's been doing some research, and has reached the uncertain conclusion that a Reform synagogue might be more accessible to Cathy—and more comfortable for him than a Christian church. "What I would hope is that we could find one thing that we could all share," Zach says. "But I don't see that happening. I could never convert. Well, why should I expect her to convert when I could never convert?"

For her part, Cathy has no theological conflict with Judaism, and is somewhat less stressed juggling two religions in their home. "It would be great if he was Christian, but I'm just glad he's religious in any way," Cathy says. She puts an upbeat spin on their situation, but there are moments when her concern for Zach, and the strain this places on her, comes through. When they got together, Zach's Judaism didn't really mean anything to her, but over time she has come to recognize it as an important part of who he is, and thus an important difference between them. "We've had more things to work out than I first realized we would. I feel like I've kept him away from Judaism, like he would've been more involved if I were Jewish. This bothers me and I feel guilty about it, even though I know it was his decision that it was okay to marry a Christian. I feel as though the differences in our backgrounds are obstacles to overcome."

For Cathy and Zach, intermarriage is no religious cop-out. There are no bad guys in their story, no one to blame. Quite simply, their desires to be together, to be true to the faiths they were raised in, and to create a unified home, bring them into deep, even agonizing turmoil. There are no easy answers for Cathy and Zach, and the conclusions reached by them and others like them—that is, interfaith couples who take their religions seriously—will have crucial consequences for the Jewish community of the future.

Cathy and Zach are an unusual young couple, as thoughtful, probing, religious people of any age generally are. Cathy fits the profile of the gentile siren as poorly as Zach fills the bill as her helpless prey. But while Cathy and Zach quietly contend with the real stuff of intermarried life, popular culture periodically spits out alternative American versions of the myths about Jewish men and gentile women, and glib solutions to their predicaments. For young people who find traditional ideas about interfaith liaisons hopelessly dated, the silver screen offers updated stereotypes—or the chance to be stranded between old myths and new.

The Celluloid Shiksa

Just as in Jewish tradition, when relationships between Jewish men and non-Jewish women are portrayed on film, they are slanted from the man's perspective. His life is center screen, along with the stasis, erotic, romantic, and otherwise, from which he suffers. Invariably, the dilemma posed is whether he will have the nerve to use a woman who would seem to be his mismatch to free himself from his deadlock. Representing the all-American schizoid notion of individuality, these films advocate ditching any aspect of Jewish identity that interferes with the pursuit of happiness—that is, with disappearing inside a homogenous non-Jewish identity. In their glib mix of Old and New World mythology, the gentile woman still promises unleashed sexuality. But instead of trapping a Jewish man, that sexuality will liberate him from the Jewish community that has him in its clutches. Two examples of the genre are *White Palace* (1990) and *Keeping the Faith* (2000).

In the earlier film, Max, twenty-seven, is an advertising man two years into mourning his wife, who died in a car accident. Childhood sweethearts, the two grew up together in the St. Louis, Missouri, Jewish community in which Max still locates himself socially. There is no trace of spirituality or even ethnic culture in this world. Being Jewish in Max's sphere means being monied and vapid, mouthing liberal sentiments while being served a holiday meal by an underpaid servant, and continually, insensitively pressuring anyone single to pair off within the circle. About Max's wife we learn little, though in an ironic twist, her photograph shows a blond and classically WASPy-looking young woman. We know only that she was in all respects appropriate for Max and that he is crushed by her loss.

Enter Nora Baker, forty-three-year-old fast-food worker. Nora is Hollywood's classic low-income "real" person, a role often (but not here) filled by a nonwhite. Independent and outspoken, Nora has had a gritty life. She has suffered and, made of less sensitive stuff than Max, survived. She is aggressively sexual and despite their inability to relate to each other out of bed, she will bring Max back to life. In fact, she will inspire him to start a new life, leaving his job, his home, and his vacuous Jewish community while being transformed into a spontaneous, unrestrainedly sexual person his late wife probably wouldn't recognize. *White Palace*'s gentile woman isn't really very different from traditional Judaism's model: she's oversexed, uncontrolled, and animalistic. But here these qualities have uses the sages never envisioned.

Set in New York City, *Keeping the Faith*'s equally unlikely scenario concerns thirty-year-olds Jake and Anna. Inseparable as children, they've been out of touch some sixteen years, and meet up again when Anna returns to New York as a successful, workaholic businesswoman. In her absence, Jake has become a rabbi dedicated to revitalizing a dormant congregation and, it is implied, a moribund religion. Of course he immediately falls in lust with Anna.

In an updated spin on the shiksa goddess, Anna is endowed with the best—or at any rate most sought-after—qualities traditionally ascribed to both the gentile and Jewish woman. She is tall, blond, lithe, and all-American, utterly free of ethnic characteristics, family, or social ties of any kind. At the same time she is smart, warm, and, unlike the humorless (!) Jewish women Jake encounters, funny.

As a rabbi, Jake can't marry Anna, but they can have an illicit affair. Unlike *White Palace*'s Max, Jake isn't pining for a soul mate. But as an assistant rabbi gunning for the top job at his synagogue, being single is a liability, and until he has a wife, his congregants are going to keep forcing him to date inappropriate women. Jake can singlehandedly rejuvenate the Jewish world, but he can't be expected to marry one of its stale female caricatures, a fate he likens to life in a cage. "Pandas don't mate in captivity," he comments.

Though Jake and Anna share a certain camaraderie, once they begin sleeping together their relationship appears to be something that can take place entirely between the sheets. As an executive with no life outside her corner office, Anna is an unlikely choice to save Jake from his uptightness and his stultifying Jewish milieu, but then she is no more unlikely than the gospel choir Jake brings in to rev up his congregation one Saturday morning. Like *White Palace*'s Nora, both Anna and the gospel singers play Princess Di to Jake's House of Windsor: fresh blood for the suffocatingly inbred. But in its facile and surreal end, *Keeping the Faith* parts company from earlier Jewish films in that this time, a Jewish man gets to have it all on-screen. Jake won't leave his community, he'll become head rabbi, with aspiring convert Anna at his side.

How influential are stereotypes of gentile women offscreen these days? According to Rabbi Sanford Selzer, who served as the first director of the Commission on Reform Jewish Outreach, "Old myths about non-Jewish women and why Jewish men prefer them are far less prevalent today, but those kinds of myths die hard."

Not long ago, Selzer says, "if the non-Jewish woman was blond, well, that explained it immediately." On the other hand, he adds, the gentile woman has also been seen as the less demanding, more accommodating alternative to the so-called Jewish princess. He recalls this moldy joke about Jewish brides: "What does a Jewish girl make for dinner? A reservation."

Men coming of age today may not expect their partners to serve up domestic bliss with a square meal. But a visit to the place where teens and twenty-somethings congregate—the Web—would indicate that the shiksa, object of desire and derision, survives in the imaginations of young adults with amazing persistence. Let's look at a few examples.

Reviewing *Keeping the Faith* on the Web site Leisuresuit, a desperately hip critic writes: "Ah, the lure of the blonde shiksa Goddess . . . Many a nice Jewish boy has heeded her call and found his heart dashed on her cold, rocky shores. Yet still she compels us, and every year thousands are lost to her Tiffany-like siren song." Responding to the review, another young single quips that watching the movie was like seeing his own life on-screen.

Among college students, sexual fantasies of non-Jewish women are also alive and well. One pubescent Philip Roth wannabe recently wrote of his longing to sleep with shiksas in a Brown University publication called *Clerestory*, while a Northwestern sophomore dreamed in print about possessing a shiksa goddess in *The Daily Northwestern*.

While it would seem that these Jewish boys just want to have fun, the laughs may be on the girls who try to form serious relationships with them. Go Ask Alice, a health-issues question-and-answer Web site provided by Columbia University, contains a distraught letter from a graduating senior who signs herself "the Shiksa." Though she has declared her willingness to convert before their wedding, this gentile woman reports, her boyfriend's parents are hostile to their relationship, evidenced by such tactics as their efforts to keep his ties to previous—Jewish—girlfriends alive. Meanwhile, her boyfriend tells her the problem is all in her head. The young woman believes that her boyfriend and his parents have a good relationship and she doesn't want to weaken it. In order for their marriage to succeed, she feels, the parental conflict must be resolved.

Even the high school set seem to be inheriting musty clichés about non-Jewish women. The Dr. Martin Luther King Jr. Writing Awards gave an honorable mention in 2001 to an essay called "Shiksa," by high-schooler Carolyn Elliott, who writes that being a gentile girl meant being trivialized and finally dumped by a Jewish boyfriend.

What some young Jewish men want may be summed up by a concept I've encountered in conversation with twenty-somethings as well as on the Web: the Virtual Shiksa. This golden girl is tall, slender, and blond, gentile in appearance and demeanor in every way, yet capable of satisfying the parents: she's actually Jewish.

A few years ago Rabbi Toby Manewith, of the George Washington University Hillel, hired "a drop-dead, knockout, blond, thin, young woman" to fill a job usually held by someone Jewish. In a role that brings her into heavy contact with Jewish college men, Manewith had already observed that, "Young men are single-minded, and what you hear about non-Jewish women is how they look: tall, thin, blond." So it probably wasn't surprising that her young constituents repeatedly questioned her employee's pedigree, to which Manewith repeatedly explained that the woman was Jewish. "Well, she doesn't look Jewish," was the remark she heard again and again. "Sorry," Manewith would tell them. "I didn't mean to hire someone so pretty."

Twenty-six-year-old Jorie Ryder has had her own experiences with Jewish college men. A nonpracticing Irish Catholic, Jorie graduated from a predominantly Jewish college. The school had exactly the academic programs she was looking for, and to Jorie's untrained eyes, the smattering of Orthodox students on campus made it look like a place where it would be cool to be different. To some extent, she was right. Jorie had a great time at college, until it came to dating.

"With the majority of the guys I knew who were attracted to me, there was just this assumption that I was off-limits. The most hurtful would be cavalier because I didn't need to be taken seriously. It almost felt like I was being played with." In *Keeping the Faith*, Jake sees Anna as a strictly sexual toy, and is astounded when she suggests the relationship could be something more, only changing his mind when he is assured that Anna won't mar his standing in the Jewish community. Jorie describes a similarly callous treatment from young Jewish men at a college where interdating, unlike most campuses, is still considered taboo. Male students flirted, maybe asked her out, then abruptly dropped her because she was, in the end, "untouchable" as a non-Jewish woman. It was impossible for these young men to see her in anything but sexual terms. While her women friends were all Jewish, the nonromantic friendships she had with men on campus were exclusively with non-Jews.

Throughout these stories, we've looked at the complex links between sex and religion, and how they are inextricably bound up with Jewish identity. We've heard the reasons gentile women were associated with sex, and sex with religious assimilation, at the dawn of Jewish time. In part, Jews defined themselves into existence in opposition to the pagans around them. While their neighbors engaged in cultic sexual rites, Jews would be the people who sanctified sexual relationships between human beings on the one hand, and the spiritual relationship between humans and God on the other, by separating the two.

The Torah and the rabbinical writings that followed it institutionalized a dread of gentile women as powerful and insidious undoers of Judaism who would ensnare Jewish men with the arsenal of erotic, even demonic weapons at their disposal, as illustrated in Proverbs' caution, the legends of Lilith and the story of Cozbi. At the heart of these examples are the paired archetypes of an aggressive, evil-intentioned gentile woman and a passive, helpless Jewish man. These paradigms, deeply embedded in the Jewish psyche, may come into play even now when a community like Sharon Bascom's synagogue closes ranks against an outsider, or in the expectation that without a Jewish wife, a man will do little to keep his Judaism alive. Even when seduction and entrapment are not involved, as in a politically or socially advantageous marriage sought by a man or his family, tradition holds that intermarriage is bad news for Jewish survival, as Exodus warns—"their daughters . . . will cause your sons to lust after their gods"—and as Jezebel and Ahab's example makes clear.

Like every group, the Jewish people builds its muscles by
pushing back against whom and what it calls Other. For Judaism,
the non-Jewish woman is always a candidate to fill this role,
handy because she is found so close to home. In fact, she's found
at home. As already noted, rather than blending into their pagan
neighbors, the Israelites may have incorporated many of them,
just as local women have since joined Jewish families in most, if
not all, the times and places they have lived. Jewish men have
married out despite the prohibitions and sometimes no doubt
because of them. Most young men are not scared off by the
warning that a woman is so highly sexed that she will make a
man forget who he is, and in any case, romantic love is a time-
honored method of rebellion.

Yet despite her presence in Jewish families and participation
in communal life, the sense of gentile woman as Other persists.
Jewish history has incorporated gentile women's bodies, lives,
work, and children, but not their voices and perspectives. Their
collective experience has been blanketed by a silence that even
today it may be difficult to break, while the tradition continues
to recycle old myths and antipathies without ever really looking
at them. I've sat in synagogues in which it would be unthinkable
to read a biblical passage condemning homosexuals or vilifying a
long-vanished ethnic group without discussion to distance ourselves, modern readers, from the attitudes reflected, but where
dire warnings against the evils of gentile women are placidly
read without comment.

We've seen how the vestiges of traditional ideas about gentile women play out in some contemporary lives. For Sharon
and for Jorie Ryder, being gentile meant that Jewish men would
never have to say they were sorry, or respect them. Corrosive
suspicion also cost Sharon her place in a religious community,
while Winnie Marks was finally shut out by two different men
when she failed to fit herself into their Jewish worlds. Those
who are opposed to intermarriage may crow over these victories, but old prejudices against gentile women are much more

likely to alienate couples from the Jewish community than they are to stop marriages. For Mary Rosenbaum, the second-class status of a non-Jewish bride, particularly a Catholic one, made her an object of derision in her husband's family, at the same time as she bore the blame for "dragging him down" into practicing a religion—his own. Valerie Paulsen was told that she was destroying her husband's family by marrying into it, and is now ignored by most of his relatives. Their hostility, combined with the anti-Semitism she was raised on, has inspired in her an intense antagonism to Judaism that ensures the marriage will never be a comfortable place for her husband to be Jewish or for children they may have to be raised as Jews. When Grace Lewis decided to stop jumping through the Jewish hoops set up by her husband's folks, she also gave up on the connection she'd made to Judaism, accepting her in-laws' dismissal of her Reform conversion. When she has children, she plans to keep them away from her husband's family.

Though young Jewish men still seem to count shiksas before they fall asleep at night, married men like Rick Bowers tend to deny that a partiality for gentile women played a role when they chose non-Jewish wives. What about the women? Jewish tradition, Philip Roth, and Barbara Bartlett's *The Shiksa* would have us believe that there are gentile women who can't get enough of Jewish men. What do gentile women want?

Women like Valerie and Cathy say their husbands' backgrounds are incidental. Attracted to peers who seemed very much like them, they only discovered later on that their husbands' Judaism isn't akin to a divergent taste in food or music but is a difference with real consequences for the relationship. I've also spoken with a number of women, ranging in age from midtwenties to early sixties, who report that they are specifically drawn to Jewish men or to the qualities or way of life they represent. For some there is a religious motivation toward Judaism; for others, the appeal is entirely secular. Winnie finds the traits she values most in her Jewish friends, and is well aware that nearly all the significant relationships of her adult life have been with Jews. As we've seen, attraction to a man's Judaism doesn't necessarily win a gentile woman points in the Jewish world, where the stereotypes about her continually trip each other up. While one mind-set insists that a gentile woman with a sincere interest in Judaism is a contradiction in terms, another calls her a troublemaker who will make her man "too Jewish" for his own family to recognize.

Whether gentile women and Jewish men have a thing about each other, or whether they come together because these days, they are simply each other's boy and girl next door, the reality is, they do come together—often in happy, successful relationships. Most gentile women probably aren't out to assimilate Jewish men, though many may help to bring about that result, just by being who they are. If Valerie had been warmly welcomed by Jed's family, she might now be an active participant in the building of a Jewish home—or she might be clinging to her father's anti-Semitism regardless of her in-laws' reception. By practicing a religion of her own, Cathy, sincere and well-meaning, presents an even tougher dilemma. From a Jewish point of view, she can't express her spirituality, much less pass it on to her child, without harming the Jewishness of Zach's life, his family, his home. She is aware of this, and is troubled by it, at the same time as she is not to blame.

In Israel, where few punches are pulled and issues of Jewish identity and survival are played out on a grand scale, these problems are seemingly resolved with a single stroke: interfaith marriage is against the law. To be more specific, marriage is under the jurisdiction of the rabbinate and can only take place between two people with valid Jewish credentials. Of course, some Israelis leave their country to tie the knot elsewhere, and some, evidently, are led astray by foreigners. Some kibbutzim, agricultural collectives, have voted to bar non-Jewish volunteers in an effort to halt the influx of Nordic women they said were coming to work the land and making off with kibbutz sons. Like prohibitions against intermarriage in American Jewish communities, this may keep non-Jewish women out, but it doesn't stop men from leaving. And if a man marries a non-Jewish woman abroad, he will think twice before bringing his family home with him.

As in the Book of Ezra, some Jewish communities are loath to accept non-Jewish brides. Others argue that newcomers revitalize the tradition with fresh ideas and enthusiasm. What everyone agrees on is that ethnic infusion causes change. Therapist Esther Perel sees Jewish life today as "multiracial, multicultural, very global, if you like. Not as many large organizations can talk for all Jews." The meaning of group identity itself is changing, Perel says. "You make the group fit the individual."

But Jewish identity is never a completely individual affair, any more than it's solely about the past and the present: to speak of one person's Jewish identity today is to speak collectively and in the future tense, about the generations of Jews whose existence hangs in the balance. As we'll see over the course of the next two chapters, the effect gentile women have on the Jewish community will be judged by the children they raise.

3

Children for Molech: Matrilineal Descent

"Of thy seed thou shalt not give to pass through to Molech."
The text speaks of an Israelite who has intercourse with a
[foreign] woman and begets from her a son for idolatry. . . .

— *MIDRASH LEVITICUS*

I ONCE read an article in a Jewish publication detailing what the
writer saw as key issues brought about by the proliferation of
non-Orthodox Jewish day schools. Some of these schools, he
noted, admit the children of gentile mothers. From a traditional
perspective, these children are not Jews. If they grow up to
marry their classmates born of Jewish mothers, their Jewish
schools will have created intermarriages.

In the days of biblical patriarchs and kings, Jewish identity
was part of the inheritance a father passed on to his children.
But for much of the past two thousand years, Jewish status has
been determined matrilineally. According to rabbinic law, communities are to recognize and include only those children born
to a Jewish mother. In this view, the child of a Jewish woman
and gentile man is Jewish; the child of a Jewish man and gentile
woman is a gentile.

83

While the Orthodox* and Conservative movements continue to cling to a matrilineal definition of Jewishness, the Reconstructionist and Reform movements now embrace any child with either Jewish parent who is raised as a Jew. In 1983, when the Reform movement, Judaism's largest denomination, chose to recognize a father's ability to pass on his Jewish identity to his children, the resolution caused a kind of seismic ripple through the Jewish world. Robert Gordis, who edited an issue of the journal *Judaism* in 1985 devoted to a consideration of the ruling, noted in his introduction that "The decision aroused passionate controversy in many quarters, particularly in those committed to traditional Halakhah [Jewish law]." In one of the essays included in the volume, Walter S. Wurzburger wrote, "Few religious controversies have so polarized the Jewish community as has the patrilineal descent issue."

Why all the fuss? By delineating the boundaries of Jewish identity, the issue of matrilineal descent goes right to the core of who is, and is not, a Jew. In the recent past, an obsessive concern with rooting out Jewish ancestry was the stuff of anti-Semitic genocide, used against Jews to ensure that no one with even the slenderest strain of Jewish lineage got away. Today, at a time when the Jewish community looks at its dwindling numbers and rightly fears extinction, it is a small number of Jews who are concerned with determinations of Jewish ancestry—ironically, with the aim of keeping people out.

"In the Orthodox community we don't accept anyone who isn't documented as halakhically Jewish, and married to some-

---

*Of the four major movements in American Judaism, *Reform Judaism* has historically maintained the loosest connection to traditional observance, adapting Jewish practice to conform to modern (Christian) social norms. With its emphasis on social justice and relatively welcoming stance toward secular Jews and non-Jews, it claims the largest share of American synagogue membership. Second most popular, *Conservative Judaism* adheres more closely to Jewish law as well as to a more socially and politically conservative outlook. *Orthodox Judaism* purports to maintain adherence to all aspects of Jewish law, and, although there are variations from one sect to another, represents the most socially, politically, and religiously conservative strain in American Judaism. The smallest and most recent of the four movements, *Reconstructionist Judaism* is an outgrowth of the Conservative movement that promotes a humanistic, socially conscious Judaism in which religious practice plays a meaningful but unrestrictive role.

one who is documented halakhically Jewish," says Rabbi Solomon Rybak, a New Jersey congregational rabbi who is chair of the committee on conversion for the Orthodox Union's Rabbinic Council of America. "The established Orthodox position is that a person is Jewish if he is born of a Jewish mother or if he converts." Rybak allows that matrilineal descent is not spelled out in the written law, identifying it as a received oral tradition. "The Orthodox Jew since antiquity has lived by the oral law and the written law," he explains, noting that matrilineal descent is part of a category of laws "without reason." And is it a good law? Rybak laughs. "We don't presume to have that divine knowledge." According to Rybak, the great medieval scholar Moses Maimonides "very often tried to rationalize different laws, but even he never tried with that one. If he wasn't going to, I'm certainly not."

In this chapter, we'll try to question the issue more deeply. I believe that Jews owe it to ourselves —our families and our communal survival—to examine matrilineal descent very closely. We'll take a look at the research on the origins of matrilineal descent, and hear from those who argue both for and against maintaining this definition of Jewish identity. We'll consider the intersection of matrilineal descent and deep-seated prejudices against gentile women. Is matrilineal descent a product of those attitudes? Are the attitudes partly the result of matrilineal descent? A matrilineal definition of Jewishness places the sole responsibility for the survival of Jewish lineage on Jewish women, despite the genetic evidence, discussed in the Introduction, that Jewish communities have always relied in part upon gentile women to create and keep them alive. In a male-dominated tradition, do Jewish women view matrilineal descent as a crucial source of power, or a burden they alone must bear? We'll consider what the matrilineal principle says about the role of fathers in the Jewish family, and its effect on the children of Jewish fathers and gentile mothers. In short, we'll consider the question Rabbi Rybak shied away from: Is matrilineal descent good for the Jews?

In my conversations with gentile women, I've found matrilineal descent to be among those issues that arouse the strongest feelings. Interestingly, the subject tends to inspire an emotional response across the board, from women intensely involved in raising their children within Judaism to those maintaining the greatest distance between themselves and the Jewish community.

"In my heart I feel they're Jewish," Lucy Porter says of her children, who are being raised as Jews without either Lucy or her Jewish husband taking a very active stance in their religious education. An agnostic of Christian descent, she grows heated the moment the question of matrilineal descent is raised. "I don't give a shit if I'm Jewish or not, and I just think any congregation that would reject them based on the fact that I'm not Jewish is not worthy of having them in its hold."

Some of my informants identify the matrilineal principle as a key source of alienation and pain. For a woman deeply committed to raising her children Jewishly, matrilineal descent can feel like a pointed rejection, Judaism's way of saying that no matter what she does her children are tainted by their close association with her—ironically, the parent who may be doing as much as or more than her Jewish husband to raise their children as Jews.

Felicia Cruz, whose story we'll hear more of in the following chapter, describes matrilineal descent as "pitting my womb against yours. My womb is no better or worse than someone else's." A mother of three, she plays more of a leading role than her Jewish husband in creating a Jewish home, without having formally converted herself. She expresses frustration that her children would not be considered Jews by some facets of the Jewish community, while children in families with two Jewish parents, in which Judaism is not practiced at all, would be. "I would definitely challenge that, especially when I see a lot of Jews by birth who don't even do half of the things I do, and not to compare, but in a way it's like, how dare anyone look down on me when I have such a clear mind of who I am and what I'm doing in my home? For me actions speak louder than anything, and I feel pretty secure about what we're doing."

The fact that Jewish tradition doesn't recognize their children can play an important role in a couple's decision about whether to raise them Jewishly. For the non-Jewish mother in such a family, the sense that the Jewish community doesn't want her children may come as a relief.

"I think it's curious, but it's actually made things easier for me," says Marta Hernandez, a practicing Catholic and mother of two young children. "If the Jewish community in general defined my children as Jewish, I would feel more of an obligation to go above and beyond in giving them a Jewish education." Thanks to the matrilineal principle, Marta says, her husband, Alex, "wrestles with his semioutsider status as the only Jew in the family," and struggles to define what, if anything, he should do to Jewishly educate children he's been told not to consider Jewish.

Early Jews from Abraham and Sarah, father and mother of the Jewish people, through the Israelites of the second century of the Common Era, would be baffled by Alex's problem. Judaism is a patriarchal religion, and for biblical Jews, identity was handed down patrilineally. When God selects Abraham to found the Jewish people, the rite of passage stipulated is circumcision, the only conversion ritual that would exist for many generations, until the introduction of immersion in a mikvah, or ritual bath, for both men and women in the rabbinical era. There is no ritual to transform Sarah into a Jew; it is simply taken for granted that she will go along with her husband.

God's covenant with Abraham passes to his and Sarah's son, Isaac, and from Isaac to his son, Jacob. Isaac's wife, Rebekah, and Jacob's wives, Rachel and Leah, are cousins who worship pagan gods. The women enter the homes of their husbands' families and are absorbed by them, giving birth to the children who will carry on their fathers' line. Maybe the women become monotheists and join their husbands in worship, maybe they don't. Either way, their children belong to their husbands, body and soul, and there is no question that they are Jewish. Bereshit, Genesis, recounts that matriarch Rachel couldn't let go of her father's idols when she left his house, and tradition has it that she inadvertently brought about her own death by hanging on to them. Yet it has never been suggested that her illustrious son, Joseph, or her younger son, Benjamin—two of the twelve founders of the tribes of Israel—weren't Jews.

When was matrilineal descent instituted and why?

History as Mystery

In his book *The Beginnings of Jewishness: Boundaries, Varieties, Uncertainties,* biblical scholar Shaye Cohen set himself the task of tracking down where, when, and why a matrilineal definition of Jewish identity replaced patrilineal descent in Jewish life and law, only to conclude that none of these things can be known for certain.

Cohen establishes that the notion of matrilineal descent was unknown in biblical Judaism, in the Christian New Testament, and among Jewish writings of that era. "All of these texts appear to be familiar with a patrilineal system. The Mishnah, however, states the matrilineal principle . . . as if it were agreed upon by all, and provides no reason or justification. It appears in the Mishnah like a bolt out of the blue." Compiled early in the third century C.E., the Mishnah is the six-volume work with which the rabbis codified Jewish law. Cohen notes that in the Middle Ages, scholars looking for a "scriptural hook" on which to hang matrilineal descent managed to find it in various biblical passages. But these are—often highly convoluted—justifications after the fact, not sources of the law.

Cohen considers and dismisses a number of possible explanations for why the rabbis broke with tradition to adopt the matrilineal principle. He notes that matrilineal descent is classified with a host of laws delineating types of people who may not marry each other, and the social status of a child born to two people of unequal social strata. Here, non-Jewish women are classed with slave women as unacceptable marriage partners, and the children of both are to be considered less than legitimate members of the community. However, this tells us nothing about why non-Jewish women and their children were abruptly given this status.

Similarly, he points out that matrilineal descent may reflect the rabbis' distaste for the intermingling of different types, in particular, their feelings about sexual interchange between humans and animals. Cohen notes that Maimonides, the medieval scholar too modest to take on matrilineal descent, wasn't so shy when it came to this subject. Maimonides, he writes, ruled that "a gentile woman who has had sex with a Jewish man should be stoned 'like an animal'—that is, just as we stone an animal with which a person has had sex." Again, such a statement makes very clear what Maimonides thought of gentile women, but not why rabbis who lived generations before him broke with established practice and decided that the children gentile women bore to Jewish men were not Jews. Commenting on the disturbing implications of Cohen's theory of forbidden mixtures, Judaic studies scholar Robert Goldenberg asks, "If . . . the implicit premise of the matrilineal principle is that Jews and gentiles constitute diverse species, do we really wish to continue embodying this premise? I cannot believe that most of us do; we know too much of previous Jewish experience with such a premise in our time."

Other explanations for the matrilineal principle that Cohen finds implausible are the notion that the rabbis suddenly wished to legally recognize the emotional bond between a mother and her children—something they had never ascribed much importance to—and the equally unlikely idea that the new law was intended to comfort Jewish women raped by Roman soldiers, by saying that the children that resulted from those rapes would be Jews. Though Jewish, such offspring are classified as *mamzarim* (illegitimate children only permitted to marry other *mamzarim*), which in a sense is a worse fate than being a non-Jew; while a non-Jew can convert, a *mamzer* is a *mamzer* forever. Again, this explanation doesn't reveal the source of an exclusively matrilineal definition of Jewishness: a Jewish woman's right to transmit Jewish identity needn't be at odds with a Jewish man's right to do the same.

Since it was the usual practice at the time for a woman to join her husband's family and go to live with them, it's odd that the rabbis chose to make the children out-marrying Jewish women bore to non-Jewish communities Jews. Of course, declaring the children of non-Jewish women gentiles might deter Jewish men from bringing home non-Jewish wives. As we saw in the previous chapter, Ezra's expulsion of foreign wives and children demonstrates the extent to which a community might feel threatened by an influx of foreign women and their children. But Cohen refutes the argument put forward by some scholars that Ezra introduced matrilineal descent in this incident, because patrilineal descent continued to be the norm in later texts. Further, he insists that intermarriage was not a significant concern in the Jewish world at the time matrilineal descent was instituted.

Though he makes no claim for proving the hypothesis, the guess Cohen likes best is that the rabbis may have decided to take on a Roman custom when opting for matrilineal descent, since the Jewish version echoes then-current Roman law. But why? Refuting Cohen's suggestion, Robert Gordis argues that, "It is difficult to believe that they would set aside the age-old tradition of patrilineal descent and follow the law of the Romans, whom they regarded not merely as oppressors and pagans, but as steeped in licentiousness and unnatural practices." Cohen himself admits that even if we could determine that the rabbis had modeled themselves on the Romans, we still wouldn't know why.

> The matrilineal principle has had enormous social conse-
> quences for modern Jews, and it is easy to believe that the
> rabbis in antiquity must have been compelled by some socie-
> tal need to institute it. But there is little evidence to support
> this belief. Intermarriage was not a severe problem in rab-
> binic society, and even it if was, the logical response would
> have been the institution of a bilateral system, requiring both
> a Jewish father and a Jewish mother for an offspring to be
> reckoned Jewish by birth. Perhaps elsewhere the rabbis were
> legislators listening attentively to the demands of their con-
> stituency. In their statement of the matrilineal principle,
> however, the rabbis were philosophers, and, like most
> philosophers, they did not always live in the real world.

This stunning statement suggests that Jewish identity has been, is, and, if traditional opinion holds sway, forever will be determined on the basis of an obscure philosophical whim.

As Rabbi Solomon Rybak has already explained, Jewish law rests upon the Torah and the oral culture recorded hundreds of years after it. In many instances, later law elaborates on what the Torah has at least alluded to. In the case of matrilineal descent, of course, it contradicts what has been clearly spelled out. Not only was patrilineal descent the biblical norm but to this day clan affiliation is passed down from father to son, with tradition designating members of the priestly (Kohein) or subpriestly (Levite) class men whose fathers are members. If Jewish law is written in stone, on this matter it must be said that it is written, from opposing views, in two stones.

Rabbi Phillip Sigal writes that "the primary biblical ha-lakhah approves Judaic status to the children of non-Jewish mothers and Jewish fathers. . . . [T]he rabbinic departure from this clear biblical view was an innovation based upon a culturally determined and historically limited bias. Contemporary culture and history calls for halakhic innovation which would reclaim and integrate thousands of Jewish children. . . ."

Robert Goldenberg agrees, arguing that inflexible adherence to an outmoded ethos only calls the viability of Jewish law into question. "[I]f we wish to see halakhah as the authentic behavioral expression of our deepest religious values, then we must form our halakhic norms in full consciousness of these values, and we must remain conscious that such values are always formed under the influence of the world in which we live and function."

Can Jewish law accommodate innovation? Judith Hauptman, a scholar of the Talmud, the most important collection of oral traditions interpreting the Torah, says yes. Hauptman, who opposes recognition of patrilineal descent for reasons we'll look at later, writes, "There is no question that halakhah can change. Any openminded student of the Talmud knows that the underlying issue on nearly every page of Talmud is change—reinterpretations of Scripture or Mishnah to meet shifting realities."

While these scholars see an evolving Jewish legal system in which change has always played a role, others see an eternal but highly fragile structure that any alteration threatens to bring down.

Who's Afraid of Patrilineal Descent?

For Conservative Alan Silverstein matrilineal descent is a given. "We do not accept patrilineal descent," says Silverstein, a New Jersey rabbi and the Conservative movement's unofficial spokesperson on intermarriage and related issues, "because that's been the traditional position."

In response to the suggestion that the Conservative movement has felt free to diverge from tradition in other areas, for example, the ordination of women, Silverstein replies that such changes were made "in the context of Jewish law," while a return to the biblical recognition of patrilineal descent would constitute stepping outside it, something Silverstein says he "suspects has happened in rare cases." Conservative Jews, Silverstein says, "practice halakhah, something we regard as a sacred system. The clear reason is that is the way Jews have practiced for thousands of years. For the Reform movement, halakhah is not binding and change is easy; for us, change isn't easy."

When asked what he would say to families who feel shut out by an exclusively matrilineal definition of Jewishness, Silverstein laughs. "It's also discussed that patrilineal descent in Reform has caused a decline in conversion, it has also caused a disconnect with world Jewry and Israeli Jewry! There are people who feel it's the only way to go, people who feel the opposite. I suspect that there are a lot of interfaith families who disapprove of rabbis who won't officiate or co-officiate at intermarriages, who won't stand up in a church with a priest and co-officiate on a Saturday. But remember, the purpose of our religion is not to have beliefs and practices that please other people."

When Silverstein contrasts "our religion" and "other people," the implication is that those who take exception to the law of matrilineal descent are not Jews, certainly not Conservative Jews. What is interesting is that Conservative and, to a lesser extent, even Orthodox rulings on matrilineal descent do not necessarily reflect their constituents' attitudes on the issue. While Reform and nondenominational Jews overwhelmingly accept patrilineal as well as matrilineal descent, they are not alone. A study conducted in 1986 by Steven Cohen found that 12 percent of Orthodox Jews and 47 percent of Conservative Jews accept patrilineal descent. Reflecting on these findings, demographer Egon Mayer writes that "less than half the Conservative respondents in Cohen's sample subscribed to the standard of their movement on the issue." A Jewish Outreach Institute (JOI) study conducted in 1990 asked rabbis and Jewish lay leaders whether they would consider their own grandchildren Jewish if they were born of non-Jewish mothers. Ninety-five percent of Reform grandparents and 65 percent of Conservative grandparents said they would. When JOI put the same question to Jewish philanthropists in 1993, 96 percent of Reform, 72 percent of Conservative and 18 percent of Orthodox respondents said they would consider their grandchildren Jewish if born of a Jewish father and non-Jewish mother. These findings were born out anecdotally in my conversations with the Jewish grandmothers of children born to gentile women, not one of whom hesitated to claim a Jewish birthright for her grandchildren. Asked her opinion of the rule of matrilineal descent, one woman particularly knowledgeable about Jewish law exclaimed, "I think that's ridiculous!"

If the majority of Jews accept patrilineal as well as matrilineal descent, it begins to seem as if the tremendously influential belief that only the child of a Jewish woman is a Jew is actually held by a shrinking minority, a small and isolated contingent of Orthodox Jews and Conservative leaders who are the advocates for excluding the children of non-Jewish women from the Jewish community. As we've seen, many Jewish communities would not exist without these women and their children. The genetic codes imbedded in Jewish populations all over the world tell the stories of Jewish men—escaping persecution, making a living as traders, driven by sheer wanderlust—who traveled to places where no Jew had gone before, and of non-Jewish women local to these places who married the travelers and with them founded communities culturally, religiously, and genetically identifiable as Jewish today. Perhaps reflecting this reality, the Lemba, a South African tribe whose long claim to Jewish ancestry has now been validated by genetic research, allow *only* women to convert and join their Jewish community.

If non-Jewish women have always procreated for the Jewish people, why not simply acknowledge this fact with official recognition of their children, and move on?

It's impossible to say that the rule of matrilineal descent is a direct result of the negative attitudes toward non-Jewish women imbedded in Judaism, but it is of a piece with them. The origins of matrilineal descent are a mystery, and as we saw in the previous chapter, there is ample evidence that antipathy toward gentile women long predates the time when the Jewish community began disowning their children. However it can be said that a matrilineal definition of Jewishness could not exist without that antipathy. We have seen that the gentile woman occupies a special place as Other in the Jewish imagination despite her long presence in the community. Extending the classification of Other to her child, matrilineal descent intensifies—in a sense, codifies—her reputation as a disruptive force within Judaism.

Humorously, demographer Egon Mayer characterizes the traditional view, which he doesn't share, of gentile wives and their children: "What is she bringing us? She's bringing us non-Jewish children that we now have to deal with, and that's a problem!"

In deadly earnest, Talmud scholar Joel Roth expresses his own opinion this way:

> Numbers aren't everything. There is much to be said in favor of potential quality as against simple quantity. Given the fact of the intimacy of motherhood, it is unlikely that significant numbers of children of gentile mothers will be very dedicated to traditional Jewish values and especially to traditional Jewish observances. How unlikely is it, after all, that a Jewish father who was willing to violate a cardinal tenet of the faith by intermarrying in the first place would exert so great a counterbalance to maternal influence as to result in a committed Jewish child?

Given "the intimacy of motherhood" it might be supposed that a Jewish woman "willing to violate a cardinal tenet of the faith by intermarrying" would also come up short as a Jewish model for her children. But neither this writer nor anyone else that I am aware of advocates according gentile status to the children of Jewish women and non-Jewish men. For Roth, including the children of non-Jewish women and Jewish men in the community constitutes swelling Jewish ranks with inferior goods—choosing quantity over quality. His statement suggests that this issue represents an intersection of misogyny and racism in Jewish thinking: the non-Jewish mother bears a taint that she passes on to her child; her male counterpart is either not stigmatized in this way or keeps his stigma to himself, so that his child is not marred by it.

Roth comments that a Jewish father needs to outweigh "maternal influence." Here he assumes that, as a matter of course, a non-Jewish mother will attempt to influence her child away from Judaism, perhaps toward another faith. In essence, his argument is that the child of a gentile mother shouldn't be considered Jewish because the child of a gentile mother will never be Jewish. His thinking puts me in mind of a comment made by Grace Lewis, who we met briefly in the last chapter. "I've been expected to overcompensate for not being Jewish," says Grace, whose Reform conversion was dismissed by her in-laws. "And the matrilineal theory makes that impossible."

While Roth makes no attempt to disguise his distaste for the children of gentile women, some who argue in favor of a strictly matrilineal definition of Jewishness are not quite so direct. Scholar Judith Hauptman, who believes that change is nothing new in Jewish law, opposes a patrilineal definition of Jewishness on the grounds that it would "confer acceptability upon intermarriage" and "reduce the pressure on Jewish men to seek a Jewish mate." Since statistics tell us that Jewish men and women intermarry in equal numbers, matrilineal descent presumably confers acceptability on the out-marriages of Jewish women, lessening the pressure they might feel "to seek a Jewish mate." Addressing this point, Rabbi Phillip Sigal writes that "if an argument is to be made that, by excluding [patrilineally Jewish] children, mixed marriage will be deterred, then children of Jewish mothers and gentile fathers should also be excluded." But again, no one appears to be arguing that the children of intermarried Jewish women should be stripped of Jewish identity, for this or any other reason. Meanwhile, the gentile women I speak with are keenly aware that in the eyes of some, their children have no Jewish identity to lose.

"My children would be considered beneath the kids with Jewish mothers," says Valerie Paulsen, whose story we heard in the last chapter, explaining why she will not encourage Jewish involvement for any children she and her Jewish husband may have.

"It's like original sin!" exclaims Clara Townsend. Clara, an ex-Catholic whose story we'll encounter in the next chapter, practices Judaism without having formally converted. She says her children, eleven and fourteen, sometimes express anxiety that as patrilineal Jews, they won't be accepted everywhere in the Jewish world, despite the fact that "they see me going to temple more than they go, I'm fully engaged, in their minds we are a Jewish family." Clara and her husband try to reassure them that at least in the synagogue they attend, they needn't worry. "We point out that it really depends on what community you're in," says Clara. "I'm so happy to be at our synagogue, where they don't have to feel that they're not full citizens."

In the modern state of Israel, the citizenship of patrilineal Jews is very much at issue, and definitions of Jewishness have consequences in death as well as life. Many Israelis were born in the former Soviet Union, where a non-Jewish mother or grandmother didn't save them from the special persecution reserved for Jews. But in Israel, these immigrants discover, some for the very first time, that a non-Jewish maternal relative can be enough to make them gentiles. For many, arrival in Israel is an intensely emotional homecoming from generations of exile and oppression—until they are informed that Israeli law doesn't consider them Jews, and stamps this opinion on the identity cards all Israelis must carry. In recent years there have been many much-publicized cases of young people denied Jewish status under Israeli law. The most poignant of these, and the most notorious, involve soldiers who are killed defending their new country, only to be denied burial in Jewish cemeteries. Stories of patrilineally Jewish immigrants who seek to gain recognition as Jews through formal conversion also abound in Israel. Since nothing is simple in this embattled country, and since conversion, like marriage, is controlled by the Orthodox rabbinate, these people often find themselves enmeshed in protracted and bitter struggles to prove their sincerity and their strict observance of religious law in an overwhelmingly secular society.

In the United States, the conversion of children born to non-Jewish mothers is not so arduous a process, at least within the Conservative movement. When an intermarried Jewish man joins his synagogue, says Rabbi Alan Silverstein, "We explain that if he wants to raise his children as Jews, we are happy to help them be converted." He maintains that the reception of all intermarried families is "identical in everything, except that when the non-Jewish partner is female, the children have to convert."

The question then becomes whether the need to have their children converted will look like a minor detail to an interfaith couple, when it is obviously much more than that to the community that requires it. Philip Graubart, a Conservative rabbi in southern California, says, "My personal feeling is that if the child has a non-Jewish mother and is brought up Jewish, conversion confirms a choice that they've already made. I think that what's happening in introducing patrilineal descent is that it creates offensiveness about asking someone to convert. It's not questioning someone's Judaism."

Graubart articulates the Conservative position with sensitivity for the feelings of families affected by it. But the reality is that only someone whose Judaism is questionable—in fact, someone who isn't Jewish—needs to convert to Judaism. As Marta Hernandez noted earlier, parents may not feel prompted—or permitted—to raise a non-Jewish child Jewishly. How many parents of any kind feel obligated to give a child a religious education in a religion to which that child does not belong? A woman who is told that her children are not Jews would have to be extraordinarily motivated toward Judaism to have them formally converted. For many, the sense that her children are stigmatized by their association with her would be enough to quash such motivation before it could flower.

It must be said that not all non-Jewish women are put off by the issue of conversion for their children. Three of the women I've spoken with come to mind. One, Julie Schulman, whom we'll hear more from in the next chapter, overcame an initial unease in agreeing to the conversion of her six-year-old daughter. Megan Taylor, a thirty-two-year-old woman living with her Jewish partner in Nebraska, is studying for her own Conservative conversion, and has no qualms about taking her infant daughter with her to the mikvah. Mary Rosenbloom, who we met in the previous chapter, was surprised, but not unhappy, when her daughter announced her desire to formally convert at the tender age of fourteen. "We just knew that halakhically they weren't Jewish," Mary says of her children. "I sympathize with the Reform movement [in recognizing patrilineal descent] but I can see that it's creating a lot of practical problems. On the other hand, there is biblical evidence for a very ancient non-matrilineal descent."

Has the Reform movement created "a lot of practical problems" with its recognition of patrilineal descent? Graubart believes that matrilineal descent doesn't "serve any purpose" except that "it is a definition, it's a traditional definition. Patrilineal descent hasn't really played out that well in the Reform movement. There's now a class of Jews not considered Jews by segments of the community. It creates confusion, division. The thing that's tricky is that there's no standard."

Rabbi Steven Mason, who counsels intermarried couples in Connecticut and describes himself as "a little bit left of Reform," argues, "It's not the womb that counts!" Yet he admits that the Jewish community is "still breaking heads" over the issue, and that in the Reform movement, "Patrilineal descent is accepted under chaotic situations and nobody knows what that means."

Modernity and Tradition

Dru Greenwood feels she knows exactly what the Reform movement's 1983 ruling means. "It doesn't seem chaotic to me at all," says Greenwood, who is director of outreach for the Reform movement. "If a child has one parent who is Jewish, the child is under presumption of Jewish identity if the child is identified as Jewish. When it was passed, the feeling was that we knew that there were a lot of children of Jewish fathers and non-Jewish mothers and we wanted to be able to include them without a formal conversion."

Unlike the introduction of matrilineal descent in the Mishnah, which Shaye Cohen describes as "a bolt out of the blue," the Reform decision to embrace the children of Jewish fathers could be seen coming for a long time. The movement's leadership, the Central Conference of American Rabbis, grappled with the issue in 1947 and again in 1961, inching toward the 1983 decision that equalized all children with a single Jewish parent, whether that parent was the father or mother. The decision states, "Since the Napoleonic Assembly of Notables of 1806, the Jewish community has struggled with the tension between modernity and tradition. This tension is now a major challenge, and it is within this specific context that the Reform movement chooses to respond. Wherever there is ground to do so, our response seeks to establish Jewish identity of the children of mixed marriages."

Rather than explicitly instituting patrilineal descent, the ruling speaks instead of all children of intermarriage, declaring that "It can no longer be assumed a priori . . . that the child of a Jewish mother will be Jewish any more than that the child of a non-Jewish mother will not be. This leads us to the conclusion that the same requirements must be applied to establish the status of a child of a mixed marriage, regardless of whether the mother or the father is Jewish."

The ruling calls for the Jewish identity of such a child to be "established through appropriate and timely public and formal acts of identification with the Jewish faith and people," specifying these acts as "acquisition of a Hebrew name, Torah study, Bar/Bat Mitzvah, and Kabbalat Torah (Confirmation)." By positing these requirements, says Dru Greenwood, the movement is demanding more than traditional matrilineal descent. "In some ways it's more strict, because you don't have the situation where someone doesn't have to do anything but is still Jewish—where Khrushchev's grandchild is Jewish, and Ben Gurion's is not." Greenwood uses the family situations of these Soviet and Israeli leaders to illustrate a curious side effect of the matrilineal definition of Jewish identity. A person who can trace his or her maternal line back to a Jewish grandmother, no matter how distant, is Jewish under Jewish law, even if that person disavows all connection to Judaism and the Jewish people, even if he or she is committed to another faith; while a gentile maternal ancestor can make a non-Jew of even the most Jewishly raised and identified.

As Judaism's largest movement in the United States, Reform made a splash when it issued its decision in 1983. Yet it wasn't the first movement to recognize the children of Jewish fathers. The tiny Reconstructionist movement, an offshoot of the Conservative movement representing 1 percent of American Jews, got the jump on Reform in 1968 when it ruled that "conversion is unnecessary if one parent is Jewish," says Rabbi Amy Klein, the Jerusalem-based director of Israel programs for the Reconstructionist Rabbinical Assembly. In 1968 the movement stipulated that the child of a Jewish father and non-Jewish mother must be raised and educated Jewishly in order to assume Jewish status, and be circumcised if male. In 1984, the movement reaffirmed the earlier decision, but changed the wording so that it now applies to the child of either a Jewish mother or father, "for the sake of full gender equality and to better reflect the sense in which Jewish acculturation today is voluntary."

The decision lists a number of factors that went into Reconstructionist thinking on the issue. Like the Reform decision, it refers to the biblical precedent for patrilineal descent, but most of what it has to say is very much about the present. The ruling calls the matrilineal principle harmful to Jewish life in that it discriminates against fathers, noting that recognition of patrilineally Jewish children gives a divorced father legal grounds on which to fight for a say in his children's religious education. It notes that "Jewish identity is cultivated by Jewish life," says Klein. "The life that is being lived is most important." The decision also states that Jewish law must be sensitive and humanitarian if it is worth preserving, and that "an interpretation of Judaism that insists it is a static system" does not accord with Reconstructionist thinking.

As we'll see next, Reconstructionists aren't the only ones rejecting the notion of Judaism as a static system.

What Kind of Continuity?

In recent decades, the greatest challenges to the etched-in-stone view of Judaism have come from Jewish women demanding new interpretations of their roles in the family, the synagogue, in every aspect of Jewish life, ritual, and law.

"There's a value to continuity," says feminist scholar Susannah Heschel, "but what kind? I hope that Jewish feminists will transmit a new kind of leadership to the next generation."

Jewish feminists have their own opinions of the role matrilineal descent plays in the dynamic between Jewish men and Jewish women. In theory, Heschel says, matrilineal descent confers a certain power on Jewish women. In reality, it doesn't do much of anything at all. "It says to Jewish men, 'If you want a Jewish child, you have to marry me.' On the other hand, no one pays attention to it." Heschel recalls that when the Reform movement issued its decision recognizing patrilineal descent, she was upset by it and not in favor of the change. "It was supposed to create equality, but we're so far away from any kind of equality between men and women in Judaism. In an ideal world, it's great to tell Jewish men, 'You need us if you want a Jewish child.' But most men don't care."

Reconstructionist rabbi Amy Klein argues that even in theory matrilineal descent has nothing to offer Jewish women. She says she understands a reaction to patrilineal descent like the one Heschel initially had, "But I have a visceral reaction of my own. Matrilineal descent says that women's place is in the home. Traditionally, boys went to school and learned about the ritual aspects of religion at home, so Orthodox apologists say the woman has such an important role in the home. Matrilineal descent plays into tradition."

The arguments in favor of a strictly matrilineal definition of Jewishness are indeed bound up with an ardent belief in the Jewish woman as the essential core of the Jewish family, the conduit singularly capable of transmitting Judaism to future generations. But Paula Hyman, a scholar of Jewish history, refutes the claim that this version of the Jewish family ever existed.

> True, the Jewish mother wielded enormous moral influence over her children, and provided the proper atmosphere for Jewish celebration. However, the transmission of Jewish culture does not really lie in cleaning the house, baking *hallah*, lighting candles, or even urging children to be good Jews.
>
> Religious celebrations within the home were presided over by the husband and father. Moreover, learning and teaching were central to cultural transmission within the Jewish community, and both were the preserves of men. . . .

According to feminist writer Letty Cottin Pogrebin, Jewish women's bodies have also been the preserves of Jewish men, and the matrilineal principle is all about keeping it that way. "Matrilineal descent appears to confer power on women," argues Pogrebin. "But it's a mirage." Like Hyman, Pogrebin insists that Jewish continuity is women's work "only in terms of home based rituals, the ambience of Shabbat and holiday observance, and the cheerleading role that Jewish women are expected to play for Jewish men in the world. When it comes to intellectual, scholarly, communal, political and religious expressions of Jewish identity, continuity is still largely the responsibility of men." Rather than reflecting a key role for women in the transference of Judaism, Pogrebin believes that the matrilineal principal is an outgrowth of men's need to be certain of their children's paternity. "Matrilineal descent does not exist in a vacuum but rather in the context of halakhic constraints on women's virginity." Since those constraints include a husband's ownership of his wife's sexuality and reproductive capacity, in Pogrebin's view, matrilineal descent declares that "a Jew is a person born of a Jewish woman whose virginity and sexuality are by law controlled by a Jewish man who thereby can be assured that, most importantly, his sons are his."

The fact that feminists offer this critique of matrilineal descent doesn't, of course, necessarily mean that it is so summarily dismissed by the Jewish woman in the street—or in the locker room. Robin McMann, a Catholic who has three sons with her Jewish husband, had this confrontation over the issue of her children's lineage while changing out of her swimsuit at the local Y.

"I was talking with a religious woman who has since moved to Israel," Robin recalls. "I had just had a baby, and we had had a bris for each of the boys. She elicited the stories of each bris, and then when I was finished said, 'Well, why did you even bother, because your children are not Jewish?' She made nasty remarks and said, 'Oh, I love these secular Jews who think they're going to raise their children as Jews.' I was naked in the locker room!"

Reflecting on this experience, Robin asks rhetorically, "Why shouldn't the children also be what their father is?"

That, of course, is the question matrilineal descent poses to all families of Jewish men and gentile women. Orthodox Judaism's insistence that children are *not* like their fathers is oddly inconsistent in a religion that otherwise disowns its mothers in so many aspects of ritual and lineage. The traditional version of the Amidah, the central prayer of Jewish worship, invokes the names of the patriarchs, Abraham, Isaac, and Jacob, omitting the matriarchs Sarah, Rebekah, Rachel, and Leah (whose names have been added in contemporary egalitarian liturgy). When a man is called to the Torah during a traditional service (where only men *are* called) he is identified as the son of his father, while his mother's name is forgotten. And as already noted, clan affiliation is passed on patrilineally. As Alexander Schindler, who was president of the (Reform) Union of American Hebrew Congregations in 1983, wondered then, "If the father is good enough to bequeath priestly status, why isn't he good enough to bequeath Jewishness?"

We saw in the previous chapter that much of the received wisdom concerning Jewish men and non-Jewish women depicts men as helpless, and rather witless, victims, who, once snared, will allow their gentile mates to call the shots. Jewish men are not expected to assert their own religious and ethnic identities in an intermarriage, and matrilineal descent makes a similarly negative statement about the role tradition anticipates they will play in their children's lives. Yet according to Jacob J. Staub, a past editor of *Reconstructionist* magazine, "Sociological data indicates that large numbers of children are being raised as Jews even though their mothers were not Jewish at the time of their birth."

Where do the contradictions leave the children?

Zachary Dresher, the young father we met in the last chapter, wonders what effect matrilineal descent will have on his two-year-old daughter's future. "It bugs me that if she decides to be Jewish, how is the religion going to view her?" Harry Meade, whose daughter is now in her twenties, has worried about the same thing even as he and his non-Jewish wife have watched their daughter's Jewish identity flourish. "She has serious Jewish friends she's been shocked to find eat bread [which is forbidden] during Passover, something she wouldn't do," Harry comments. Once, when his daughter was dating a Conservative Jewish man, and had been invited to his home for Shabbat dinner, Harry warned her that his family might not consider her Jewish. "She said, 'No one's going to tell me I'm not Jewish.'" Harry himself is not so sanguine.

What impact does matrilineal descent have on the children of Jewish fathers and gentile mothers? When I began giving talks on the role of the gentile woman in Judaism, I discovered that a significant presence among those concerned with the subject identified themselves as the children of gentile women and Jewish men—and weren't at all sure what to call themselves. By defining who they are, these are the people, men and women, boys and girls, who are, in fact, most affected by the matrilineal definition of Jewishness. As we'll see, from biblical days through the present, Jewish lore has not been so busy issuing opinions of gentile women that it hasn't found time to have something to say about their children as well.

Children for Molech

Among the biblical passages sometimes used to justify a matrilineal definition of Jewishness are these lines from Vayikra, or Leviticus: "From your seed do not offer up to Molech" (18:21), and, "Any man among the Israelites, or among the strangers residing in Israel, who gives from his seed to Molech, shall be put to death" (20:1). Since Molech was a pagan god to whom children were sacrificed, it's not much of a stretch to assume that God is stipulating here that the Israelites are not to sacrifice their children to Molech, or perhaps, by extension, that they are not to allow their children to enter into idol worship of any kind. However, in the midrash on these statements, the rabbis conclude that God's message to the Israelites is that Jewish men are forbidden to copulate with foreign women because the children that result from such unions will be pagans, not Jews. Ingenious, if a bit cryptic, the explication becomes a handy justification for the matrilineal principle.

In fact, it is a matrilineal definition of Judaism that creates children for Molech—not biblical-era idol worshipers but non-Jews. Those who argue most strenuously for matrilineal descent claim that the children of non-Jewish women aren't Jews no matter what they do, then trot out statistics to demonstrate that the children of non-Jewish women are insufficiently Jewishly identified. They may be helping to create the end they decry—Jewishly alienated children of intermarriage—but those who hold to these views don't feel they have much to lose. Insisting on the pernicious influence of gentile women, they don't expect good things from their children.

Throughout most of the twentieth century, intermarriages took place primarily between Jewish men and gentile women. Since the children of intermarriage were by and large the children of gentile women, matrilineal descent effectively made non-Jews of almost all children of interfaith families. Needless to say, until quite recently, these children would not have met with a warm reception in almost any synagogue or Jewish community; certainly not in the congregation led by Canadian rabbi David Kirshenbaum, who published a book in 1958 called *Mixed Marriage and the Jewish Future*. In a sense, Kirshenbaum's book is prescient, predicting that intermarriage will become a pressing concern for North American Jews. His argument is a near-hysterical polemic, in which he casts himself as a Cassandra-like figure attempting to warn an oblivious Jewish community of the devastation to come. About the children of intermarriage he has nothing but bad news, writing of them that, "Jewishness remains a sort of superfluous afterthought, with considerable effect, albeit of a negative nature, on their characters. There develops a strong antipathy against the Jewish side of their ancestry—a feeling which often turns them into anti-Semites."

It is to be hoped that contemporary opinion no longer expects the children of gentile women and Jewish men to grow into anti-Semites. But as we've seen from scholar Joel Roth's essay, the Jewish community may still not expect them to become good Jews. In 2001, the Jewish Outreach Institute and Lights in Action, a Jewish student organization, surveyed college students from mixed family backgrounds. Of the 205 respondents, all but ten said that they identified as Jews, despite the fact that half had been raised in both their Jewish and non-Jewish heritages. Half the students reported participation in synagogue life, and said that they had taken or were planning to take Judaic studies classes. According to Lights in Action program director Kent Kleiman, the biggest problem respondents complained of was feeling excluded by the Jewish community when encountering "a rabbi critical of intermarriage," or by being labeled a "half Jew."

Of course, if those with non-Jewish mothers venture into a Conservative or Orthodox milieu, they will not be recognized as any kind of Jew at all. Perhaps in that situation they will learn to keep their family backgrounds to themselves, as Natalia Moss has done.

Natalia Moss

"My sister and I pledged a moratorium on speaking about our family," says Natalia Moss. "We were tired of being judged, and we got too many questions."

Despite the curiosity she says it arouses, Natalia's Christian-Jewish heritage is not unusual, and, as Jewish demographers keep reminding us, becoming more common all the time. Natalia, thirty-eight, lives with her Jewish husband and their two small sons in France, where they count themselves members of a socially circumspect Jewish community. The French milieu suits her, Natalia says, because people aren't expected to share intimacies about their backgrounds.

Natalia and her sister grew up in Cleveland, the daughters of a Unitarian mother and a Jewish father who worked hard to distance himself from his Florida family, despite their relatively accepting stance toward his wife. "Daddy tried to distance himself from the Jewish community in general," Natalia remembers. "He had been married to a Jewish woman before who his family hated. Once my grandmother told me 'Your mother may not be Jewish but she's good for Dave, and that's all that matters.'"

Natalia thinks that things went smoothly in the family in part because her father chose to keep his relatives at both a physical and emotional arm's length, and in part because her mother "wasn't really Christian and agreed to certain conditions." That is, there were no Christian symbols in their home, though Christmas was celebrated as a nonreligious holiday. Since her father hated holidays and special occasions of all kinds, and refused to celebrate them, her mother, who liked Passover, made a practice of taking her two daughters to her Unitarian church's observance of it. She continued the practice after their father died when Natalia was ten, ironically—given his nonparticipation—in his memory.

Reform Jews, Natalia's paternal relatives considered her and her sister Jewish. Among their mother's relatives, who were Episcopalian, and their Catholic stepfather's extended family, their identity was never in doubt. "Everyone was very nice to us, very kid-glove, as they knew we were Jewish." Natalia says she considers Christianity part of her cultural inheritance but has never felt any emotional attachment to it. "We may not have been religious growing up but I always felt that connection to Judaism."

In the Jewish world outside her family, things weren't always so simple, and Natalia recalls being turned away from Jewish camps and youth groups because of her gentile mother. Thanks to this, and her father's complete lack of interest in Judaism, she received very little Jewish education, and still regrets her limited knowledge of Hebrew and Jewish liturgy. But despite her family background and the rejections from the Jewish community, neither Natalia nor her sister grew up alienated from Judaism. Both became actively involved with Reform Judaism in college, and Natalia eventually spent time as a volunteer on a kibbutz in Israel. Beating the odds—those predicting that the child of a gentile woman and a Jewish man will have a nebulous Jewish identity, if one at all, and is unlikely to marry a Jew and have Jewish children—Natalia has made her choice for Judaism, and she and her husband are raising Jewish children. Natalia is comfortable with all of this; the only thing she isn't comfortable with is having it known that her mother isn't Jewish.

"It might be controversial, but I don't tell everyone my background. They don't need to know this, especially in the generally conservative community I now find myself living in. The French are very private so it fits into the culture. I have a girlfriend who also has a Jewish father and husband. We never talk about it."

In addition to the sense that the Jewish community would disapprove of her gentile mother, Natalia says she feels pressure from interfaith couples not to talk about her Jewish-Christian background—even within the anonymity of Internet discussions. "Recently I saw a message from another woman with a mixed background, and I said, 'Hi, seems most people here are part of mixed couples.' I got blasted! They thought just saying this is rude."

Natalia feels that because she didn't receive a Christian education growing up, her background isn't really all that "mixed," and that she doesn't actually have much to hide. In fact, she is critical of couples who try to impart two religions to their children. "The Great Solution is to have a bris *and* a baptism, a rabbi *and* a priest at the wedding. It seems to me that this is a nonchoice, and undermines the very meaning of these ceremonies."

It's ironic that in these sentiments, and in her concern for the future, Natalia's voice would not be out of place among those in the Jewish community who would be most eager to deny her, the daughter of a gentile woman, a place in the fold. "I've seen a lot of parents raise their mixed children effectively but the real moment is when they become adults," Natalia says. "The real choice is made in the next generation. It seems that they didn't think that far ahead. What will the grandchildren be?"

Given his aversion to his family and community, and his total unconcern with giving his daughters a Jewish education, it may be assumed that Natalia's father didn't think very far ahead. Perhaps he wasn't worried about the ethnic and religious affiliations they would choose for themselves as adults. Or maybe, if he thought about it at all, he hoped they wouldn't choose Judaism. Because he died when Natalia was only ten, the portrait she is able to draw of him is far from complete. But based on what we know, he would seem to have been the very father those who argue most strenuously in favor of maintaining matrilineal descent expect—even insist—all intermarrying Jewish men will become. When Natalia asks "What will the grandchildren be?" this segment of the community would readily answer that what the grandchildren of such a man *won't* be is Jewish. Yet Natalia's children, as well as Natalia and her sister, defy their grim expectations. Making no distinction between matrilineal and patrilineal Jews, psychologist Mark Sirkin says that the children of intermarriage "comprise one of the fastest-growing segments of the Jewish population, yet very little is known about their needs, attitudes, and commitments to Jewish life." There may be more about patrilineally Jewish children than meets traditional leadership's eye.

Edmund Case, president and publisher of InterfaithFamily.com, an on-line journal devoted to the day-to-day issues of interfaith family life, raised two Jewish children with his non-Jewish wife. He says, "I hope someday, and it's probably not going to be in my lifetime, that all the branches of Judaism will get together and recognize my children. It's probably not going to happen, but I want to fight for it."

Case may not be the only member of his family interested in fighting for patrilineal recognition. A couple of years ago, his son, Adam, a senior in high school at the time, wrote a piece for InterfaithFamily about how he feels visiting Israel, aware as he is that the country doesn't consider him Jewish. "The thing that troubles me most is that the very land that I feel such a connection with is the same state that would not recognize me as a Jew," wrote the younger Case, noting that matrilineal descent is the standard of Jewish identity in Israel. Describing his strong religious education and current allegiance, he declares that he doesn't feel "any less Jewish than anyone else."

Are Adam Case and Natalia Moss anomalies? Adam received a solid Jewish education, Natalia Moss did not; both are called gentiles by traditional Judaism, and both call themselves Jews. Adam reports that his most recent trip to Israel, organized by a Jewish youth group, included at least nine other children of intermarriage—all of whom were treated, along with the rest of their peers, to their group leader's homily on in-marriage as the way to create Jewish children. If these young people and their feelings could be overlooked in the intimacy of a group tour, it is to be expected that theirs is an equally invisible presence within the larger Jewish world. Yet it would be pointless to argue that most young people will lay claim to Jewish identities in defiance of Jewish law, particularly if their upbringing is as indifferently Jewish as Natalia's was. Like Holly Burns, whom we'll meet next,

many patrilineally Jewish children will hear that they don't belong in the Jewish community, and simply grow up believing it.

Holly Burns

When a college application form asked for her religion, Holly
Burns wrote "JAP/WASP." Many years later, in her role as a research librarian for a large Connecticut university, she heard
that a patron was searching for an essay whose title included the
words "the Ultimate Shiksa." Her first reaction was, "Oh, I always think that's me!" What both these responses demonstrate,
says Holly, thirty-five, is that, "I really don't fit. I really don't belong anywhere."

When they immigrated from Eastern Europe to the United
States in the late 1880s, Holly's paternal relatives wanted to fit
into American culture, and leave their ethnic and religious heritage behind. Growing up in Westchester, New York, Holly
didn't hear much about the family's origins, but she did know
that when her grandfather died, his widow changed her own
and her young sons' names from Bernstein to Burns and "the
whole family tried to become as 'American' as possible. As far as
I know, none of them observed any Jewish traditions, and I
don't think they ever went to temple."

Two of the Burns sons, including Holly's father, married
Christian women from the South, while the third remained single. When Holly and one of her cousins cleaned out their unmarried uncle's apartment after his death, they were stunned
to find a card from a rabbi indicating that the anniversary
(*yartzeit*) of their grandmother's death had been ritually observed. In Holly's memory, this is the only connection between
any member of her father's family and the Jewish religion.

Holly's father and mother, a nonpracticing southern Baptist,
were left-wing intellectuals who celebrated Christmas as a nonreligious holiday and nothing else while Holly was growing up.

After her parents divorced, her father remarried a German woman who Holly says celebrated Christmas German style. "He had been a POW taken by the Germans after parachuting into Normandy," Holly comments. "He hated Germans, and then he married one."

Holly's mother embodied some contradictions of her own. Holly has picked up hints that her mother's family was not pleased with her decision to marry a New York Jew. Though a liberal, her mother retained some of the prejudices with which she was raised. "I remember one derogatory comment she made about Jews. I was eleven or twelve and was offended, and I told her that I was offended." On the other hand, Holly also recalls how upset her mother was when she came upon Holly at a younger age, perhaps eight or nine, drawing a swastika. "I was just trying to draw the shape without being aware of its meaning," Holly remembers. "She let me try to draw it and then explained its symbolism and said I should never draw it again. I was struck at the time by how seriously she took the issue and never did attempt to draw it again."

With very little religion of any kind in the household, it's not surprising that an incident pivotal in shaping Holly's sense of her religious identity took place outside it. In her early teens she attended a summer camp in the Adirondack Mountains in New York, where the majority of the kids came from Jewish families. Though the other campers weren't religious, a strong ethnic affiliation prevailed. "I remember a conversation about Judaism and who was and wasn't a Jew," Holly recalls. "Someone emphatically told me that because my father was Jewish and not my mother, I wasn't and couldn't ever be considered a Jew. As a young teenager, I didn't question this. I felt *horrible*. It felt like I didn't fit in with my friends, I could never fit in. It was like getting a door slammed." It didn't help that there was no one in her family whom Holly felt free to ask about what she had been told. "I didn't explore it because it wasn't okay."

Twenty years later, Holly still doesn't feel free to explore

Judaism, despite having always had Jewish friends and feeling drawn to Jewish religion and culture. She laughs when she recalls that her husband, who is not Jewish, was initially attracted to her because he thought she was. "Both of us are attracted to Judaism," she comments. Holly doubts that she and her husband will have children. If they do, she says that based on her own experience it would be better to introduce them to some religion than none. Since she feels she couldn't legitimately offer a tradition of her own, she imagines that she would probably raise them as Unitarians by default.

"I have thought about learning more about Judaism, possibly attending services or something, but I always feel awkward in a synagogue," Holly says. "Mostly, I suspect, it's because I don't know enough of the traditions and practices, and I'm afraid I'll do the wrong thing. Partly, though, it's because I feel torn about my own heritage. Am I half-Jewish or am I not Jewish at all? Where does such knowledge come from, anyway?"

Where does such knowledge come from? Most people know that they are Jewish because they were raised to know it, they have always known it, and it is an essential element in everything else they know about themselves. For some, knowledge of Jewish heritage comes suddenly, with the dramatic revelation of a family secret. According to rabbinic law, if such people can trace Jewish lineage back to a matrilineal ancestor, no matter how distant, no matter what the family's recent religious affiliation has been, they are Jewish. Judaism is wonderful in embracing its far-flung children in this way.

It's ironic that traditionally, the community is equally committed to casting away the children, no matter how Jewishly raised and identified, who don't meet the single rabbinic criterion for Jewish status, a Jewish mother. As we've seen, a Jew was once defined as the child of a Jewish father. For reasons which have so far proven impossible to uncover, the postbiblical rabbis who codified Jewish law chose to change this definition. At the opening of this chapter, we heard about a Jewish writer troubled that the children of gentile mothers are admitted to some Jewish day schools, where they may "intermarry" with the children of Jewish mothers. According to Rabbi Phillip Sigal, "The self-styled 'orthodox' have no halakhic grounds" on which to base such a concern. The claim that matrilineal descent is a sacred, God-given commandment is contradicted by the central texts, the books of the Torah, upon which halakhah is based. Halakhah is a mutable system that has been changed in all sorts of ways throughout the past two thousand years. Matrilineal descent is one of those changes. Recognition of both patrilineal and matrilineal descent can, in our generation, become another.

As Robert Goldenberg writes, "To isolate the halakhic from everything else we know . . . is to reduce the moral gravity of the halakhic to intellectual formalism, and that would be a catastrophic impoverishment of Jewish life."

Currently, the Jewish community chooses to impoverish itself to the extent that it excludes some of the children of intermarriage. While matrilineal descent apparently sanctions intermarriage for Jewish women, it penalizes Jewish men who marry outside the fold. It places no stigma on gentile men and embraces their children, while keeping gentile women and their children beyond the pale of traditional communities, denying them participation in some synagogues, camps, and schools. It creates fathers who feel they don't have the right to raise their children Jewishly, and adults who feel similarly unentitled to lay claim to Jewish identity. Matrilineal descent is a definition of Jewishness defended exclusively by those who are not themselves affected by it, and who are, moreover, entirely unable to offer a single convincing argument in favor of maintaining it. But no convincing argument is offered because no convincing argument can be offered: *matrilineal descent doesn't serve the Jewish community*. It can serve only those who would see the Jewish community, or all but a tiny segment of it, disappear. By

CHILDREN FOR MOLECH: MATRILINEAL DESCENT

recognizing patrilineal descent, the Orthodox and Conservative movements could create thousands more Jews in one fell swoop.

Scholar Trude Weiss Rosmarin writes, "Far from weakening the Jewish community, emancipating the Jewish father by conferring upon him the right of transmitting his Jewish identity to his children, with the non-Jewish mother's consent, will increase our numbers and thus add strength to our Jewish survival potential."

Is the survival of matrilineal descent more important than the survival of the Jewish people? Should those who would answer yes to this question call the shots that will determine the Jewish future?

Given that the law results from an obscure human decision, given that it creates a gender dichotomy in Jewish life, and willfully rejects thousands of potential members of the community, those who support matrilineal descent need to look very closely at exactly what it is they are arguing for. They must open their eyes, their hearts, and their minds to the reality taking place in the Jewish community today, where, despite every effort to push them away, countless Jewish children are being raised in Jewish homes by Jewish fathers and non-Jewish mothers.

It is these families that we will look at next.

4

Not-So-Jewish Mothers:
Gentile Mothers in the Jewish Family

I ONCE attended a very heated panel discussion concerning the role of non-Jewish members in the leadership of a synagogue. Joe, an eloquent, forty-something father of teenagers, felt strongly that non-Jews should be excluded from leadership positions. Among other things, he feared that the inclusion of non-Jews would send a message to the synagogue's young people that intermarriage was acceptable: after all, non-Jewish members were, by and large, the partners of Jews. Joe believed it was the synagogue's responsibility to let its children know that intermarriage was *not* okay.

In answer to a question from the audience, it was established that interfaith families comprised half the membership of the synagogue. In his desire to discourage intermarriage, was Joe thinking of the 50 percent of young congregants with gentile fathers or, as in most cases, mothers? Was he aware that what he wanted these children to understand was that the synagogue disapproved of *their* families—in fact, of their very existence?

Survival anxiety is built into Judaism, a faith of small numbers and hostile neighbors. Since the dawn of Jewish time, this anxiety has been played out in Judaism's contradictory relationship to the gentile women in its midst, with the tradition voicing strong objections to intermarriage—and countering those objections with heroic images of gentile wives and mothers even in the very first Jewish families. As we'll see in the stories of contemporary non-Jewish women that follow, the contradictions still touch lives, sometimes having a pivotal impact on whether and where families choose to locate themselves within Judaism.

Like it or not, intermarried families are a part of most Jewish communities. As we've seen, according to the law of matrilineal descent still adhered to by Orthodox and Conservative Judaism, only the children of a Jewish woman can be considered Jews without formal conversion. Yet the reality is that gentile women are giving birth to the Jewish community's next generation in significant numbers. First, let's look at those numbers.

As already noted, according to the findings of the National Jewish Population Survey for 2000–2001, the Jewish community is both shrinking and aging. It is also failing to replace itself: the survey found that Jewish women reaching the end of their childbearing years had an average of 1.8 children, below the replacement level of 2.1. How might these figures improve if the non-Jewish partners of Jews who are—or could be—raising Jewish children were counted? Clearly the Jewish community needs them, given that it is widely accepted as fact that roughly half of all Jews are choosing partners from outside the faith. Until recently, these unions nearly always involved Jewish men and non-Jewish women.

Jody Rosenbloom, a Jewish educator who has spent a two-decades-long career at Temple Israel in Minneapolis, Minnesota, a Reform congregation of 2,200 families, and at the 350-member Reconstructionist Jewish Community of Amherst, Massachusetts, offers a typical observation: "Before the last ten years, when you referred to an interfaith household, nine times out of ten it was the father who was Jewish. In the twenty years of my experience with families, the non-Jewish parent is nearly always female."

It is estimated that some 1.3 million children are currently part of interfaith homes, while a recent Jewish Outreach Institute study concluded that more children under twelve belong to interfaith than to all-Jewish families. With women accounting for nearly all the gentile partners in interfaith unions formed prior to the past couple of decades, and at least half of those involved in interfaith marriages being formed today, it is safe to assume that more—perhaps a good deal more—than half a million children are being raised by gentile mothers and Jewish fathers.

To those concerned about Jewish continuity and the religious identification of the children of intermarriage, statistics tend to paint a grim, if erratic, portrait of the Jewish involvement among interfaith families. Most estimates of the number of children of interfaith families being raised as Jews range from 20 to 33 percent overall, though a recent study reported that three-quarters of families in which the mother is Jewish and slightly less than half in which the father is Jewish, are raising Jewishly identified children.

Why do so few gentile mothers choose to raise their children as Jews?

Some in the Jewish community, most notably Reform movement leaders, have asked themselves for years how to engage the non-Jewish partners, usually the wives, of Jews and their families. It is a crucial question: *Jewish survival depends, in part, upon non-Jewish mothers.* As we'll see in the stories ahead, mothers tend to be decisive in children's religious lives. The goodwill and generosity of gentile mothers agreeing to raise their children as Jews will be a determining factor in the size and vitality of the American Jewish community of the future. But perhaps before the question can be meaningfully addressed, a little soul-searching is in order.

Is the Jewish community unambivalent in its desire for these children? What role does Judaism's attitude toward gentile women play in keeping mothers—and their children—away?

According to conventional belief, gentile women are the

archenemies of Jewish continuity. They entice Jewish sons into severing their roots, bear children Jewish law doesn't recognize as Jews, and then, adding insult to injury, whisk them off to the baptismal font, where they are lost to Judaism forever.

One thing wrong with this scenario, of course, is that it woefully overlooks the role played by Jewish men and their relationships to their own identities. "If the man is well socialized in Judaism, rooted in a synagogue, this is a good situation for the children to be raised as Jews," says Rabbi Steven Mason, the therapist who has counseled intermarried couples in the Hartford, Connecticut, area since 1986. "If the Jewish man is disconnected from all this," Mason adds, "anything goes."

Jewish educator Jody Rosenbloom sees problems that run still deeper than disconnection. "The Jewish father may be very ambivalent about being Jewish, and therefore was attracted to being with somebody who wasn't Jewish, or he can be self-hating," says Rosenbloom. "There's a whole range. Some Jewish men are sincerely committed to their Judaism, and their interfaith marriage, if it was accepted within the man's larger extended family, continues to foster a Jewish identity." If the marriage wasn't accepted, she adds, "It can be a lot more difficult for the whole household," and decisive in whether a gentile mother feels "welcomed or ostracized within the whole network" of Jewish communal ties.

In our first story, we'll visit Monica Cassia's Chicago home, where Jewish observance has certainly been characterized, more than anything else, by ambivalence: her husband's.

Monica Cassia

When Monica Cassia, a graphic designer in her midforties, was growing up, her father's international career required them to live in Italy for a number of years. In Rome, Monica met three popes and received Catholic confirmation from one of them.

The family moved often, but Monica and her siblings attended parochial schools whenever they lived in places that provided them. "I just really feel that I had my big hit of religion," Monica says. "It was not a good thing for me."

When Monica got involved with Will, who is Jewish, she let him know that spiritual life was, quite simply, something she had opted out of. Still, she was ready to go along with any Jewish practices he cared to introduce into their home—provided that *he* took the initiative.

But Will's feelings about Judaism were—and are—anything but simple. For years he avoided synagogue membership. Then he joined a temple to attend services for the High Holy Days of Rosh Hashanah and Yom Kippur, only to report each year that the sermons were diatribes against intermarriage. At one point, Monica and Will considered putting their first child, Nate, now thirteen, into the synagogue's religious school. The withering response Monica's Italian surname received at the school's open house reception changed their minds.

Will has since joined a liberal congregation where he feels less alienated but no more inclined to become an active member, and his attendance at services is still a twice-a-year occurrence. He has spoken with the rabbi about his doubts, gone through a fitful period of reading Buddhist texts, and continues to remain tortured over exactly what his beliefs consist of.

"I've asked him a lot of questions about the Jewish feeling about one thing or another," Monica comments, "and he'll say, 'I have no idea.' I don't know if that's because he has no idea or because there isn't really a Jewish answer." Monica believes that deep down, Will loves Judaism, but that "the more his mom pushes him to go in that direction the more he wants to put on the brakes, and say, 'No thanks.'"

Whether or not Will's mother plays this crucial role in his feelings about Judaism, she does loom large in Monica's. Before she met Will, Monica had been seeing another Jewish man whose family had welcomed her with open arms. But when she and Will got together, she recalls that she was "overwhelmed, crushed" by the negative reaction his mother, Sophie, had to the relationship. "He's her one and only boy and I'm not sure if any girlfriend of his would have been exactly welcomed. But the fact that I wasn't Jewish was a big problem, partly because of the fact that the woman needs to be Jewish for the kids to be Jewish, at least in the old way."

Monica has come to see Sophie as "a very intelligent, very tough, very domineering, intense woman. She's also an incredibly loving grandmother to the kids, which I really appreciate, and a good person." At the same time, she feels Sophie holds her responsible for the family's lack of strong Jewish identification, manifested in such choices as Nate's decision not to have a bar mitzvah, the coming-of-age ritual customary for thirteen-year-old boys (bat mitzvah is the equivalent ritual for girls). "I think it will be convenient for her to say, 'It's Monica.' I wasn't talking the bar mitzvah down, but I wasn't spearheading it. I think her disappointment is with her son, but it's more convenient to blame me."

Monica and Will have been together for twenty years. What happened over Nate's bar mitzvah is part of a long pattern, in which their skittish relationship to religion and culture gets played out at times that are important occasions for many couples. They didn't marry until Nate was a preschooler, because Monica felt that any kind of service, religious or civil, would be meaningless. When they did tie the knot, so that Will could receive health insurance through Monica's job, it was strictly a mechanical affair without friends or relatives. And there were no celebrations for the births of Nate and Daisy, eight, though Monica still gets upset recalling Will's unexpected insistence that his son be circumcised.

"I thought that we would read everything available to us about circumcision, and make a decision based on all the facts that we had amassed. Then Will, after a lot of back and forth, said, 'I'm sorry, but I'm a Jew and I feel like the circumcised penis is a very important part of that and I don't think I can go with an uncircumcised kid.' So we went ahead and did it, but that kind of rocked me a little bit because I felt sort of left out." Even so, Will didn't want a brit milah for Nate, only a hospital procedure.

Monica's ironic and edgy delivery becomes wistful when she speaks of these missed opportunities for marking significant events. "I think that I've spent my whole life tossing off these things that don't have meaning for me, but not necessarily replacing them with stuff of my own." Nate's choice not to have a bar mitzvah again saves the family from having to locate themselves within a tradition. Monica predicts that Daisy's choice will be different. "She loves the synagogue school, she comes home singing the songs and telling the stories. I'll bet she'll want a bat mitzvah."

Despite Monica's hands-off stance, she feels supportive of the children's involvement in Judaism. Most of the family's friends are Jewish, and Monica is as comfortable at Will's synagogue as she is likely to be at any. When they celebrate Shabbat, the Jewish Sabbath, in their home on Friday nights, it's because Monica has remembered to buy the traditional candles and the challah, the braided loaf of bread. They spend Jewish holidays with Will's mother, but one year, when it wasn't feasible to be with her for Passover, Monica offered to have a seder, a Passover dinner, at their house. She told Will he would only need to provide her with the necessary guidance. Will's response? "Never mind."

"I've been thinking lately that women are often the ones who continue traditions," Monica comments. "It's humiliating to keep going to your parents for holidays, how old do you have to be to have your own holidays? But he's not put himself in a position where he's keeping stuff alive, and I don't think I should play a starring role in this."

Which makes it all the more striking that Monica is the only woman I've spoken with to raise the question of what she would do if that starring role was suddenly forced upon her. "I think if something happened to Will, if he died, I would try to keep it up," she says slowly. "It would be kind of sketchy, I mean maybe that would make me want to find out more. But I can't imagine ever converting, and I don't think I was duplicitous, I think I was very clear from the beginning about where I stood. I just don't think he was really clear about where he stood."

It's safe to assume that her children's Jewish education is probably the last thing a woman worries about when she contemplates the loss of her husband or the dissolution of her marriage—but Jewish leaders are another story. According to Rabbi Sanford Selzer, former director of the Commission on Reform Jewish Outreach, the way a gentile woman feels about a commitment to raise Jewish children may be very different out of marriage than in it. "We have a growing incidence of divorces where the non-Jewish partner, usually a woman, no longer wants to abide by that agreement after divorce. If she's widowed and remarries someone who is not Jewish, then what?"

On the other hand, educator Rosenbloom cites some "extreme examples" she's seen of divorced or widowed mothers going to great lengths to champion their children's right to a place in a Hebrew school, despite the opposition or indifference of their synagogue. Maybe, like Monica, some of these women would have preferred to remain backstage in their children's Jewish lives, but stepped forward when there was no one else to take the lead.

What everyone agrees on is that even in intact homes, mothers are still the linchpins in the religious and cultural lives of families: it's a point made or implicit in nearly every conversation I've had about the subject with gentile women and Jewish leaders. "I see a very significant role for non-Jewish mothers," says Selzer. "All the psychological data maintain that mothers still play a more profound role than fathers in the child's life and in the home."

In the synagogue, too. "It happens to be a sociological fact that I've noticed that mothers are more concerned with children's religious life," observes Philip Graubart, a Conservative rabbi at Congregation Beth El in La Jolla, California. "Generally, it's the non-Jewish mother who's more active than the Jewish father."

Rosenbloom agrees. While she says that she has never known a non-Jewish father to be an active agent in his child's Jewish education, she's witnessed a range of positions taken by non-Jewish mothers, beginning at one end of the spectrum with women like Monica: "Some mothers make it clear, they're not Jewish, they have no role. But I've seen a lot of mothers go above and beyond with carpooling, trying to monitor their kids' behavior and participation in class, being willing to have their kids teach them Hebrew, or to learn Hebrew on their own in order to facilitate their kids' education."

How are these mothers and their families received within the constellation of synagogues, Hebrew schools, day schools, and camps that make up the social parameters of Jewish family life?

"Inevitably, there's friction," says Graubart. "Sometimes a Jewish member will question how a non-Jew has been allowed to become so involved or be in a leadership-type position." Not necessarily an *actual* leadership position, Graubart explains. On occasion a gentile mother veered dangerously close to chairing the school committee at Congregation B'nai Israel, a Massachusetts synagogue where Graubart worked previously. That situation would have required a communal policy decision—perhaps public forums like the meeting Joe, above, spoke at—and Graubart was careful to lead his congregants away from such a mandate. "It would have divided us."

In our next story, we'll meet a woman who has felt those divisions.

Clara Townsend

Clara Townsend, forty-seven, a pediatrician in the Washington, D.C., area, and her husband, Mark, are the parents of Ethan, fourteen, and Sarah, eleven. In the early years of their marriage, Clara and Mark were members of a Conservative synagogue that some of Mark's family attended.

"Weird things happened," says Clara. One evening, she got a call from a doctor in the community engaged in fund-raising that specifically targeted physicians. "He was hoping that as a physician I would have a deeper pocket and would reach into my deeper pocket. But then in that same week the community was voting on something, and we got a letter laying out the laws that Mark, as a Jew, could vote, but I couldn't." The congregation, Clara felt, was trying to have it both ways. "You can't call me as a member of the community and ask me in particular for money and then say that I can't vote. That's like taxation without representation. We don't do that here!

"I never really recovered from that," Clara continues. "I just felt like I wasn't a whole member and I felt kind of taken advantage of too. It was two different groups sending out two different signals, but I just felt like they hadn't looked at that issue, they hadn't looked at how that would feel. I felt excluded and like my kids were not going to be complete citizens either."

That sense of being an incomplete citizen was something Clara grew up with. Her father, a Catholic, was barred from receiving communion after his marriage to Clara's Protestant mother. Though he dutifully took his children to mass each Sunday, Clara felt the Church never really accepted them—and she returned the compliment. "I always remember feeling Catholicism rub against my grain," she explains. "I have a very vivid memory of learning about original sin [the belief that babies are born in sin] in the third grade and thinking, 'This religion is all wrong, it isn't right for me.'" Clara laughs. "In hindsight, that was my first inkling that I was a child advocate, that I would be a pediatrician."

For his part, Mark's upbringing had emphasized strong Jewish cultural ties but had pretty much left out religion. Mark's father welcomed Clara into the family as a daughter, but with his mother the situation was quite different. "For his mom it was really a problem that I was a shiksa, and I was clearly a shiksa. Thank heavens I was a doctor, and she would tell you so much, 'At least she's a doctor.' To her the fact that I was a physician saved me, and over time she came to accept me."

Clara's differences with her mother-in-law were often matters of temperament and taste, yet in Clara's mind, all of these things had a way of getting folded into religion. Clara grew up in middle-class suburbs. She likes to spend her free time running and hiking, and her preferred wardrobe reflects this: running shorts and sweats, no makeup or high heels. Mark's family are fashion-conscious, wealthy New Yorkers whose idea of a bat mitzvah party climax is to have the girl of honor jump out of a ceiling-high Bloomingdale's shopping bag to the tune of Madonna's "Material Girl." "I know that if I was with an upper-crust family of another religion, I would feel just as alienated," Clara says. "But I've always felt like the shiksa from the country."

These differences didn't translate into an antipathy toward Judaism itself. When Mark made it clear before their marriage that their children would have to be raised as Jews, Clara, very much in love and no longer a practicing Christian, found it easy to agree.

What exactly that would mean for their family life has evolved slowly over the years, and is still in flux. Like many gentile women, Clara's first brush with Jewish religious practices came when she and Mark sought out a rabbi to marry them, and discovered that most can't (Orthodox and Conservative rabbis) or won't (a majority of Reform and Reconstructionist rabbis) officiate at weddings between Jews and gentiles. Unlike any other stories I've heard, Clara and Mark also met with a bizarre response from some rabbis in their search. "We spoke with rabbis who said they wouldn't marry us for the regular price, but if we paid a little bit more they would. Whoa! That was a turnoff."

Nevertheless, Clara explored the possibility of conversion before the wedding, and found a rabbi she really liked. But eighty-hour weeks as a medical intern made the classes and meetings the rabbi required impossible. In any case, since Mark's attachment to Judaism at the time was purely ethnic, Clara didn't think her conversion would have all that much meaning to either of them.

They joined the synagogue that some of Mark's family belonged to despite the rabbi's inability to marry them, and stayed after his refusal to assist with the baby-naming ceremony they wanted for Ethan in lieu of a traditional circumcision. Their tenuous membership was brought to a natural close when they moved south to a more remote coastal community.

There Clara discovered a tiny Reform Jewish congregation where she was not only welcomed as a member but actually allowed to teach in the religious school's youngest classrooms. "It was all volunteer and we'd just kind of get together and bake and do arts and crafts and sing songs," she recalls. "That was really nice. I definitely felt like a full member of that community."

After a few years, Clara and Mark moved back to their old town. This time they opted for a more liberal synagogue unaffiliated with any of the major Jewish movements. Though she hasn't become as involved as she was in her previous community, Clara says she feels at ease there. She and Mark particularly found themselves engaged by the spiritual preparations for Ethan's bar mitzvah: the family meetings with the rabbi, the community-service responsibility Ethan took on and still continues. "Developmentally, we were ripe, feeling a midlife draw toward spirituality. We really like the group prayer, and feeling that sense of community is so grounding. We really didn't reach this point until Ethan's bar mitzvah, and now I want to keep that experience full and give it some context. To show Ethan by our weekly life that it wasn't just a party."

Clara and Mark have begun attending Friday night synagogue services regularly, and Clara is struggling with her work schedule to get home early enough on Fridays to make a family ritual of Shabbat dinner. She and Mark are bringing Jewish books into the house, and discussions of their contents to the dinner table. Like other gentile women I've spoken with who are trying to create Jewish homes, Clara doesn't feel that the term "interfaith" describes her family, because they are unified by the practices of a single religion—almost. She is still negotiating with Ethan and Sarah to let go of the minimal Christmas observance they grew used to as younger children. She's considering conversion again, too, but still questions when she would find the time, and whether her family's connection to Judaism would be deepened by it. "The kids already feel like I've converted," she says. "They see me going to services more than they do."

While Monica probably wouldn't warm up to religion in any circumstances, for Clara, as for other non-Jewish women, taking Judaism gradually into heart and home has been a natural outgrowth of family life.

Initially, Clara's love for Mark translated into an openness toward those things that were important to him. Now she recognizes spiritual needs of her own and has a sense that Judaism can satisfy those needs—a sense that has everything to do with her reception in specific Jewish communities, with feeling accepted "as is." But like other, though by no means all, women in her situation, her interest, perhaps her feeling of entitlement, is still very much tied to her connection to Mark and her responsibilities as a mother. Her family, she reports, doesn't need her to convert; in fact, conversion would represent an independent relationship to Judaism that she has no compelling drive toward.

Clara has been hurt when treated as an outsider in the Jewish community. But it must also be said that she has had to struggle at times against her own inclination to see that community as alien, by labeling individual or class traits she finds distasteful the products of ethnic values. When she describes her in-laws' materialistic excesses, she hovers just this side of anti-Semitic caricature, as she is well aware.

Many women searching for a place in the Jewish community as non-Jews or potential converts get hung up on the idea of Jewish ethnicity from another angle entirely. Despite Jewish law's insistence to the contrary, they feel—and some Jews encourage them to feel—that Jewish parentage is the only ticket to inclusion, that a "real" Jew is an ethnic Jew. If that's so, then many of the figures the Jewish people considers its forebears weren't actually Jewish at all.

In the Beginning

When the Jewish people recalls its origins, three patriarchs and four matriarchs are acknowledged as its founders. There's Abraham and Sarah, their son Isaac and his wife, Rebekah, Isaac and Rebekah's son, Jacob (also called Israel), and Jacob's two wives, the sisters Rachel and Leah. The central prayer of Jewish liturgy, the Amidah, traditionally opens with a clarion call to the God of Abraham, Isaac, and Jacob. Thanks to the efforts of Jewish feminists, egalitarian prayer books also address the God of Sarah, Rebekah, Rachel, and Leah, the four mothers of the Jewish people, and, in the case of Rachel and Leah, the specific mothers of the twelve sons of Jacob from which the twelve tribes of Israel spring. There's only one problem: Rachel and Leah didn't give birth to their twelve sons all on their own. They had help.

When Rachel's maternity is delayed, she has Jacob impregnate her handmaid, Bilhah, and Bilhah's two sons, Dan and Naphtali, are counted as Rachel's. When Leah decides her first four sons are not enough of a lead over childless Rachel, she gives her handmaid, Zilpah, to Jacob and adds two more sons, Gad and Asher, to her side of the register.

In other words, four of the twelve tribes of Israel descend from the sons of gentile women.

A surprising number of gentile mothers appear in the Torah. While the matriarchs are prone to faulty fertility, the non-Jewish slaves in their households have no such trouble. When all else fails, a gentile servant girl can be pressed into service (no pun intended) producing a patriarch's offspring. It's a relationship introduced in the original Jewish family of Abraham and Sarah, in which the Torah demonstrates that the situation of such a "birth mother" is no picnic—particularly if she and her child become expendable.

Unable to conceive (biblical infertility is always a female problem), Sarah decides that Abraham should cohabit with her Egyptian slave, Hagar. The arrangement is not a ménage à trois made in heaven. Once pregnant, Hagar exhibits a sense of superiority over her mistress, and, not surprisingly, Sarah finds her servant's attitude intolerable. When Sarah blames Abraham for the position she finds herself in with Hagar, Abraham tells her to treat Hagar as she pleases. Sarah abuses Hagar and Hagar runs away into the wilderness, where she becomes the first biblical woman to be personally addressed by God. God tells Hagar to return to Sarah, to put up with her harsh treatment and await the birth of a son who will found a great people.

Hagar gives birth to Ishmael in Sarah's house. Then Sarah herself conceives and bears a son, Isaac. Now it is Ishmael who becomes a threat in Sarah's eyes. Sarah doesn't want Ishmael to grow up alongside Isaac and she tells Abraham to send him away. When Abraham demurs, God instructs him to do as Sarah wishes. Hagar and Ishmael are banished into the desert. Isaac and Ishmael are parted, and their children, the Jewish and Arab peoples, are severed in a family split whose painful consequences reverberate to this day.

It's interesting to speculate what all of these biblical women, both gentiles and Jews, would make of the modern arrangements of surrogacy and adoption.

In the late 1980s, the "Baby M" case brought surrogacy to explosive national consciousness, when a Jewish man named Robert Stern, the son of Holocaust survivors, had a child through contractual arrangement with a gentile woman, Mary Beth Whitehead, artificially impregnated by him. The notoriety of the case publicized the murky emotional and legal terrain crossed by those on either side of such an arrangement. Surrogacy has not caught on as a popular remedy for childlessness, and those who do pursue it tend to do so quietly.

Much more common is adoption. From 15 to 20 percent of American Jews experience fertility problems, and more than 3 percent—some 60,000—of the children in Jewish homes have been adopted. Overwhelmingly, the children who enter the Jewish community through adoption, both domestic and international, are born to gentile mothers. They have no place in the Jewish community, yet, through their children, these mothers are a kind of shadow presence within it.

"Whoever brings up an orphan in his home is regarded as though the child had been born to him," declares the Talmud, a postbiblical work of Jewish law, neatly severing the tie between a birth mother and her children. In the Jewish community, an adopted child sheds a biological mother and is reborn as a Jew— or so adoptive parents hope. According to Shelley Kapnek Rosenberg, author of *Adoption and the Jewish Family*, some families feel that despite Jewish law, an adopted child is greeted with "a subtle undercurrent of wondering, an attitude of 'Does this child come from good stock?'"

That's an attitude that gentile mothers raising the children they've given birth to in the Jewish community have been known to encounter as well. "Are they *Jewish*?" Monica Cassia has been asked about her children by Jews recoiling from the Italian half of their hyphenated surname. For some women, being told that their children must undergo conversion in order to be accepted as Jews communicates that kind of suspicion. For others, as we'll see in the next story, it's a minor stumbling block, if one at all.

Julie Shulman

Two years ago, when Julie Shulman relocated from New York to a small midwestern city with her husband, Ted, and their then five-year-old daughter, Laura, the new start seemed like a good time to rethink their decision about how Laura would be raised.

"When we were getting married we decided that our children would be baptized because I was Catholic and we would make everyone happy," says Julie, thirty-four. "Then they would have both religions, celebrate everything, and we would allow them to decide. It was that misconception that we were going to allow our children to decide what they would like to be. When you look at that realistically, it sounds so stupid that you could have even thought that that would be possible."

For Julie, her daughter's baptism and other gestures toward her Catholic background were expressions of her attachment to her parents, not to her religion. As a child she had found Catholicism's practices, such as confession, "humiliating," and its worship of multiple figures, including the Virgin Mary, confusing. Because her best friend was Jewish, she grew up familiar with Jewish ritual, and always found herself drawn to the Jews in her social milieu. As an adult, she was attracted by Jewish values and by Judaism's emphasis on monotheism. Maybe this was the religion that she wanted in her daughter's life.

They visited the synagogue nearest their new home, which happened to be Conservative, and were told that in order for Laura to be considered Jewish by the congregation, she would have to be formally converted. "It shocked me at first," Julie recalls. "I wondered why that would be necessary." But despite her initial reaction, Julie accepted that conversion was Conservative Judaism's condition of admittance for the child of a gentile mother. Julie and Ted decided to send Laura to the synagogue's Hebrew school for a year and then see if conversion felt right to them.

Many of the gentile women I've spoken with echo Clara Townsend's report of meeting with a warmer welcome at Reform, Reconstructionist, and unaffiliated synagogues than in Conservative congregations. But temple culture varies so much from one community to the next that generalizations are highly unreliable. Julie has never felt uncomfortable at her family's Conservative synagogue—though she admits that with her husband's surname, her New York accent, and no obvious indications to the contrary, many members probably just assume that she is Jewish. In any case, Laura had a particularly sensitive and supportive Hebrew-school teacher, and Julie was very involved in her daughter's first year of Jewish education. At the end of that year, just a week before she spoke with me, Julie took her daughter to the mikvah, the ritual bath that completes the process of conversion.

"It had seemed so far-fetched to me, and yet when I was standing there watching her immerse herself, it felt very right. It didn't seem so strange or foreign."

The difficult part for Julie was a sense of disloyalty toward her own parents. "They said, 'It's okay, we support you, it's not what we would want for you but we will sort of give you our blessing.' Sort of. Kind of." Julie laughs.

Laura's conversion has, of course, pleased her Jewish grandparents, and seems to have resolved any hesitations they may have had about Julie. Like Clara, Julie encountered a father-in-law who voiced no opposition to his son marrying a non-Jew. "But his mom was raised in a kosher, very observant family, and I think that she would have wanted a Jewish woman for her son." This despite the fact that Ted's upbringing had not been particularly observant. "After the kids had bar mitzvahs, they just didn't follow through very much," Julie says of her in-laws. "Ted is actually remembering prayers now that he'd forgotten. Kids make you come back."

Because her part-time work as a private duty nurse allows her a lot of time at home, while Ted is often away Julie plays a much more active role in Laura's Jewish life. When people ask Laura about her mother, she tells them, "Mommy isn't Jewish yet."

"I think she feels a lot of the time that I'm more Jewish than her father, because I'm the one who teaches her and reads to her and tries to help her make sense of things," Julie says. "I've had my own issues, having to get used to a whole new thing, and understand what was happening to me and the family. But I feel welcomed into the community. There's a faith in our lives, the symbols are there in our house."

Though Julie has taken classes and is educating herself about Judaism, she knows that her parents would consider her conversion a terrible blow. "Because of my parents, I don't think that I can do it. But I do practice, we go to services together. Whether I convert or not, I'm still worshipping."

In biblical times, before the introduction of formal conversion, worshipping was enough. That is, for a woman. A man who wished to become Jewish had the questionable distinction of a circumcision requirement. In the earliest of its archetypal stories of non-Jewish women marrying into the Jewish family, the Torah expects that, much like Julie, wives will simply adopt their husbands' customs. No questions are asked about how the children they give birth to will be raised; it goes without saying that they will grow up in the faith of their fathers. Yet several of these women must prevail over seemingly insurmountable obstacles to bring Jewish children into the world in the first place. For sheer chutzpah, none offers a more striking tale than Tamar.

Tamar the Trickster

Judah has three sons, Er, Onan, and Shelah, and as a wife for Er, he chooses a Canaanite woman named Tamar. But for unspecified reasons, Er displeases God and God takes his life.

When a man dies without a male heir, the law of levirate marriage (*levir* is Latin for "brother-in-law") dictates that his brother marry his widow and produce a son that will be counted as the dead man's. Accordingly, Judah has Onan marry Tamar. But Onan is indifferent to the demands of family continuity: he'd rather not have children than father his dead brother's child. When he cohabits with Tamar, Onan allows his seed to spill on the ground rather than impregnate her. This displeases God, and God takes Onan's life as well.

Reluctant to tempt fate with his third and final son, Judah sends Tamar back to her father's house, telling her to wait there for Shelah to grow up. But a long time passes, Shelah is grown, and Tamar is not called to be his wife. One day, she hears that Judah will be traveling her way for the annual sheep-shearing. Her father-in-law having failed to fulfill the law of his people, Tamar now takes that responsibility into her own hands, with a risky and desperate act that nearly costs her her life.

Trading her widow's garb for the disguise of a prostitute's robe and veil, Tamar stations herself in Judah's path. When Judah expresses interest in the prostitute's services, Tamar demands to know how she will be paid. Judah replies that he will send her a sheep from his flock, and she requests his seal, cord, and staff as a pledge. Upon returning home, Judah attempts to send the sheep and redeem his pledge. But the woman cannot be found and he is told that there has been no prostitute in the place where he met Tamar.

About three months later, Judah learns that Tamar is pregnant, and orders that she be burned to death as a harlot. Tamar has laid her plans with precision, a flair for the dramatic, and a

supremely cool head. Waiting until she is actually being dragged
from her home to be put to death, she sends her father-in-law
this message: "I am with child by the man to whom these belong. Examine these: Whose seal and cord and staff are these?"
Judah recognizes his things and knows at once that Tamar was
driven to her act by his own procrastination. He recognizes
something else as well, something Tamar has known all along:
his interests and hers are not at odds. Tamar gives birth to twin
boys, Perez and Zerah, as Judah's wife, though the couple won't
resume an intimate relationship that would not be sanctioned in
light of her previous ties to his sons. Not only are her actions
vindicated, they appear to be part of a divine plan. Perez will be
an ancestor of King David, from whose descendants it is believed the Messiah will one day come.

As a Canaanite, Tamar is a member of a people the Israelites view with suspicion, the inhabitants of the land God has
directed them to take for themselves. When Abraham is ready
to marry off his son, Isaac, he summons a bride from his own
people rather than choose a Canaanite for him; Isaac, in turn,
sends his son Jacob to his mother's birthplace to find a mate,
telling him, "You shall not take a wife from among the Canaanite women." Jacob and Leah's son, Judah, exhibits no such scruples. He is happy to marry two of his sons to Tamar. When those
sons die, his attitude changes. Now when Judah looks at Tamar
he sees death: the annihilator of his children and of his entire
family line.

But Tamar rejects this role, along with the widowhood and
childlessness it condemns her to. That she brings life, not death,
to Judah's house is hinted in her name: *Tamar* means "palm
tree." According to Psalm 92, "The righteous flourish like the
palm trees," and in Jewish liturgy the palm tree symbolizes what
flourishes in a barren land. By her actions, Tamar frees the family she has married into from the stalemate of Judah's fears.

For thousands of years, the gentile woman has represented
death to the Jewish people. Like Tamar, who does nothing to

harm Er and Onan, she has been a convenient scapegoat for a dwindling Jewish family. Yet the Torah is remarkable for its psychologically acute understanding of the range of human possibility. In Tamar's story, it offers the Jewish family a vision of hope beyond its fears, a model of steely courage and tenacity in the form of a gentile woman who finds a way, against all odds, to help her Jewish family thrive.

The arrival of a non-Jewish daughter-in-law isn't often cause for celebration in a Jewish family. But sometimes, like Tamar, the woman who seems to threaten a family's Jewish survival turns out to be its friend.

Felicia Cruz

Holocaust survivors, Felicia Cruz's in-laws didn't envision a Puerto Rican ex-Catholic when they imagined a wife for their son. But then, there are so many reasons why they couldn't have imagined Felicia. Like Clara and Julie, Felicia practices Judaism without having undertaken a formal conversion, and she comes to her practice with a singular passion. For Felicia, descriptions like "non-Jew" and "gentile" are fighting words.

"I have a relationship with God through Judaism that nobody can question," she says. "I am raising my children this way, but also, as an adult, it has clicked something in me. I might not be considered Jewish in terms of the law, but this beautiful religion has given me the chance to establish an exquisite and unique relationship with God, and that relationship is something nobody's supposed to interfere with and nobody's supposed to judge. It's disrespectful to refer to me as a non-Jew when I have requested not to be referred to that way."

Felicia, forty, is a social worker currently staying at home in suburban New Jersey with her three children, Marcelo, eleven, Claudio, three and newborn Ana. With its classes and reading lists, conversion, she feels, would be like going to graduate school all over again, and her family life doesn't leave her time or energy to take that on.

In contrast to many of the stories I've heard, Felicia describes her husband, Joel's, attachment to Judaism as religious, "more spiritual than cultural," a fact which may have influenced Felicia's own spiritual connection. That his Judaism was important to Joel was something Felicia knew from the start of their relationship—he told her on the day they met that his children would have to be raised as Jews. "My first reaction was, 'If that's your intent and it's really a requirement, then why aren't you dating a Jewish girl? Hel-*lo*, this is our first date, how do I know? Let's see if you're worth it.'"

Once she decided that Joel was worth it, it was a given that if her children were going to be Jewish then so was she, even if only in her own eyes. "I feel that in order to do it with your kids, you need to practice it. How can you be a model—and a good one—and not practice it?" Felicia didn't have a religious attachment of her own to stand in her way. Growing up in Puerto Rico, what Catholicism meant to her was joyous family gatherings for holidays like the Epiphany, not spiritual practice. Since that was the aspect of her background that she would miss, the solution has been to make Jewish holidays as festive as those she enjoyed as a child.

In her own family, Felicia's marriage to Joel and their decision to raise Jewish children caused no problems with her devout mother. Her brother was more hesitant, but Felicia was efficient at overcoming his misgivings. She also initiated a dialogue with her in-laws about their disappointment in Joel's choice to marry a non-Jew.

"I don't think in the beginning they would have chosen me," Felicia says of Joel's family. "That's one of the things that I have accepted. I don't think it should be an excuse not to be welcoming, but I do understand that some people have a lot of issues with people mixing. Now I feel that they love me, we spend a lot of time with them, we have a lot of fun with them. I don't see any difference in the way they treat my children and the way they treat the other children in the family."

Her experience in larger Jewish communities has been mixed. As new parents living in Boston, she and Joel received a warm welcome at a Reform congregation that, despite its vast membership, felt intimate. Then they moved to Puerto Rico for a time, where going to synagogue felt like coming home to Felicia. Now living in the town where Joel grew up, they are members of a congregation Joel's parents helped to found, and where the rabbi's refusal to marry them years before still rankles—as does the generally chilly social climate.

"I don't feel that the people there are particularly embracing, and I have no idea what it has to do with. It could be that I'm Puerto Rican, it could be that I'm dark-skinned, that I'm tall, anything. I can tell you that there are not that many dark-skinned people at the synagogue, and historically, here in the north, not that many dark-skinned people are Jewish."

Despite the lack of institutional support, Felicia has made friends with a few synagogue members. It is she who pushes the family to attend services if someone they know is celebrating a bar or bat mitzvah, she who reviews the work her oldest child, Marcelo, does in Hebrew school. And in her home, Felicia has achieved a kind of Latino-Jewish fusion. Every Friday, the family light Sabbath candles, eat the challah she has made, and sing songs, while Jewish holidays are spent with Joel's extended family. At the same time, Felicia chose Latin names for each of her children. And while Marcelo and Claudio had Jewish circumcision ceremonies when they were eight days old, she gave her daughter "a Puerto Rican bris," piercing her ears on her eighth day of life.

Just as she is adamant about her own connection to Judaism, Felicia is unequivocal about her children's identities: "My kids are Puerto Rican Jews."

Felicia's resolve to define herself and her children in defiance of Jewish law would make many Jewish leaders unhappy. Her comfort with her choices and her unshakable confidence would make many gentile women envious.

Her stance raises knotty questions about who has the right to determine Jewish identity, and how a Jewish community should respond to a person who takes that right for themselves. But controversy ends outside Felicia's door. In the circle of her family, there is calm self-assurance, lively celebration, and an absence of the anxiety and ambivalence that characterize the issue of religious identity in so many Jewish, as well as Jewish-gentile homes.

What enables one gentile woman to feel at ease in a Jewish milieu entirely foreign to her, while another never sheds an excruciating sense of being out of place? In Felicia's case, one answer may lie in the spiritual connection she and Joel have to Judaism. Those who think of Judaism as an ethnicity, rather than a religion, have the most trouble accepting—or becoming—non-ethnic Jews. Defining themselves as religiously Jewish leaves plenty of room for Felicia and Joel to express their family's Puerto Rican cultural identity, and places no demands on Felicia to shed the part of her background that is important to her: Judaism and Puerto Rican ethnicity are not at odds.

But comfortable or not, is it really possible for a mother to raise a child in a tradition to which she herself does not belong? How does a woman who will not convert make a choice to create difference, if not distance, between herself and her child? These are questions with answers as numerous—and as openended—as there are families living them out. They are also the questions very much on Jane Woo's mind.

In Jane's story, we'll meet a woman who feels like an outsider to Judaism to a degree that Clara, Julie, and Felicia have never felt, a woman more ill at ease over religious identity than Monica. We'll meet a woman whose painful experience in a Jewish family may be more common than many in the Jewish community would like to think.

Jane Woo and the Book of Ruth

A San Francisco Bay Area native in her midthirties, Jane Woo's scant experience with the Jewish people has been dominated by her relationship with her mother-in-law, Nora. And that, Jane says, "is the relationship from hell."

During the first years of Benjamin and Jane's marriage, Nora made it a practice to talk over or interrupt Jane whenever she spoke, and never apologized. If Jane tried to enter a conversation on a Jewish topic, Nora informed her in no uncertain terms that she couldn't possibly know what she was talking about. When Benjamin referred proudly to Jane's work in public relations, Nora was quick to make fun of it. On one occasion when Jane, whose grandparents were from China, prepared some of her family's dishes for Nora, Nora voiced explicit anti-Asian slurs. Benjamin's reaction made it clear that this time Nora had gone too far. After that, Nora limited herself to sneering and oblique remarks at any mention of Jane's ethnic background or of her parents.

Given all this, Jane assumed that Nora wouldn't be eager for grandchildren. If Nora agreed with traditional Jewish law's stance on matrilineal descent, Jane and Benjamin's children would not be Jewish. "Even if she didn't, they'd still be Chinese as well as Jewish. And worst of all"—Jane pauses for mock-dramatic effect—"they'd be *mine*."

So Jane was unprepared for Nora's ecstatic reaction to the news of her first pregnancy. She was dumbfounded when Nora sent her a card thanking her for making a dream of Nora's come true. But she was really confused when her son was born and Nora visited with some of her friends to see him for the first time.

Jane stood holding Sammy in her doorway as Nora and her friends approached. The moment they arrived, Nora asked, in a voice laced with both pain and sarcasm, if she could hold the baby. Her tone made it clear: she shouldn't have to ask, Jane was already remiss in not handing him over. Jane at once complied. Minutes later, again in a tone that expressed the absurdity and injustice of needing permission, Nora asked Jane if she could take off Sammy's hat. Again Jane assented. Nora untied the cap, and turning to her friends, joked, "He can't be my kid, he has hair!"

"Everyone laughed," Jane recalled. "Benjamin and his brother were bald when they were born, and now Nora had a baby with hair. But I wasn't laughing. I was thinking, 'Huh? He's *your* baby?' She kept making these remarks like she thought he was her's. She still does."

Nora's enthusiasm for her grandchild hasn't spilled over into any new warmth toward Jane. As she was once aggressive in negating Jane as a person, she now denies Jane's role in Sammy's life. She declares him identical to Benjamin, and breaks in when Jane tries to point out evidence of her share in the boy's gene pool. During his infancy, she disliked Jane nursing the baby, and begged to be left alone with Sammy and a supply of formula or sugared water. When Nora's own women friends make a strained but valiant effort to compliment Jane on the way she's decorated Sammy's room, and tell her she's doing a good job as a mother, Nora assumes a tight-lipped expression and turns away.

In short, Jane feels she's simply been cut out of the equation. Sammy has no mother, or rather, Nora is his mother, though Nora's attitude toward Jane now includes a subtle, grudging acknowledgement that Jane has done her a service. When Nora comes to visit, Jane says, "I feel like a surrogate mother, a body for rent. I mean, she said it herself: I made her dream come true."

During the first year of their son's life, Benjamin and Jane began celebrating Jewish holidays together more actively than they had done before. Jane entered into these occasions with mingled curiosity and reluctance. She didn't have Monica's alienating experience of religion; she had almost no religious experience at all. Her parents consider themselves Methodists but had only distant ties to a church while Jane was growing up. With nothing to stand in her way, Jane felt intellectually attracted to Judaism, and to Jewish values. But on a personal level she couldn't imagine that she would ever see any reflection of her own experience in this exotic tradition and its enigmatic tales. That is, until she encountered the Book of Ruth. As Jane discovered, Ruth had a mother-in-law, too.

The Book of Ruth is an exquisite work of literature, a love story—or a story of unrequited love—and the Torah's problematic masterpiece on conversion to Judaism. It introduces Naomi, a Jewish woman whose husband and two sons have died and left her utterly bereft, grief-stricken and penniless in Moab, the foreign land to which her family had once fled in a time of famine. She has decided to return to her home in Bethlehem, and says good-bye to her sons' non-Jewish widows, Orpah and Ruth. The younger women cling to Naomi but—apparently originating the three refusals traditionally given to the gentile who comes seeking entry into the Jewish people—Naomi tries three times to send them away. After Orpah has left them, Naomi again tells Ruth to return to her family, and it's in response to this final attempt to dismiss her that Ruth gives voice to some of the most beautiful words of devotion ever written:

> "Do not urge me to leave you, to turn back and not follow you. For wherever you go, I will go; wherever you lodge, I will lodge; your people shall be my people, and your God my God. Where you die, I will die, and there I will be buried. Thus and more may the Lord do to me if anything but death parts me from you."

Ruth accompanies Naomi to Bethlehem, where she marries Boaz, the man Naomi chooses for her, and bears a child. Boaz is a kinsman of Naomi's late husband, a "redeemer" for Naomi's family according to the tradition of levirate marriage. (He is also a descendent of Perez, Tamar's son.) His and Ruth's off-spring will perpetuate Naomi's family line, and ensure Israel's royal and messianic lineage as well, since their son, Obed, will be the grandfather of King David, from whose seed the Messiah is to come.

Viewed symbolically as a convert, Ruth is a woman in love with Judaism, longing for the acceptance of Israel as for the encompassing embrace of a mother. But Naomi never acknowledges Ruth's value, never reciprocates her extraordinary devotion. Without a word, Naomi receives Ruth's declaration of love, her compliance in carrying out Naomi's risky plan for winning Boaz, the food she works to supply, as if all these were her due, just as, in the end, she receives her child. Even when a chorus of her women neighbors plead Ruth's case, "Your daughter-in-law . . . loves you and is better to you than seven sons," Naomi has nothing to say.

Ruth's determination, expressive speech, hard work, and canniness are all employed to bring her to this point in the story where the women declare her "better than seven sons" to Naomi. Once there, this most eloquent of women becomes a silent vessel. Ruth gives birth and disappears from the text, while Naomi and her neighbors assume center stage. "Naomi took the child and held it to her bosom. She became its foster mother, and the women neighbors gave him a name, saying, 'A son is born to Naomi!'" If Ruth's value to Naomi and her people is limited to procreation, procreation is also the beginning and end of her role as a Jewish parent: to realize her dream of becoming a daughter, she relinquishes her rights as a mother.

To Jane, this looks a bit like the deal Nora is offering her. In Ruth and Naomi's story, Jane feels she's discovered that she and her family are living in an archetypal matrix she hadn't even known existed. "I'm not equating myself with Ruth," Jane says. "But Naomi *is* Nora."

In Naomi's silences, Jane hears Nora's icy withholding of approval. When Naomi holds Ruth's son to her bosom, she sees Nora's jealousy of her breast-feeding and her flagrant efforts to shut her out of Sammy's life. In the chorus of women neighbors, she sees Nora's friends, supporting Nora's claim to the baby on the one hand while offering Jane tokens of kindness on the other. Are Jane's situation and Ruth's story, separated as they are by thousands of years, both manifestations of a cultural norm?

The Book of Ruth offers a glimpse of what appears to be a very stable Jewish world, a world in which Ruth's path is to blend invisibly. For an initiate in such a world, Ruth's way could, conceivably, map a viable path home. And though she may pay a heavy price for her acceptance, her family and her community unquestionably benefit from what she has to give. Our own time is very different: there is no Boaz, no redeemer, waiting in the wings for every Jewish family fallen into despair. In our world, does the Jewish community benefit from a mother who relinquishes the role of active parent to her child? Who stands to gain when an articulate supporter—or potential supporter—of Judaism disappears between the lines of her own story?

Some biblical commentators point out that, as a convert, Ruth received an extraordinary honor in being permitted to play a role in the birth of King David. These commentators don't remark on Ruth's loss of her baby, whether real or symbolic. It seems that Ruth, Judaism's model convert, is to feel grateful for the honor bestowed upon her, and grateful, too, for finally gaining a place in Naomi's world, regardless of the terms of admittance.

What, then, can Jane conclude about the kind of mother Judaism intends its non-Jewish daughters-in-law to become? Sammy is now three, and the question of how he will be raised remains unresolved, as does Jane's own attitude toward Judaism. Benjamin would like his son to be a Jew, but he's made it clear that Jane's vote will be decisive. What sort of role can Jane, who may never convert, hope to play in her son's Jewish life, assuming he has one? Is Ruth's story telling her that allowing her child to be raised as a Jew means giving him up?

No: it's clear that's the way Felicia, Julie, and Clara would answer Jane's question, as would many women living out a concrete choice to raise their children as Jews. Some mothers negotiate a perch for themselves on the periphery of their children's Jewish involvement in which they feel quite at home. In households in which Judaism is not a significant commitment, some decide that religion is an aspect of their children's lives they don't need to share.

But while the details of Jane's story, and in particular her identification with a biblical precursor, might make her experience look unusual to some non-Jewish mothers, others would have no trouble recognizing her estrangement and her strong sense of being judged—and found wanting—by the Jewish community. Highly sensitized to scrutiny, gentile women often find it necessary to maintain a defensive posture when it comes to Judaism, and to recognize red flags when particular issues are raised. There are mothers, for example, who react with distress, even anger, at any suggestion that their children are being raised with Christian, as well as Jewish, traditions. Then there are mothers like Celia Flemming for whom it's the opposite presumption that offends, mothers who feel that if Judaism has to be all, it had much better be nothing.

Celia Flemming

Celia Flemming felt welcome at her husband's Boston-area temple—too welcome.

"Because we went to the synagogue, there was the assumption that we were raising the children exclusively Jewish, and not in my faith or my tradition at all. The assumption was that one religion was better than the other, that I really wasn't proud or wanting to pass on my experiences."

That attitude and their own lack of conviction about raising their four children in any particular faith resulted in Celia, a full-time mother in her late thirties, and her husband, Alan, withdrawing from synagogue membership. Unlike Felicia, who is able to edit the Christian aspects out of the Puerto Rican heritage she wants to keep alive, Celia retains a more general allegiance to her Irish Catholic background. For Alan, whose Jewish connection is not very spiritual, yet who once led children's services at the temple, the decision to withdraw from religious affiliation isn't entirely satisfying. He'd like to be involved in a Jewish community, but in the crush of work and family life, he hasn't made it a priority.

Still, as Celia notes, "Judaism is something you can bring into the home, you don't have to go somewhere to do it." If they all happen to be at home on a Friday evening, Alan will light Shabbat candles with Alan Jr., eleven; Daniel, nine; Noah, six; and Caitlin, two. They celebrate Jewish holidays with friends, and Christian holidays with Celia's family. And if she is at her mother's house when her mother is leaving for church, Celia might go with her.

Now and then they visit Alan's family, who live in California, for a Jewish holiday. But for Celia, a trip to California is no vacation.

"When we were getting married, nothing was said overtly but there were so many problems that I think were because I wasn't Jewish." One hears echoes of Jane when Celia recalls the day she and Alan were married: "His mother invited no one to our wedding and then said, 'If you had told me that you were going to have a lovely wedding, I would have invited people.'"

Alan's family, like the synagogue members Celia encountered, conveyed an absolute expectation that their children would be raised as Jews. Not surprisingly, Celia's commitment to passing on some of her own traditions hasn't gone down well with them. There was open hostility over their choice of a Gaelic name for their youngest child. And in contrast to Celia's mother, who gives the children presents for both Jewish and Christian holidays, and who has her son-in-law light Hanukkah candles at her home when Christmas and Hanukkah coincide, Alan's family never acknowledge that Celia has special days of her own.

"We've been out there for Passover when it's also Easter and they don't mention it. If we do anything, we have to do it in our hotel room, where they don't know anything about it, and Alan tells the kids they can't bring their Easter candy to his parents' house."

The tension is inevitably communicated to the children, despite Celia's attempts to keep it from them. She recalls an incident when their plane was landing in California and Alan Jr. became suddenly frantic to remove a chain that held both a cross and a Magen David, or Jewish star, from around his neck before his grandmother could see it.

Celia admits that when her own family upsets her in some way, "I forgive them easily, while I hold on to the things Alan's mother says." Still, it's hard for her to accept that while her mother can brag about grandchildren who are "Jewish and Irish and Catholic," Alan's family will never feel the same.

This is a point raised, in very different ways, by most of the women I've spoken with. Some, such as Celia and Jane, believe that their non-Jewish backgrounds make their presence in a Jewish family or community undesirable, threatening, perhaps shameful. They experience a distinct pressure to keep a low profile, to avoid the kind of attention to who and what they are that a Chinese meal or a handful of Easter candy brings. When children are involved, they see a similar pressure communicated to them as well—to suppress the aspects of themselves that represent their mothers.

Like Celia and Jane, a woman may confront a Jewish family or community's disapproval—whether of herself as a gentile woman, of her efforts to create a Jewish home, or, conversely, of her determination to have her family life reflect its dual heritage—with anger and pain. Or, like Alice Harper Goldsmith, whom we'll meet next, she may insist that centuries of Jewish persecution and the need to safeguard Jewish tradition and continuity in our time excuse any personal rejections they might experience. It's easy, these women argue, for Christian families and faith communities to welcome an outsider into the fold: their survival isn't at stake.

Alice Harper Goldsmith

"We're not talking about two equivalent religions," says Alice Harper Goldsmith. "It doesn't mean the same thing to the Christian community to have a Christian marry a Jew. One religion is very inclusive, the other needs to be exclusive for many very good reasons."

Alice, thirty-nine, lives in southern California, where she is an English professor and is working for a Jewish organization to create an interfaith program. Brought up a Baptist, she is now an Episcopalian, married to Jon, a Reform Jewish man "who was not raised to be very religious." The couple are bringing up their one-and-a-half-year-old, Molly, in both their religious traditions.

At one point, Alice attended a meeting of an advertised interfaith group, "and realized that my religion was not of interest. Jon wasn't a Jew married to an Episcopalian but a Jew married to a non-Jew." The experience, Alice adds, left her with no hard feelings, "just more realizations about what interfaith means." As for their families, neither side evinced any hesitation about their marriage. "Though," Alice says, "there are certain assumptions like Jon's mother being polite in not asking me to say Hebrew blessings when I know them better than she does."

Alice belongs to a progressive Episcopalian church, Jon to a similarly liberal Reform synagogue. Each feels comfortable accompanying the other to religious services, and to observing both faiths in their home. Alice says she feels "pretty overwhelmed at the level that I am welcomed at our Reform temple. I'm a member, I worship there as often as I please, probably twice a month." They were disappointed but understanding when the rabbi was unable, in keeping with synagogue policy, to co-officiate at their wedding. By contrast with most rabbis, she was willing to marry them solo, but that was something Alice and Jon wouldn't agree to. In the end, Alice's priest married them under a chuppah, a traditional Jewish wedding canopy.

Similarly, Alice describes their negotiations with the rabbi over their choice to have dual welcoming ceremonies for their daughter as "a learning experience." Molly was baptized in the Episcopalian church, then blessed by the rabbi at home. "It wasn't appropriate to have the baby-naming in synagogue, and at the same time, the words that would have included her in the covenant of Abraham and Sarah were not said because that preludes other commitments, and she had been baptized."

Their long-term plans for Molly are to give her a Jewish education at a synagogue Sunday school, then the equivalent experience in Alice's church. "Maybe the Jewish part first, so it's not too confusing for her."

They see their religions, Alice says, "as two very distinct things that we want to share with her. We are each a different religion, but as a family, we're definitely both."

"The synagogue is happy to let her in," says Rabbi Steven Mason of temples like the one Alice and Jon attend. "But then how far will this go?"

Mason, the interfaith counselor, is raising a point about the turbulent and changeable nature of synagogue policies regarding the presence and participation of non-Jewish women and their children. Practices vary from one movement to another, one congregation to the next, from case to case. How far should a congregation—or a family—go to include a non-Jewish member in Jewish spiritual practice?

Alice inadvertently touches on a particularly sensitive issue when she refers to her mother-in-law's assumption that she won't be familiar with Hebrew blessings. Unlike Felicia, Alice isn't looking for acceptance as a Jew—she is unambiguous about her Christian allegiance. Yet her knowledge of Jewish ritual is a matter of pride to her; nothing would surprise Alice more than to learn that for some, a Hebrew blessing on the tongue of a non-Jew makes a mockery of the entire notion of Jewish peoplehood.

All blessings begin with the words *Baruch ata Adonai Eloheynu Melekh Ha'Olam,* "Blessed are You, Ruler of the universe." Many continue, *asher kid'shanu b'mitzvotav v'tzivanu* . . . "who sanctified us with Your commandments and commanded us . . ." The repetition of "us" underlines the message that it is Jews who have been sanctified and commanded in this way. Does a reinterpretation of that "us" to include anyone who cares to say the blessing strengthen or weaken the community? It's a matter of hot debate.

"I don't like the non-Jewish parent saying blessings," comments Jewish educator Jody Rosenbloom. "What kind of message is that conveying to the child? If you chose not to convert you can't mirror that authentically."

For years, I myself lived in a home in which blessings were regularly spoken, and, until my conversion, never felt licensed to say them. On Friday nights, in particular, when my husband fulfilled the traditionally female role of lighting and blessing the candles that usher in the Sabbath, I was acutely aware that ours was a home with no Jewish woman to perform this ritual act. "Jewish women and girls light Shabbat candles at such-and-such a time," the little advertisement on the front page of the *New York Times* read each week. I'll never forget the first Friday night after my conversion, when I realized that I could now include myself in that designation.

Of course, there's a before and after to my story. The fact that saying the blessings as a non-Jew didn't feel right only made the transition conversion represented the more profound. But most of the women whose stories we've heard have no plans to convert, and most, if not all, feel pained and pushed away when they encounter manifestations of Rosenbloom's stance.

To avoid rejection, some women stay away from the Jewish community. Others, like Elizabeth James, stay under wraps.

Elizabeth James

Elizabeth James is one of a number of women I've spoken with who say most people in their husbands' congregations don't know they aren't Jewish, and most don't need to know.

Like Alice Harper Goldsmith, Elizabeth, a forty-two-year-old museum curator in Providence, Rhode Island, is a practicing Episcopalian raising a single daughter in both her own and her husband's faiths. But unlike Alice, whose daughter is a baby, Elizabeth and her husband, Rob, have nine years of experience in what it means to juggle Judaism and Christianity in their home.

One thing it means is a very busy Sunday. Lily's morning starts with religious school at her father's synagogue, followed by mass and afternoon religious school at her mother's church. Occasionally the family attends Friday night Shabbat services, and together they celebrate the Jewish holidays of Rosh Hashanah and Yom Kippur, Hanukkah, Purim, and Passover, along with Christmas and Easter.

"The rhythms of the year are pretty much settled," says Elizabeth. "We haven't really gotten into the theology yet, but this past year at Easter, Lily started asking more questions." Answering Lily's questions about their theological differences, Elizabeth and Rob walk a kind of tightrope of frankness and respect: this is where Mommy and Daddy's religions coincide, this is where they absolutely part company. "From my perspective, Judaism is also part of my faith tradition," says Elizabeth. "Certainly from Rob's perspective, Christianity cannot be part of his faith tradition. That may be the hardest thing for Lily to figure out for herself. Deep down, it really doesn't concern me that Lily may not choose to be a Christian. I can't speak for Rob."

Rob may hesitate to speak for himself. Like most of the women I've met, Elizabeth describes her husband, who is the son of a Holocaust survivor, as having an attachment to Judaism that is more a matter of cultural and historic identity than religion. Several stories she relates suggest that Rob might be uncomfortable making claims for his Judaism.

When the two met as graduate students at an Ivy League university, religion was never an issue. Even planning their wedding, Rob expressed no preferences about the venue. Instead, he startled her with the sudden revelation that if they were married in a church, his parents and family would not attend. Similarly, he asked for no commitment from Elizabeth that their children be given a Jewish education. But when, with great difficulty, they found a rabbi willing to co-officiate at the wedding with an Episcopalian priest, the rabbi had no such hesitation.

"At that point," Elizabeth recalls, "I made a pledge that I'm obligated to fulfill. Rob didn't ask for it, but I think he really wanted it."

Living out her pledge to educate her children Jewishly, while "at the same time not wanting to leave them without access to my own faith and tradition" has sometimes proved a challenge in her family's busy schedules. It hasn't been a source of conflict, perhaps because, to some extent, Elizabeth has been careful to protect herself from it.

Her own pastor has been very supportive of how Lily is being raised, but neither she nor Rob have confided in their rabbi. "Maybe at the back of my head, I suspect that the rabbi would not approve and I want to avoid encountering that," she admits. Like Alice, early in her marriage Elizabeth attended an interfaith event at another synagogue, only to discover that its sole purpose was to attract gentile partners to Judaism. That was the only off-putting experience she has had as an acknowledged

Christian in a Jewish milieu; it's the only experience she's had of any kind.

"Earlier on I could have been looking for more acceptance for who I was from a Jewish community. I wondered if there was going to be a place for me. But I've never wanted to identify myself as part of an interfaith couple at Rob's synagogue. I haven't seen an outreach or an effort, and I've come not to expect it. For me, as someone on the edge, it would be presumptuous, and I guess I'm afraid that under the surface there might not be openness or acceptance. If I brought it up, and said, 'This is what I'm doing,' someone might say 'It won't work.' After I've put all this effort into it, I'm not sure I'd appreciate that."

The staff at the synagogue school, however, do know that Lily is also receiving a Christian education: when she started classes there she told them herself, a fact that was noted on a progress report. "I noted that it was noted," Elizabeth says. "I don't want Lily to be in a position where she needs to defend herself."

Lately, Elizabeth has observed that Lily has stopped referring to herself as both a Christian and a Jew. She considers herself Jewish, and both she and her father expect that she will have a bat mitzvah at thirteen. In Elizabeth's view, Lily is a child of God, whether she opts for Christianity or Judaism. But there's a touch of sadness, perhaps inescapable in a woman deeply committed to her faith, when Elizabeth says that the future she imagines for her daughter is a Jewish one.

"I guess to some extent I'll always be on the edge of Rob and Lily's engagement with Judaism. That's my choice—if I don't convert or really throw myself into the synagogue, I guess that really has been my choice."

Choice. These days, religious practice, even religious identity, is a choice, not a given. That's true for everyone, and something a partner in an intermarriage is unlikely to forget. Even Felicia

Cruz, whose husband announced on their first date that his children would be Jews, describes her choice to accept that condition. Even Celia Flemming, holding Judaism at arm's length, says her children could have more of a Jewish life if their father made it a priority to create it for them.

The eight women whose stories we've heard are all making their own choices. They are individuals, each with her own history and perspective, and they're not intended to represent the full range of gentile women raising children in, or on the edge, of the Jewish community. Yet when I ask Jewish leaders to describe the situations typical of gentile mothers with some connection to Judaism, they offer a spectrum consistent with this group of women.

They mention women whose commitment to raising Jewish children is mirrored in their own attraction to Judaism, yet who hesitate to convert out of a fear of wounding their parents (Julie Shulman) or a sense that formal conversion is somehow unnecessary (Clara Townsend and Felicia Cruz). They mention women rooted in their own religions (Alice Harper Goldsmith and Elizabeth James) who facilitate a dual spiritual education for their children, women uncomfortable with all religious expression (Monica Cassia), and those who feel alienated by the Jewish community (Jane Woo and Celia Flemming) and fear that Jewish involvement for themselves or their children would constitute a tacit agreement that their own backgrounds are inferior.

It's striking how many women refuse to let discouraging experiences entirely estrange them from Judaism. At a time when Jews often turn their backs on a Jewish establishment desperate to welcome them, many gentile women weather the indifference of partners, the derision of in-laws or off-putting receptions from synagogues to link their families to the Jewish community. They take on the responsibility of promoting a tradition not their own, appreciate in-laws for what they have to give, describe warm friendships and shared holidays with Jewish friends, and remain open to finding the congregation where they might feel more at home. For many there is the sense that something important is at stake—for the Jewish people, for their children, maybe for themselves as well.

Monica, an outsider to any kind of spiritual life, believes the lighting of Shabbat candles is a nice ritual for her children. Elizabeth, juggling Christian and Jewish observances and struggling to keep all the balls in the air, says, "Being part of an interfaith couple and being able to tag along on some of the services and rituals has been very enriching. That has been an unexpected bonus."

Becoming a mother can have the effect of heightening a gentile woman's sense of herself as an outsider in a Jewish family or community—or of giving her an opportunity for exploration and inclusion that she never felt before. Her children may bring her into contact with a wider Jewish world beyond her husband's family for the first time. They may inspire her to seek out a place where she will be accepted as what one woman called "a practicing non-Jew."

In fact, educator Rosenbloom says that if she has one piece of advice for non-Jewish mothers, it's to shop around: there are many "Judaisms," and chances are there's one out there to fit a family's needs.

Rosenbloom also has some advice for the Jewish community. "I would like to see cultural places and nontraditional congregations where people could explore what they want Jewishly. If the only option is a traditional congregation that is very closed, I think you lose people who could potentially make Jewish choices and contribute to the community in very positive ways. I also think it's very shortsighted. The Jewish community has always had a percentage of converts and relationships with non-Jews."

Which circles back to one of the questions we began with: Does the Jewish community want the children of gentile mothers? That depends on which Jewish community you ask.

Rabbi Sanford Selzer, the former Reform outreach commission director, says yes. Rabbi Edward Feld, Rabbi in Residence at the (Conservative) Jewish Theological Seminary in New York, says maybe. "The Conservative movement is ambivalent. I think each synagogue is behaving in different ways and there's no consistency. My own feeling is that without outreach, we've condemned the Conservative movement to being just a minority of a minority."

According to Feld, Conservative Judaism has declined from 38 to 30 percent of all American synagogue membership in recent years and Orthodoxy from 15 to under 10 percent, with most of the remainder accounted for by Reform Judaism and a small fraction by Reconstructionist and other Jewish movements. Feld says the Conservative defense is that less is more. "There are those who argue that there is strength in purity. It's important to keep up standards so that people will be clear what is required."

It was that point of view that held sway when the Conservative movement decided to bar the unconverted children of gentile women from attending Camp Ramah, its summer camp affiliate, a policy Feld calls "offensive." But devotion to purity has its limits. At one Camp Ramah in New England, children with non-Jewish mothers started being admitted when the camp failed to fill its enrollment without them.

For many in the Jewish community, such a pragmatic response to the composition of today's Jewish households sets off an alarm. There is a fear that, step by step, such small inclusions will cause the dilution—and dissolution—of a people historically shielded by ghetto walls and ethnic boundaries. But as we saw in the biblical chronicles of Judaism's earliest families, pragmatic inclusion has always been a part of Jewish survival. If a matriarch can't conceive, her non-Jewish handmaid can produce the next generation. When a son dies childless, his foreign wife may prove as loyal to keeping his name alive as any daughter-in-law could be.

It is apt that these archetypal stories of Judaism's creation are family stories: Judaism was, and still is, an intensely family-centered religion. It's not surprising that gentile women are often significantly influenced in their ideas about Judaism by their encounters with their husbands' families. And for many a woman, describing those encounters means talking about one person: her mother-in-law.

We've already seen how Jewish tradition characterizes Jewish men as the helpless victims of gentile women and their assimilating influence, and the way that matrilineal descent discounts a father's role in his children's lives. In many of the stories we've heard here, death or divorce might have taken a husband's father from the scene before a gentile daughter-in-law's appearance, but for the most part, these men seem to be passive witnesses to their own family dramas. "His father had no opinion," one woman said about her husband's decision to marry outside his faith. From the pages of the Torah through four thousand years of recorded Jewish history, women are too often notable for their absence; now, in this most patriarchal of traditions, it seems that men have become the silent partners in their families' religious lives. Whether and why American Jewish men are as disaffected from Judaism as they appear to be are questions that lie outside this exploration. But gentile mothers are unquestionably implicated when Jewish continuity is deemed women's work.

In a very real sense, Jewish women are not merely responsible for Jewish continuity, they *are* Jewish continuity. This is reflected in the law of matrilineal descent that makes women the sole endowers of Jewish genes, and in a tradition that has long relied on women's devotion to Jewish education, volunteer organizations, home life. It is reflected in the stories of disengaged husbands and fathers content to leave their children's Jewish identities to their wives—even to wives who aren't Jewish. It is reflected in the crackling tensions between many Jewish mothers and those threats to cultural stability, their non-Jewish daughters-in-law.

Not all relationships between gentile women and their Jewish mothers-in-law are strained, and strained relations between mothers and daughters-in-law are known in cultures everywhere. But Monica's, Jane's and Celia's encounters with their mothers-in-law all beg the question: Are Jewish mothers and gentile daughters-in-law natural enemies? Monica believes herself the most visible and convenient scapegoat for her husband's failure to raise their children with strong Jewish identities. In the behavior of their mothers-in-law, Jane and Celia see a desire—perhaps a cultural dictate—to wipe them altogether out of their children's inheritance in the interests of Jewish cohesion.

We'll look more at these issues in the next chapter, as we explore the complicated ties between Jewish and gentile women. For now, let's acknowledge that gentile women often experience their husbands' mothers as disapproving, even brutally rejecting keepers of the gate in Jewish families. Let's acknowledge that if Jewish mothers are charged with the survival of the Jewish family—of Judaism itself—it seems unavoidable that they assume a well-guarded stance toward the outsiders cast as its destroyers. To get beyond this impasse, gentile women will need to understand the acute pressures—historical, psychological, religious— brought to bear upon their mothers-in-law. Jewish women will need to appreciate that, in the Jewish family as a whole, someone else *is* shouldering some of the responsibility for Jewish continuity: their gentile daughters-in-law.

5

Rebekah's Bitterness, Miriam's Banishment:
Rivalry and Rancor Between Jewish and
Gentile Women

God is one but the goddess who is part of him, is two.

— *RAFAEL PATAI*, THE HEBREW GODDESS

IT'S HARD to talk about the gentile woman in the Jewish world
without talking about the Jewish woman in the Jewish world. In
the myths and stereotypes about them, the feelings and expectations they inspire, Jewish and gentile women often seem to be
two sides of the same coin.

Gentile women are sexually available, Jewish women are
withholding. Jewish women are excessively demanding and materialistic, gentile women appreciative and easy to please. Gentile women are tall and blond, Jewish women are not. Jewish
women are emotive and boundlessly possessive, gentile women
cool and a little remote. Jewish women are the heroines of the
Jewish family, gentile women are its destroyers. Gentile women
lure Jewish men away from the Jewish family, Jewish women
drive them away. What all the clichés have in common is that
they view Jewish and gentile women entirely in relation to Jewish men. And if they seem to contradict each other—or reality—that's because they do.

Shiksa

We saw in chapter two that Jewish mysticism envisions a male God pulled in opposing directions: toward the Shekhinah, the female aspect of the Divine and God's rightful mate, and toward Lilith, fatally sexy she-demon. In the mystics' take on the Jewish Diaspora, the Shekhinah clings to her people, accompanying them into exile, but God does not, opting instead for a little cosmic coupling with the Shekhinah's usurper, Lilith.

Historically, the American Jewish community has viewed itself within the parameters of a similar dynamic. While the gentile woman beckons Jewish men away from their roots, the Jewish woman is the indivisible heart and soul of the Jewish family and by extension the Jewish community, and is accountable for their rise and fall. For the Jewish man, family and community are options. Support his people or succumb to the lure of gentile America and abandon them, the choice is his—and is both enacted through and symbolized by the woman, Jewish or gentile, at his side.

This is not to say that Jewish men have not been subject to a communal mandate to marry within the tribe. However it's a curious fact that while Jewish men have formed the avant garde of assimilation, the shedding of religious and cultural ties, and intermarriage, it is Jewish women—and of course, gentile women—who have been blamed for it.

We've discussed the multifaceted way in which the gentile woman has long appeared to menace the Jewish family and community, a view that would seem to champion the Jewish woman as the sole protector of Judaism. As we look at the internal workings of the American Jewish family, a more complicated picture emerges.

The link between the enclosed, all-Jewish family at one end of the spectrum, and the interfaith relationship between a Jewish man and gentile woman at the other, is the Jewish man. According to a mind-set that is both anti-Semitic and misogynist,

Jewish men marry out because their mothers model an image of Jewish womanhood that sends them rushing into the arms of the nearest gentile woman, while Jewish women in general frighten or turn them off with emotional and material rapaciousness, sexual coldness, or an inability to conform to WASP modes of female beauty. As already discussed, the notion of a passive, Jewishly disconnected man is deeply imbedded in conventional expectations of relationships between Jewish men and gentile women. The sense is that such a man will not—perhaps cannot—take charge of his own spiritual life, the Jewishness of his home, his children's religious identities, the survival of his community. Once he has chosen to entangle himself with a non-Jewish woman, nothing more, Jewishly, can be expected of him. Curiously, the same might be said of the Jewish man who chooses a Jewish woman as his mate. With this one act, he acquits himself of his Jewish responsibility.

Within the Jewish community, this dynamic sets up a dichotomy between the Jewish and gentile woman, positioning the Jewish man as the static third point of the triangle. For the Jewish woman caught in that matrix, what sort of feelings does her gentile counterpart inspire?

"Definitely there is tension," says feminist scholar Susannah Heschel. "It's coming from the kind of jokes that have been made about Jewish women, it's coming from men, Jewish men. This Jewish man chooses a gentile woman over a Jewish woman, and it entails a kind of rejection. The Jewish man feels insecure in his sexuality, or whatever—I'm not interested. The woman gets blamed, even though he did it."

The Jewish woman has a venerable history of getting blamed. Historian Paula Hyman argues in "The Modern Jewish Family: Image and Reality" that since the midnineteenth century, Jewish communities have been subject to social, economic, and geographic upheavals that have resulted in an obsessive concern with the family as the sole means for maintaining Jewish continuity and keeping tradition alive. Within this context, it is Jewish women who are held responsible for the actions of all members of the family, and it is their particular failure if children come up short as Jews.

> . . . Jewish women bore the brunt of communal criticism for the flourishing of assimilation among the younger generation—this despite the fact that throughout the nineteenth and twentieth centuries it is Jewish men who have outpaced Jewish women in both apostasy and intermarriage. . . .
>
> By focussing on the failings of Jewish mothers as transmitters of Jewish culture to their children, communal leaders were able to project on women their own guilt over their inability to set limits to assimilation. In doing so, they transformed assimilation from an individual to a familial act, from activity in the public (masculine) sphere to inactivity in the domestic (feminine) sphere. . . .

Within the domestic sphere, Jewish women were increasingly going it alone. Anthropologist Riv-Ellen Prell finds that by the 1950s American Jewish men had essentially become silent partners in Jewish family life, emotional and sometimes physical absentees. "Jewish men were a problem of home and synagogue life because they were not present," Prell writes in *Fighting to Become Americans*. "But Jewish women were dangerous because they were."

Among the dangers Jewish women reputedly posed to their communities was their talent for inspiring Jewish men to marry out—by failing to be, or to raise their daughters to be, desirable brides. In his 1958 polemic, *Mixed Marriage and the Jewish Future*, Rabbi David Kirshenbaum claimed that young Jewish women were so overindulged and materialistic, they couldn't help but scare away young Jewish men. For Jewish men, Kirshenbaum wrote, "This has the effect of driving them into non-Jewish circles. Here they find friendships among non-Jewish girls who may appreciate the personal character of the Jewish boy rather than his ability to provide them with a life of luxury."

Which is not to say that Kirshenbaum had a high opinion of the non-Jewish girls themselves. Indeed, it would seem that if there was anything worse than a young woman who was raised in a Jewish home it was one who was not—regardless of whether or not she converted. Writing with distaste of the "proselyte daughter-in-law" in a Jewish family, Kirshenbaum found it proof of "the lowered level of American Jewish moral standards" that some Jewish parents expressed pride in family members who joined the Jewish community through conversion.

While Kirshenbaum is blessedly part of a bygone era, it would be a mistake to assume that attitudes like his are now safely consigned to history. Just as conventional assumptions about gentile women have enjoyed an amazing shelf life in the Jewish world, so have unflattering views of Jewish women, along with a belief in their deleterious effects on Jewish men. In her 1996 gloss on the Jewish American princess, "Why Jewish Princesses Don't Sweat," Riv-Ellen Prell finds Jewish women figured as insatiable consumers.

> When the Jewish woman might be expected to be productive—in the domestic sphere for example—her body performs no labor. She passively resists the desires of others. When her body is presented as a site for adornment, her desire is voracious. She must have it all. The passive body is one of consuming desire with no object of desire other than the self.

According with Prell's view, historian David Biale also notes that "the image of the Jewish woman often takes a vicious turn" in which she is condemned for extravagant consumerism and sexual frigidity, while the Jewish male is assigned the role of comically, lovably inept schlemiel. "Women," he writes in *Eros and the Jews*, "become the site for projections of all that seems most hateful about Jewish sexuality." But while these images of Jews are standards of American anti-Semitism, Biale argues that the notion of the Jewish American princess "appears to have Jewish origins."

If one is in search of recent anti-Semitic slurs against Jewish women generated by Jews themselves, there is no better place to find them than the work of French-Jewish critic Alain Finkielkraut. His book *The Imaginary Jew* expresses contempt for post-Holocaust Jewish men as "egocentric and infantile," "overnourished, pot-bellied," and possessing "the impotence of an overgrown baby who is pampered, adorned, cuddled and powdered until old age." And who is to blame for this lamentable state of Jewish manhood? Finkielkraut's answer may lack originality, but at least it's predictable. The villains, of course, are mothers.

> There's no dividing line in the Jewish family separating principles from sentiment. Everything is love, and everything, at the same time, is Jewishness. This confusion is a constant source of our finest neuroses and responsible for our most amazing character: the Jewish Mother.

The Jewish mother, writes Finkielkraut, is "a wounded Judaism" personified, destroying her sons with adoration, overfeeding, and emotional blackmail, creating a "brotherhood of Portnoys [who] could not pass unnoticed even if they wished." He says little about Jewish women directly, reveling instead in descriptions of their creations, Jewish sons who are no more real men than they are real Jews. In the world according to Finkielkraut, neither Judaism nor Jewish women have anything good to offer Jewish men. In his version of the Jewish family, mothers single-handedly make (or rather, unmake) sons; fathers, and men's own volition, don't come into the picture. Finkielkraut proposes nothing new but serves up all the platitudes of Jewish motherhood and family life in outsized, satiric proportions.

Though Finkielkraut is French and his portrayal extreme, American popular culture suggests that to some degree his views are bought into on this side of the Atlantic, in jokes, fiction, television shows and films that insinuate that nothing could be worse for Jews—at least, for Jewish men—than the Jewish family. Given the popularity of this opinion, it might be supposed that the Jewish community applauds those women who choose to put career ahead of family, to delay motherhood and in general to vacate the domestic post from which they have reputedly wielded such negative influence. But they are not applauded. Instead, they are censured for undermining the family and placing Jewish continuity in jeopardy. In *A Breath of Life: Feminism in the American Jewish Community*, scholar Sylvia Barack Fishman writes, "To the extent that the traditional Jewish family appears threatened today, women and the women's movement are often held responsible."

As already noted, women have been held responsible for what happens in the Jewish family for a long time. As with many Jewish family paradigms, accountability and blame for Jewish women goes all the way back to the Torah, the Jewish people's story of its creation.

Miriam's Banishment

Throughout the forty-year desert sojourn that follows their escape from slavery in Egypt, the Israelites struggle with a myriad of challenges, internal and external, on the road to peoplehood and homeland. Even the personal life of Moses, their divinely appointed leader, causes strife.

In the book of Bemidbar, Numbers, an episode is recounted in which Moses' older siblings, Miriam, the sole woman identified in the Torah by the title prophet, and Aaron, the wandering community's first high priest, protest against Moses' marriage to a Cushite woman. "He married a Cushite woman!" is the full text given of their charge against Moses and his wife, followed by an outburst suggesting that they question the notion that

Moses' high standing licenses his marriage to an outsider, or alternately, that the marriage brings into doubt his fitness to lead: "Has the Lord spoken only through Moses? Has the Lord not spoken through us as well?"

God hears their grumbling and is displeased. In language charged with poetic beauty as well as rage, God tells Miriam and Aaron that their brother is a prophet above all prophets, and above all human criticism as well. God ignores Miriam and Aaron's reference to Moses' choice of mate, without which their protest that God speaks through them, and not just Moses, would seem to be a straightforward statement of political or sibling rivalry. Yet the comment is there, and since nothing in the text refutes it, it remains standing, an apparently valid criticism lobbed at the wrong target. Moses' marriage to an outsider is tacitly sanctioned because, elevated by his relationship with God, he can't be judged by anyone else. If the relationship threatens the community, it's a threat held in check so long as a kind of don't-ask-don't-tell policy is maintained around it.

At the close of God's speech, Miriam is stricken with *tza- 'arat*, a skin disease usually translated as "white scales," or "leprosy." Aaron begs Moses to intercede with God on their sister's behalf, and Moses, in turn, addresses God with the shortest, most simply eloquent prayer of the Hebrew Bible: "Oh God, pray heal her!" Still incensed, God replies that Miriam will remain diseased for seven days, and should be banished from the assembly for this period. "So Miriam was shut out of camp seven days; and the people did not march on until Miriam was readmitted."

There is disagreement among biblical scholars over the question of whether the Cushite woman referred to here is Moses' first wife, the Midianite Zipporah, whom we'll hear a bit more about in Chapter Seven. Assuming this is not Zipporah, we know nothing about the woman; assuming that she is, we know next to nothing. Miriam and Aaron's remark doesn't tell us anything about her except that she is of an obscure non-Israelite ethnicity, and that is apparently detail enough to explain their dislike of her. Perhaps the intermarriage genuinely troubles them; perhaps they are looking for something to say against their brother, and this is a criticism they can expect to be generally understood and sympathized with. It would be today. If the rivals of a Jewish leader wanted to rock his boat, the Jewish community would have no trouble getting the message behind a similar statement: "He married a Christian woman!"

Whatever their motivation, Miriam and Aaron speak with one voice when they express disapproval of their brother, but it is Miriam alone who suffers the consequences of their disloyalty. Obviously uncomfortable with the entire incident, the rabbis (who, as we have seen, are not fans of intermarriage) go to absurd lengths to try to explain away what Miriam and Aaron *really* meant to be saying about Moses, to place the greater responsibility for the incident on Miriam, and to neutralize the very different repercussions for each of them. One commentator claims that Miriam's affliction was merely physical, forgotten as soon as it was gone, while Aaron's mental agony at seeing her so stricken, and at having to ask for Moses' assistance, was much more severe. In this view, Aaron was humbled by the episode, but Miriam had no pride to lose.

In fact, God makes it explicit that Miriam's skin disease is intended to humiliate her. When Moses pleads her case, God responds, "If her father spat in her face, would she not bear her shame for seven days?" Evidence in the Torah, and especially in Midrash, indicates that Miriam was a very prominent person among the Israelites, a revered prophet from long before Moses' rise to power. One commentary holds that the people were packed and ready to move on when Miriam was struck with leprosy, and that it was only because of her importance in the community that they stayed put until she could leave with them.

Nevertheless, the text itself isolates Miriam, much as she is quarantined from her community. We see that she is stricken through Aaron's eyes, not her own, and it is his distress that is noted. God, Moses, and Aaron each speak individually, but Miriam's solo voice isn't heard. Not only is she judged differently from Aaron, but their joint criticism of Moses boomerangs back at her with ferocious, physical effect, rendering her untouchable, unbearable to look at. Aaron reflects this when he pleads with Moses, "Let her not be as one dead, who emerges from his mother's womb with half his flesh eaten away." His words are generally assumed to refer to stillbirth, but a stillborn infant evokes anguish, not horror, while Aaron invites us to imagine a condition of monstrous and frightening degeneracy. For Miriam, taking on her brother's intermarriage becomes an utterly disfiguring exercise.

As already observed, Miriam is not the only Jewish woman to be held responsible for the actions of her brothers, or to find herself a kind of outcast among the very people whose lives are bound up with hers. This unsavory tale of a pillar of her family and community rendered bodily repugnant in the eyes of the Jewish men around her resonates in ways the writers of the Torah could never have imagined.

Though the Torah has nothing to say on the subject, it's interesting to imagine relations between Miriam and Moses' wife in the aftermath of this incident. If Miriam genuinely dislikes her sister-in-law, whether for personal or cultural reasons, and is not simply using Moses' out-marriage as a convenient mark against him, if some sort of power struggle exists between the two women, then it would seem that Moses' wife wins this round—that is, if another woman's degradation constitutes victory. In any case, it's unlikely that the episode will result in Miriam's increased affection for her sister-in-law.

As Susannah Heschel points out, situations in which Jewish women are made to feel slighted in favor of gentile women create tension. Jewish educator Jody Rosenbloom agrees that rivalry between Jewish and gentile women generates ill feeling. "If you look at some of the literature on Jewish single men and women and the dating scene over the last fifty years, there's a lot of very bitter Jewish women," Rosenbloom says. "Jewish men are not choosing Jewish women, and there are a lot of stereotypes about Jewish women and their strengths and their foibles. I come from Minnesota, so that nine times out of ten if a Jewish guy was marrying a non-Jewish woman she was tall, blond, lithe. The rest of us Jewish women were short and dark, so that there was tension around that over the years."

Rosenbloom's comment touches on the old notion, familiar well beyond the borders of Minnesota, that when Jewish men stray outside their religious circles, it's because they are in pursuit of the golden-haired and WASP-waisted shiksa goddess. But a letter printed in "The Ethicist" column in *The New York Times Magazine* indicates that gentile rivals who fit entirely different ethnic profiles may not bring much more joy to their Jewish sisters' hearts. The writer of the letter wonders whether it is appropriate for "a Hispanic woman who likes to date Jewish men" to avail herself of a Jewish Internet dating service. This correspondent doesn't mind, but reports that a female friend has bristled at the idea, saying, "they should keep away from our stuff."

Assuming that by "they" this Jewish woman was referring to all gentile women, and not specifically to Latinas, her sentiment is easy to understand. A Jewish dating service, by definition, is a place for single Jews to meet each other, not a showcase for Jews to display themselves to interested non-Jews. Theoretically, Jewish space, virtual or physical, is protected turf for insiders. The appearance of anyone else might well feel like an invasion. In some communities, this is true even if the newcomer is not a non-Jew but a convert.

In *The Ladies Auxiliary*, a recent novel by Tova Mirvis, a young converted woman wreaks havoc on a small Orthodox Jewish community in Memphis. The widow of a son of the community, Batsheva makes the naive assumption that the enclave will welcome her, and provide a haven from grief and rootlessness for her and her small daughter. She is sincere and well-meaning, but in the eyes of the local women, her long blond hair, gauzy clothes, and relaxed manner all mark her an outsider, and her unmarried state makes her a hazard to the community's young unmarried men. In this view of an observant community, men's opinion of the woman is portrayed as being of no importance. Her acceptance or rejection is entirely determined by the feelings of the women, most of whom regard Batsheva with jealousy, suspicion, and intense dislike. No matter what she does, they are determined not to accept her.

That such feelings of hostility toward a convert may exist among real as well as fictional Jewish women, and don't require the hothouse atmosphere of a enclosed Orthodox world to flourish, was illustrated in another recent advice column. Writing to the *Forward*'s "Ask Wendy," a Jewish man who signs himself "Conscripted by Convert" describes his predicament. Having married a woman who converted to Judaism, he now finds himself pressured by his wife to lead a more Jewish life than he desires. As already noted, the troublesome gentile or converted woman who urges her man to embrace his Judaism is a staple of Jewish jokes about gentile women. What is notable here is not the letter but the answer it receives.

"I'm sure it is not as simple as God getting back at you for marrying a shiksa," Wendy Belzberg writes. "But I'm afraid my response comes down to this: You made your bed, now sleep in it. Enjoy it while you can—before your wife decides to start going to the mikvah."

In one tidy package, Belzberg's response combines a breathtaking and utterly undisguised animosity for non-Jewish women and the Jewish men who choose them; sadistic pleasure at the discomfort of the man who believes he can sidestep his Jewish identity with such a marriage, only to be brought squarely back to it; and a rejection, in defiance of Jewish law, of the belief that once she has joined the Jewish people, a convert is nothing more, less, or other than a Jew.

Belzberg's last reference is to the laws of *niddah,* which dictate that a couple refrain from all physical contact, sexual and otherwise, from the onset of a woman's menstruation through seven days after its end, and that the woman undergo immersion in a ritual bath before contact resumes. Belzberg's response would seem to express disdain for this traditional practice as well as for those converts who take on a Jewishly observant way of life. She makes the unsubtle suggestion that what a Jewish man seeks in intermarriage is sex, then evokes the anti-Semitic and misogynist stereotype that Jewish women and sex don't mix, warning this husband that his wife's growing Jewish identification threatens to deprive him of erotic satisfaction. For Belzberg, intermarriage is a crime worthy of divine retribution, and marriage to a convert constitutes intermarriage. Her correspondent's wife is both "too Jewish" and a "shiksa" whose essential otherness is untouched by religious conversion and its manifestations.

What is at issue in these examples is not so much the fact that an individual Jewish man has chosen a woman who was not born Jewish but that his choice is seen as a rejection of born-Jewish women as a group. Rabbi Toby Manewith, who works with college students, says that even young Jewish men are inclined to envision non-Jewish women as more sexually attractive than Jewish women, and to pigeonhole Jewish women according to trite JAP conventions. "You hear the complaints about Jewish women being high maintenance, having monetary expectations, or expectations about how their boyfriend is dressed, or if the box is from Tiffany's—oh, totally. Truthfully, there are all sorts of men, and some of the men who make these complaints about Jewish women, the same complaints could be made about them."

Manewith says she currently has no non-Jewish women friends, a situation she attributes to a life lived within an entirely

Jewish milieu. If she did have a gentile friend, and her friend got involved with a Jewish man, Manewith says, "that would bother me."

As discussed in chapter two, Manewith's article on Ari Fleischer's marriage to a non-Jew bemoaned the loss of yet another Jewish bachelor. Manewith is not alone in feeling that a gentile woman's acquisition of a Jewish man is Jewish women's loss. Despite the Jewish population statistics that indicate that men and women now intermarry with equal frequency, there are those who still maintain that marrying out is a Jewish woman's course of last resort. Sylvia Barack-Fishman reports that some Jewish women are forced to marry gentiles because of Jewish men's tendency to choose non-Jewish women, and to marry women younger than themselves. A gentile husband, she says, can be the price a Jewish woman pays for putting education and career ahead of marriage: "The end result of such postponements is sometimes unplanned intermarriage."

Barack-Fishman quotes a successful doctor for whom romantic frustration is fused to resentment against gentile women. According to this woman, when Jewish men are threatened by relationships with the Jewish women who are their career, class, and educational equals, they turn to inferiors to assuage their egos. And there's always a prefeminist gentile bimbo "thrilled" to oblige:

> Single Jewish doctors in their forties don't marry single Jewish women their own age—they marry women in their late twenties who'll stay at home and have and raise their kids. And if they can't find Jewish women who'll fit the Stepford wives stereotype, there's always an obliging gentile nurse around who'd be thrilled to marry a Jewish doctor.

Like this doctor, some Jewish women see a cultural phenomenon when they look at Jewish men's interdating and intermarriage. But talk to the men themselves, and to the gentile women who are their partners, and you'll hear relationships described in terms of individual attraction and choice. Not surprisingly, both Jewish men and gentile women tend to reject the notion that their connection is based on what the woman is not: Jewish.

The contexts of dating and intermarriage seem to inspire free-floating rancor among some Jewish women toward the gentile women they see as all too available to Jewish men. But it must be said that outside these contexts, there is no indication that any particular tension exists between Jewish and non-Jewish women, who encounter each other in every imaginable setting and create innumerable connections with each other, including those of friendship and love. In Jorie Ryder's experience, even an acute consciousness of cultural difference didn't preclude friendship. The twenty-six-year-old describes receiving a warm welcome from the Jewish women in a milieu in which interfaith romance was considered out of the question.

Jorie Ryder

Jorie Ryder, who we met briefly in chapter two, graduated from a college with a predominantly Jewish student body and faculty. Irish and a non-practicing Catholic, she had grown up in a town located near the school, but in which everyone was Christian. College was her first taste of being an outsider in the midst of an in-group, and that experience formed an important part of her education.

Before she left for school, Jorie recalls two Jewish friends of her mother teasing her, "You're the kind of girl who goes to that college and comes home with a Jewish husband, to the chagrin of all the mothers!"

But Jorie didn't come home with a Jewish husband. In the insular world of the campus, interdating, so common almost everywhere outside Orthodox circles, is still considered taboo.

"The school attracted people who already knew each other, a bit like a big camp in a way," says Jorie. As already discussed, Jorie's encounters with Jewish male students were painful. Overall, her experience on campus was one in which she never forgot her minority status. She fit in socioeconomically, as she, like most of the students, came from an upper-middle-class home. But that was where the familiarity ended. "I came up against a lack of awareness of who I was, as someone Irish." Being a "local" at a school with poor town/gown relations was another mark of difference, as was being Catholic. "There was a lack of understanding of Catholics. People would talk about Catholics, having no idea what they were talking about."

Yet despite all of this, the relationships she formed at college with a circle of Jewish women have been the closest of her life.

"I was adopted straight out by these girls from a yeshiva, Camp Ramah world," Jorie recalls, referring to the Conservative Jewish summer camp. "I thought, gee, I feel kind of different from these girls, I'm Irish, I don't open up that easily, I'm not that physical."

Both in college and since graduation, dating and romance have provided the most pointed reminders of the differences between Jorie and her friends. The women like introducing one another to men that they know, and, none of them ever has any single non-Jewish men on tap for Jorie. Though her friends joke that Jorie knows more about Judaism than the average Jew, there's never any question of them fixing her up with a Jewish man. It isn't, Jorie says, that they are uncomfortable with the idea of her dating Jewish men—it simply never crosses their minds. And within the circle of their friendship, the group has been entirely embracing.

"I don't recall any hostility or sense of competitiveness with them at all," Jorie says. "I've definitely gotten a lot out of being with them, learning how to be more affectionate. My friends were almost entirely Irish Catholic before, and they wouldn't be happy if I got an A, they weren't nice to each other. The Jewish girls are so loving, so affectionate." Jorie remembers dorm life as a time of innocently lying with her group of six friends on one girl's bed, cuddled up together, lost in endless conversation. "It really softened my edges."

Like a college campus, for more than three decades the women's movement has brought diverse people together, into an arena in which rubbing up against each other softens some women's edges, while honing others'. Since the late 1960s, feminism has promised sisterhood and solidarity to all women. But as is often true of liberation movements, a focus on one form of social injustice doesn't guarantee the absence of prejudice in other guises. The early activists for women's rights were products of their own upbringings who brought the biases of their socioeconomic, racial, and religious backgrounds with them into the struggle for gender equality. Thus far, we've looked at the experiences of non-Jewish women in Jewish contexts, and the tensions between Jewish and gentile women that Jewish tradition may inspire. When they come together in wider spheres, such as the women's movement, it becomes clear that a tremendous force *not* of Jewish making also plays a role in relations between Jewish and non-Jewish women, and must be accounted for. That force is, of course, anti-Semitism.

Letty Cottin Pogrebin

In 1982, Letty Cottin Pogrebin wrote a penetrating and courageous article in *Ms.*, a magazine she had helped found, in which she exposed the anti-Semitism she and other Jewish women had met with in the women's movement. At the time, Pogrebin recalls, "We feminists expected more of one another. We were unprepared to encounter nationalist, racist, and anti-Semitic sentiments in women we believed would be our sisters."

In the twenty-odd years since, Pogrebin reports, anti-

Semitism has been confronted head-on in the women's movement, far more than in the culture at large. She feels that it is not a significant factor keeping Jewish and gentile women apart today. "Occasional discomfort" is the term she prefers to characterize the ripples that sometimes disturb the calm between Jewish and gentile feminists.

"For example," Pogrebin notes, "feminist groups have scheduled events on a Saturday without regard for the inability of observant Jewish women to participate." She points out that while a churchgoing Christian is not prevented from attending a conference on a Sunday afternoon, such an event entails many activities, such as traveling, carrying things, and taking notes, that are proscribed for observant Jews on Saturday, the Jewish sabbath. "Yet Saturday is when most women's conferences take place. Similarly, past meetings have been scheduled on Jewish holidays, and when this has been pointed out, the Christian organizers have been dismissive—as if the sort of Jews who care about such things are dupes of patriarchal religion and not worth accommodating anyway." When patriarchal religion is admitted to women's meetings, it can take the form of an invocation mentioning Jesus, again presenting problems for Jewish participants. The intention may be to bring a diverse assembly closer, but the reality is that "the mention of Jesus excludes Jews from the community of that sacred moment."

Pogrebin has noticed a reluctance to recognize "Jewish-American culture as distinct and worthy of historical and sociological acknowledgement under the umbrella of 'Women's Studies,'" and to accord Jewish Americans the multicultural status that has become a badge of honor among many ethnic and religious minorities. Among some non-Jewish feminists, she has encountered an inclination to see all Jews as supporters of Israeli government policies, and as personally responsible for the suffering of Palestinians. At the same time, "There is some reluctance to acknowledge Jewish suffering. It's as if there are no poor Jews, no oppressed Jews. To some Christians, the Holocaust is over-exposed and should not be discussed in feminist contexts."

Pogrebin views all of the above as glitches in cultural communication, not as evidence of enmity among Jewish and non-Jewish women. "Speaking personally during the last fifteen or so years, I've rarely experienced Christian-Jewish animosity among women." According to Pogrebin, "Two-way misunderstandings are understandable. For instance, what some Jewish women see as strong, assertive behavior may be perceived by other women as overbearing, pushy, 'New York' aggressiveness. Conversely, what some Christian women—usually WASP, non-ethnic Christian women—see as calm, reasonable, patient behavior may be seen by Jewish women as cold, secretive, or passive. Each party operates within and against stereotypes of the self and the other."

Operating within and against those stereotypes can complicate any relationship, whether it be a college friendship, a working partnership, or a political alliance. But it is when Jewish and gentile women encounter each other within the intimacy of family life, and in particular within the structure of the Jewish family, that the cultural expectations they have of each other may take on the most importance, and come into play in the most unexpectedly pointed of ways.

We have heard stories of gentile women who felt welcomed by their partners' Jewish families. We've also heard from women who encountered off-putting experiences with both parents-in-law, or whose fathers-in-law took the lead in expressing a family's disapproval of their son's connection with a non-Jew. But in my conversations with gentile women, and women converts, I've found that the relationship she has with her partner's mother is most often crucial in whether a woman feels welcomed—or rejected—by his extended family, and sometimes by the Jewish community itself.

In chapter two, Winnie Marks shared her belief that two romances with Jewish men ultimately foundered when her partners could neither overcome nor ignore their mothers' unhappiness over the liaisons. In chapter four, Monica Cassia, Celia Flemming, and Jane Woo all described mother/daughter-in-law collisions in which mutual disapproval, suspicion, and resentment predominate. Many women I've spoken with describe estrangement between themselves and their partners' mothers, and many take that estrangement entirely for granted. Some women so much expect their Jewish mothers-in-law to dislike them for not being Jewish, they don't initially think of mentioning it. When they do open up on the subject, the result can be a flood of painful memories.

As already discussed, Jewish women have historically been saddled with the responsibility for Jewish continuity and survival, and they have been blamed for Jewish men's, particularly their sons', out-marriages. At the same time, they've wielded very little actual power over the actions of Jewish men or the directions taken by their communities. Much responsibility and little power are a high-stress combination, and when a gentile woman—by tradition, the enemy of all that a Jewish woman is expected to preserve in Jewish life—is introduced into a family, it's little wonder if nerves are strained to the breaking point.

Though it arose in a very different time, with very different patterns of family life, Judaism itself seems to expect a non-Jewish daughter-in-law to make her husband's mother miserable. The model of a contentious relationship between a Jewish mother and her non-Jewish daughter-in-law is built right into the culture, in the Torah's earliest stories.

Rebekah's Bitterness

Since the beginning of Jewish time, Jewish men have exercised great latitude when selecting their mates—and have made their mothers very unhappy with their choices.

In Bereshit, Genesis, patriarch Isaac and matriarch Rebekah have twin sons, Esau and Jacob. At the age of forty, Esau marries two women from among the family's Hittite neighbors, Basemath and Judith (Judith, a common Jewish name, appears in the Torah only here, as the name of a Hittite woman). Esau's choice of brides is not appreciated by his parents. "They were a source of bitterness to Isaac and Rebekah," the Torah tells us. Rebekah in particular objects to her daughters-in-law. She tells her husband, "I am disgusted with my life because of the Hittite women. If Jacob marries a Hittite woman like these, from among the native women, what good will life be to me?"

"What good will life be to me?" Both Isaac and Rebekah are unhappy—indeed, embittered—over their Hittite daughters-in-law, but only Rebekah goes so far as to question the very basis of her life should a third such woman be added to the family. As with Miriam and Aaron's cry against Moses—"He married a Cushite woman!"—the ethnicity of Esau's wives is the sole piece of information we have about them. Again, their religious/cultural identities would seem to be enough to explain the extent of Rebekah's distress over them. And that distress is extreme.

Rebekah's hyperbolic language calls to mind the overwrought reactions to their sons' intermarriages supposedly common among Jewish mothers twenty years ago. Edwin Friedman opens his essay "The Myth of the Shiksa" with a letter from a Jewish mother to her son, following the young man's engagement to a Christian woman. The mother refers to the impending marriage as her son's suicide, and anticipates that an array of disasters, including her husband's death, and the loss of her own home and job, will result from it. In *The Intermarriage Handbook: A Guide for Jews and Christians*, by Judy Petsonk and Jim Remsen, the authors present a case in which a mother's dislike of her gentile daughter-in-law moves her to try to convince her son to leave his wife. When the couple's first child dies, she goes so far as to tell her son that God is punishing him for intermarrying.

These examples, published in the 1980s, are reported as typical of the lengths to which some Jewish women might go in responding to a non-Jewish daughter-in-law. Like Rebekah, the mother who behaves in this way is clearly saying that her own well-being, the value of her life, and the pleasure she can take in it, are threatened by her son's marriage. We can dismiss such a woman as mentally and emotionally unbalanced, yet in a culture in which a woman's worth is measured by her children, and a man's intermarriage represents the failure of his Jewish up-bringing, her conclusion actually appears quite rational. No one questions Rebekah's sanity when she declares, "I am disgusted with my life because of the Hittite women."

These days, most Jewish women no longer grow up with the belief that motherhood is their sole purpose, and many struggle against the notion that they are responsible for children's out-marriages. Yet in talking with the Jewish mothers-in-law of gen-tile women, what emerges is the sense that a Jewish woman's relationship with her son's non-Jewish wife is no simple thing. It's an association that can be fraught with deep-seated fears and expectations, in which shared values and experiences may clash with disparate ones, and miscommunication pose a constant danger to *shalom bayit*, peace in the home.

Of all the women and men who shared personal stories with me for this book, those who spoke as Jewish mothers-in-law were by far the most concerned with protecting their privacy, the most troubled by the fear that they would say something that might be misunderstood—or understood all too well—and that their daughters-in-law would recognize them. Even speak-ing under cover of anonymity, it was as if they felt they had, in the words of Elaine Seldes, "to pussyfoot around" their feelings about having non-Jewish daughters-in-law.

Elaine Seldes

"Will she convert?" "Am I going to go to your house and the kids are going to be singing, 'Jesus Loves Me'?"

These were some of the questions Elaine Seldes posed to her son, Michael, ten years ago when he became seriously involved with a Christian woman named Florence. Michael would tell his mother, " 'Don't worry, we're going to work it out.' I could never get a definitive answer, but the message was, 'Don't interfere.' "

Elaine, seventy-one, now lives in Marin County, California, while Michael and Florence make their home in southern Oregon. Elaine, who hails from a long line of rabbis, grew up in a Philadelphia suburb where she felt equally comfortable welcoming Christian friends into her *sukkah*, the booth constructed for the holiday of Sukkot in the fall, and helping to decorate their Christmas trees in December. Her family was "Orthodox but not superreligious. Judaism was always a joyous thing." Because her husband is a secular Jew who refused to play any role in their children's religious education, Elaine had to accomplish the task of raising them as Jews entirely on her own, in a small California coastal town where their household constituted the entire Jewish population. "It was a very isolating experience, and I always had to explain everything" about Jewish holidays, laws, and customs, Elaine recalls. In a way, the experience helped to prepare her for interacting with Florence. "It's like living in that town," Elaine says. "You have to explain everything."

Florence is a practicing nondenominational Protestant who was born in Korea and emigrated to southern California with her parents as a young child. She and Michael met as graduate students in statistical research, and were together for two years before marrying. Elaine found it difficult to get to know Florence, who she says likes to talk about her Christian beliefs but not her Korean background. "Maybe if she was a Buddhist or non-practicing Christian it would be easier. I remember when I first met her, she said, 'Jews aren't religious, they don't believe in God. My religion is important to me.' "

Michael and Florence's wedding was a cross-cultural excursion for Elaine. "They both wanted a religious wedding, in a non-religious setting. The minister was very sensitive, and took the liturgy from the Hebrew Bible." The wedding customs observed were primarily Korean, with two Jewish elements added: Florence made a chuppah, or Jewish wedding canopy, for the service, and traditional blessings were said once in Hebrew by one of Michael's relatives, once in English by one of Florence's. Elaine was invited to participate but felt too uncomfortable, with roughly two hundred and fifty of the three hundred guests from Florence's side of the family, and some practices, such as the breaking of a wineglass that concludes a Jewish wedding, having to go by the wayside in the largely Korean setting. "Breaking the glass would have been like throwing blood at the bride's gown," Elaine says. "They turned ashen when it was mentioned."

Michael and Florence have three young sons who are being raised with both Judaism and Christianity. The boys accompany their mother to church on Sundays and occasionally attend synagogue for child-friendly holidays such as Purim. The family light candles on Friday night, when the Jewish sabbath begins, and celebrate a few Jewish holidays at home. For a long time, Elaine says, they didn't have a Christmas tree. "Now they have one because Florence says the kids want one, and she can't say, 'We don't have one because we're Jewish, because we're Christian, too.'" Elaine doesn't visit them at Christmastime because she doesn't want to see the tree.

"It's usually the mother who imparts Judaism," Elaine says with a sigh. "I can't expect Florence to take them to Jewish school."

What is implicit is that Elaine also can't expect Michael to take his sons to Jewish school. Like his own father, Michael is not terribly involved in giving his sons a Jewish upbringing, despite Elaine's report that he was the most Jewishly active and interested of her three children. Elaine laughs deprecatingly at herself when she admits that she once entertained fantasies of Michael becoming a rabbi. "I think if he had married somebody

Jewish, he would be a lot more Jewish," Elaine says. "This is a compromise, he says the children will be exposed to both, will be comfortable with both, and they'll have to decide [whether to be Christians or Jews]. What they will be, I don't know. I feel sort of sad that they're not going to be raised as Jewish kids. I'm the grandma, but it's the parents' choice and responsibility."

Elaine points out that the boys were all given "very Jewish" first names and their father's surname at birth. But the most significant event surrounding the birth of a Jewish boy, the ritual of brit milah caused serious dissension in the family. In fact, Elaine describes it as the only religious issue on which she has strongly asserted her feelings to Michael.

"I was shocked when the first boy was circumcised in the hospital," Elaine recalls. "At that point, I did speak to my son. I didn't speak to Florence, but she didn't understand how important it was."

Elaine insisted that if the couple had another son, he be given a ritual circumcision, as mandated by Jewish law, rather than a medical procedure. When her second grandson was born three years later, the ritual was carried out, with only Michael and Florence and their parents attending, at Florence's insistence. "It was the worst bris that I've ever been to, and I've been to a lot," says Elaine. Apparently due to the incompetence of the *mohel*, the person ritually authorized to perform circumcisions, who in this case was also a doctor, the procedure did not go smoothly. "Florence started screaming, and you could see her parents thinking, 'What a barbaric custom.'" Fortunately, there were no negative consequences for the baby. Nonetheless, when her third son arrived, Florence refused to have another bris. A hospital circumcision was carried out, this time with Elaine and Michael present to say some of the blessings.

The circumcision experiences would seem to typify what Elaine means when she describes her relationship with Florence. "I don't know that I'd use the word 'tension.' It's a *strangeness*." Though Elaine says Florence is "lovely, she's a good mommy, the kids are happy," it is hard for her to bridge the religious gap between them. "She feels the Jewish Bible is very important but unfinished," Elaine explains. "She says things like, 'I don't know why Jews hate Jesus.' I try to explain that it isn't Jesus, it's what's been done in his name. It's the same thing with the cross, to her it's one kind of symbol, to Jews it's terrifying."

Like every other Jewish mother-in-law I have spoken with, Elaine wonders aloud what her daughter-in-law would say about *her*. "I'm certainly not pushing, but maybe she feels a subtle pressure," Elaine muses. "Or she may feel my disappointment."

Disappointment. Sadness. These are two of the words Elaine uses to describe her feelings about the course her son's life has taken, and the way her grandchildren are being raised. Like Elaine, other mothers-in-law I spoke with expressed surprise that a son they considered Jewishly identified had chosen to marry a non-Jewish woman, a surprise that was unmitigated by the extent to which the couple had or hadn't created a Jewish home of their own. "I didn't think you'd do it," exclaims Arthur Levy's mother in Ludwig Lewisohn's 1928 book, *The Island Within*. In chapter two we looked at the novel's portrayal of a gentile woman and her marriage to a Jewish man. Lewisohn also offers a vision of a Jewish mother sideswiped by her son's unexpected intermarriage, and expressing her surprise, disappointment, and sadness to her daughter-in-law in ways she may not even be aware of.

Arthur Levy comes to tell his mother that he has married his gentile girlfriend, and that she is pregnant. Mrs. Levy doesn't scream or weep, she doesn't tell Arthur that he has ruined himself or her. Instead, her entire being quietly expresses devastation.

> Her smile was profoundly sad. "What can a mother do? I'm sorry for Papa. And for myself, a little. She'll be no daughter

to us. Her child won't—But no, I mustn't talk that way. I promise you this: we'll all do our best." Her sadness had a very special quality. It was an elemental sadness, a sadness as of the earth, the patient sadness of those who are accustomed to bear burdens. It communicated itself to Arthur and he went out of the room and out of the house strangely warmed by his absorption into that sadness, strangely at home in that simple, gigantic patience that consented to the bearing of burdens. . . .

That "gigantic patience that consented to the bearing of burdens" is nothing less than Judaism itself. Arthur, like Alain Finkielkraut but with very different emotions, equates the Jewish mother with Judaism, an enveloping blanket of tradition, history, and suffering that envelopes a Jewish son even as he takes an apparently decisive step outside it. The Jewish woman is this element, and the Jewish man can move comfortably, passively within it, while for Arthur's bride, Elizabeth, it threatens suffocation—an early indicator that Elizabeth is made of alien stuff, and that her marriage to Arthur is doomed.

When Arthur brings Elizabeth home to meet his parents, without a word his mother enfolds the younger woman in a powerful, high-stakes embrace. Elizabeth tries, and fails, to respond. Through Arthur's eyes, Lewisohn painstakingly deconstructs the moment.

She had felt in that embrace more than a gesture of affection and goodwill. She had felt in it a subtle reaching out after her and possessing of her and drawing her irrevocably in. And against that assumption of her no longer belonging wholly to herself or her kind, but of being, by a gesture that was also ceremonial, absorbed into a community of fact and feeling and interests the very existence of which she had not suspected—against that her instincts rebelled. . . . Arthur knew that Elizabeth would have denied, and very honestly and sincerely denied, these various emotional imputations. Honestly, because any formulation in words made the whole thing intolerably gross—the thing which, in itself, was the shadow of a shadow in the twilight of the mind.

The embrace, which had lasted but a moment, had been crucial. Arthur's mother had experienced the subtle rebuff which she had expected. She would have been happy not to have felt it. But she was not, being human and a woman, wholly dissatisfied to have her foregone conclusions proved and to be able to assume the generous, unweariedly giving and slightly tragic maternal role which, ever since Arthur's announcement, she had been prepared to assume.

In Lewisohn's take on their encounter, both Elizabeth and Mrs. Levy are caught up in a situation which neither, being women, can hope to think their way out of, and which only a clear-eyed male can grasp in all its intricacies. And what Arthur sees is that his mother, enacting a complete acceptance of Elizabeth as a daughter, is nonetheless not "wholly dissatisfied" to have her expectations of rejection confirmed. Elizabeth, try as she may to respond in kind to Mrs. Levy's apparent warmth, is both out of her emotional depths and at the same time correct in her suspicion that those open arms are offering to swallow her whole.

Elizabeth's instinctive sense that Mrs. Levy wishes to draw her into something unfamiliar and inexplicable to her is reminiscent of Elaine Seldes's surmise that her daughter-in-law may feel a "subtle pressure" to create a home life based upon values and traditions not her own. Elaine's recollection of Florence telling her, "Jews aren't religious, they don't believe in God. My religion is important to me," the first time they were introduced is indicative of Florence's ignorance of Judaism. It may also suggest that Florence arrived at that first meeting feeling defensive, anticipating that she might be coerced into putting her husband's heritage ahead of her own religion.

It's interesting to consider Elaine's story and Lewisohn's fictional meeting alongside the experiences of gentile women who feel snubbed by mothers-in-law they see as judgmental and censorious. Like Elizabeth, a gentile woman may seem aloof in ways she isn't aware of, while her mother-in-law may convey disappointment far less subtly than she knows. If some gentile daughters-in-law wish for a warmer welcome from their husbands' mothers, some Jewish mothers are wary of offering an unwanted embrace, of "pushing," to use Elaine's word. "You have to have respect for people," says Bibi Waxman. "One thing I never said to my sons is, 'Your wives have to convert.'" Cast unwillingly in the role of Jewish mother-in-law to no less than three gentile women, respect for others was Bibi's starting point. Judging by what she's made of her part, it was a good one.

Bibi Waxman

"In some ways, it would have been easier if they had been Jewish," Bibi Waxman, sixty-eight, says of her three daughters-in-law. She remembers when her eldest son, Stephen, announced that he was marrying his non-Jewish girlfriend. "It was painful initially. I worried a lot. My main feeling was that it was most important that the children be educated Jewishly. I felt that they would learn about Christianity just by living in a Christian society, but Judaism would be harder, and I feared that Judaism might not win out."

Bibi's own childhood taught her how hard it can be to grow up Jewish. She was seven years old when she and her parents fled Nazi Germany, first for pre-state Israel, and eventually for the United States. Her mother's health had been ruined by their wartime experiences. When Bibi was young, the emphasis in the family was on helping her mother recover, and Judaism was only intermittently practiced in their home. As a result, she didn't grow up with what she calls the music of Judaism in her ears. What she took away from her early life was an intense concern with Jewish survival and continuity.

When her own sons were young, Bibi, who lives in Baltimore, was active in the Reform synagogue where the boys attended Sunday school, and the family celebrated Jewish holidays at home. While not opposed to a Jewish education for their sons, her husband, who had also been raised in a nonobservant home, wouldn't hear of them attending Jewish day schools or summer camps, fearing that they would lose something by being streamlined in that way. Partly for that reason, Bibi's efforts to raise the boys Jewishly, she admits, involved "more in the pre–bar mitzvah years, less after." In retrospect, she believes that she could have done more to strengthen their Jewish identities.

Nevertheless, she never expected that all three of her sons would choose non-Jewish wives. Stephen, as the first, was the biggest shock. "He was an education for the other two," Bibi notes. When her second son, Abe, married out, it was less of a surprise, and she was able to take the recent intermarriage of her youngest son, Joe, almost in stride. "You can't control their love choices," she says philosophically.

Bibi adds that what has most helped her to accept her daughters-in-law is their willingness to have Judaism as the sole religion in their homes. "Stephen says that by being the only Jewish parent, he takes a bigger responsibility for the children's religious education than he would otherwise. But Michelle, his wife, takes responsibility too. She took them on a Jewish retreat weekend by herself, when Stephen couldn't go."

Her daughters-in-law, Bibi says, are all women she likes and admires. She is closest to Stephen's wife, Michelle, because she has known her the longest, and because they live near one another, while Abe and Joe and their wives live in southwestern states. About Michelle she says, "She is a very wonderful, warm woman, an easy person to relate to." None of her daughters-in-law is a practicing Christian, and all agreed to have no Christian elements in their wedding ceremonies. "I don't know what my story would be if someone had wanted a Catholic priest," Bibi says. "I was very lucky, and I realized it." The three couples celebrate Christmas with the wives' families, but none observe Christian holidays in their own homes. Stephen and Abe and their wives are raising their children as Jews, and Joe and his wife have said that when they have children they will do the same.

But Bibi isn't taking her grandchildren's Jewish educations for granted. In her midfifties, when she discovered that she was about to become a grandmother for the first time, she reacted to the news by deciding to have a bat mitzvah. These days, many Jewish girls go through this coming-of-age ritual, which involves chanting from the Torah in synagogue, at thirteen. But adult bat mitzvot are also popular among women who missed out on the event when they were young. "I wanted to get myself educated, I wanted to know where to go if I don't know an answer," Bibi explains, adding that she plans to study with her grandchildren for their bar and bat mitzvot as well. "You must take on the mantle of a Jewish grandparent in a more serious way. You're the Jewish grandmother who formerly just made matzoh ball soup, now you're the maternal voice of Judaism."

Bibi says she is sympathetic toward parents who feel that through their children's out-marriages, "covenants are being broken," and attributes her acceptance of three gentile daughters-in-law in part to her own lax Jewish upbringing. "The absence of so much ritual in my life helped me. If you've had that, it's hard for people."

In a largely inactive Jewish family such as Bibi's, many in the Jewish community would have predicted that the intermarriage of three sons would spell the demise of Jewish identification in the family. Instead, Bibi chose to see her sons' intermarriages as a growth opportunity for herself, a chance to learn more about Judaism and reinvent the role of Jewish grandmother in the process. An important part of laying claim to her Jewish identity was opening up about the experiences of her early childhood for the first time. "I broke my silence about being a child survivor of the Holocaust. Everyone knew, but we didn't really talk about it." For Bibi there's an important link between the way she dealt with her Holocaust background and the way she might have re-acted to her sons' marriages. Just like her childhood experiences, she says, the intermarriages could have been an opportunity to close off, shut down. Instead, they opened doors she hadn't ac-knowledged were stuck. "I found in my Holocaust experience, doors were always shut. If you feel you have to hide something, it feels bad. Shut doors increase pain."

Bibi doesn't forget that if things have worked out well for her family, much of the thanks is due to daughters-in-law who are willing to make Jewish homes and raise Jewish children despite the fact that none has yet chosen to convert. When her sons first got married, Bibi says, "I don't think I could have believed how lucky I'd be now. I had anxieties that were unfounded. I say to my daughters-in-law, 'You've been very good to me.'"

For women such as Jane Woo, Monica Cassia, and Celia Flem-ming, whom we met in the previous chapter, a mother-in-law who says, "You've been very good to me" might constitute a dream come true—or a trip into the realm of science fiction. But as Bibi's story demonstrates, Jewish mother/gentile daughter-in-law relationships come in all shapes and colors. Contrary to popular belief, the women who fill these roles are not inevitable enemies. As mentioned in chapter three, Megan Taylor, thirty-two, is in the process of converting to Judaism. She says her partner, Simon, has little interest in a Jewish spiritual life, and "if it was up to him we wouldn't be doing anything about it." Si-mon's mother, on the other hand, is a real source of encourage-ment. She lives in another state, Megan says, but is always available to answer Megan's questions. "I consult her on the phone, she's wonderful."

It was suggested earlier that stereotypical expectations of gentile and Jewish women can serve to create a kind of theoret-ical triangle on which each is stuck as a fixed point equidistant from the Jewish man who unites and divides them. The family configuration of mother, son, and wife is the real-life triangle in which Jewish and gentile women most often come into relation with each other. Over this configuration hovers the specter of the once-powerful Jewish matriarch whose position has been destroyed by assimilation and intermarriage—by the influx of gentile women into the Jewish family. But some feminist historians, such as Paula Hyman, argue that this figure never really existed. If that is true, then Bibi Waxman may be creating her for the first time, not, as she says, by ladling out matzoh ball soup but by remaking herself into her family's authority on religious knowledge and learning. And what has inspired her to lay claim to Jewish authority is none other than the influx of gentile women into her family.

Bibi doesn't see herself as needing to mitigate the anti-Jewish influences of her daughters-in-law, as they are willing to play a part in raising their children as Jews. In this, Bibi's daughters-in-law may not be in the majority of gentile mothers, but neither are they uncommon. Many Jewish leaders, including Edwin Friedman, have observed that the people most concerned with Jewish continuity tend to be women, both Jewish and gentile.

As Bibi herself is well aware, her family situation is greatly eased by the absence of Christian practice in her daughters-in-laws' lives. Christianity is a stumbling block for the Jewish members of many interfaith families, as it is in Elaine Seldes's case, though it must be said that for some Jews, such as Linda Horovitz, Christianity is not the worst thing that could happen in their families.

Linda Horovitz places such a high value on a relationship with the Divine that she tries to keep an open mind about the paths to that relationship that her children may take. This has played out in behavior almost opposite to Bibi's: Linda doesn't promote Judaism because she would rather her older son and his gentile wife choose Christianity over nothing. "I really do want to free them," she says. "I would worry that they might end up having no religion because they don't want to offend me. I would hope that my grandchildren wouldn't grow up thinking that the Jews killed Jesus and were terrible, but I think it's important for children to believe in God, and I would rather have it either way than no way."

Not surprisingly, Linda, who is sixty-two and lives in Michigan, is more troubled by this son and his wife, who are thus far raising their children without any religion, than by her younger son and his wife, who live in Japan and practice Buddhism. The contrast between her experiences with her two daughters-in-law also illustrates the benefits of being open about differences in an interfaith family. With her elder son's wife, the all-American impulse toward homogeneity silences a conversation about belief before it can begin, while she and her Japanese daughter-in-law are so obviously different, they don't have to pretend to be the same.

"The dynamics of the relationships with my sons and their wives is very different," Linda notes. "With my Japanese daughter-in-law, the fact that we have such different backgrounds means we talk about it all the time, she's teaching us all the time, asking us about our traditions. I have a tendency to minimize differences with my American daughter-in-law. We don't talk about religion. Whether we're avoiding that or not, it just hasn't played a big role."

The desire to avoid "pushing" Judaism in their daughters-in-laws' homes is often expressed in conversations with Jewish mothers-in-law. Like Elaine, Bibi, and Linda, the mothers-in-law I spoke with were extremely thoughtful about the issues their sons' interfaith marriages raised. As already noted, each voiced the question of what their daughters-in-law would say about them. In very different ways, each conveyed a sense—sometimes unconsciously—that in this often charged relationship she walked a fine line between "pushing" her heritage and offering to share it, between respecting a daughter-in-law's differences and doing too little to reach out to her.

Negotiating this fine line was something almost all the mothers-in-law I spoke with described as a solitary act. Several mentioned feeling isolated by a sense of their own failure as Jewish mothers. One spoke of how she and all of her friends had felt the lack of anyone to turn to for support or advice—despite the fact that they were going through similar experiences and emotions at more or less the same time. At her synagogue, where many members' children were marrying out, Elaine Seldes suggested starting a support group for the parents of children in interfaith relationships, only to be told that there would be no interest in such a group. This liberal synagogue, whose membership also includes many interfaith couples, may have hesitated to suggest that intermarriage was a problem requiring discussion. Pain—or the desire to avoid giving or increasing it—may have shut the door in all these situations on a conversation that would at least have lessened the isolation these mothers were feeling. As Bibi Waxman says, shut doors are painful.

In the collective Jewish imagination, expectations of Jewish and gentile women have historically created a dichotomy between them, or at least between the life choices they seem to represent for Jewish men. But for the women themselves religious and cultural identity tend to be far more complex constructions than the stereotypes can contain. That the clichés are useless becomes especially clear when a single life straddles both sets of experiences—when the Jewish woman and the non-Jewish woman are one and the same.

As a Jewish woman, I find myself easily enraged by negative attitudes toward Jewish women from within and outside the Jewish community. I share a sense of urgency about Jewish continuity and the survival of Jewish religion, culture, and *am Yisrael*, the Jewish people. At the same time, I identify with the anger and pain of the gentile woman who feels dismissed or rejected by the Jewish community, who feels pressured to abandon or at least keep quiet about a heritage that is not deemed acceptable.

As a young intermarried woman, I was once shut out, off, and up by Jewish women at synagogues and seders, at social occasions in my own and others' homes. As a Jewish woman, I have experienced the gentile world's "insensitivity" to Jews, both blatant and subtle. Walking through New York's Central Park Zoo, I marveled at a tall, blond, expensively dressed young mother who could smile and playfully shush her look-alike husband when he shouted anti-Semitic remarks at my family. A week or so later, I struggled against the far more subtle form of cultural noncommunication that Letty Cottin Pogrebin describes among feminist activists when I attempted to convince a group of women's studies scholars (a quarter of them Jewish) that a lunch meeting should not be scheduled for the High Holy Day of Yom Kippur; the meeting went ahead as planned. As someone known to be writing about gentile women in the Jewish world, I've been treated to impromptu tales about Jewish mothers, stepmothers, and mothers-in-law with the expectation that I, a Jewish mother, would sympathize with the speakers' soft-core blend of misogyny and anti-Semitism.

A perspective informed by firsthand experiences of life as both a gentile and Jewish woman may be particularly attuned to the inadequacy of conventional distinctions between them. But a convert is far from the only kind of woman who will have trouble locating herself inside traditional parameters of Jewish or gentile womanhood. Indeed, it's difficult to imagine even one woman for whom either stereotype fits like a glove.

We'll look next at the experiences of gentile and converted women for whom ethnic and racial heritage makes disappearing inside the norms impossible, women whose presence in the Jewish community is so unexpected, there aren't even Jewish jokes about them.

6

Beyond Shiksa:
Are All Gentile Women Created Equal?

W*HEN I* began to think about the roles played by race, ethnicity, and class in the way a gentile or converted woman might be seen and received in the Jewish community, a phrase kept haunting me: "beyond shiksa." Where had I heard these words, and what did they mean? Why did they carry such painful connotations?

Finally, I remembered. Years ago, a Filipino woman named Marisa had told me the story of her first American boyfriend. Unable to gain entry to a U.S. medical school, he was attending a comparable program in Manila when she knew him. His interest in the Philippines was limited to getting his degree and going home. He liked spending his free time with Marisa, but he let her know that for him, the relationship was a pleasant way to while away a few years. It couldn't be more: he was Jewish, and a Filipino woman wouldn't make the grade with his parents. To them, he often delighted in telling her, she'd be "beyond shiksa."

Up to this point in her story, Marisa had been laughing, as if it amused her as much as it had her ex-boyfriend to imagine his parents' reaction to a Filipino daughter-in-law. She grew more somber describing his return to the States. They met for the last time at a café, and sat across a table from each other. Marisa stared at his face as he talked and talked, explaining to her why they would never meet again. Marisa watched his lips move, but she had lost the ability to hear his voice; she never knew what it was he'd said to her.

When a gentile woman enters into a relationship with a Jew, or attempts to join a Jewish family or community, how are the dynamics affected by her class, race, or ethnicity? Can a convert who wears her otherness on her skin find a home in Judaism?

The Jewish people has a long and complicated relationship to issues of race and ethnicity. We've already seen that one way the early Jews distinguished themselves as a group was to vehemently reject the sexual and religious conventions of the pagans who surrounded them. But prohibitions against these peoples go beyond their specific practices. Biblical law conveys the sense of an enmity between the Israelites and some of their neighbors that generations of coexistence couldn't overcome.

The basis of this enmity varies from one group to another. Those peoples residing in the land to which God directs the Israelites automatically pose the threat of assimilation. In Dvarim, or Deuteronomy, God orders the Israelites to annihilate the seven Canaanite nations, then, as if assuming—correctly—that the first command will be ignored, not to intermarry with them. Intermarriage with the Canaanites is forbidden, God tells the people, "For they will turn your children away from Me to worship other gods."

Sometimes a history of bad blood lies between the Jews and another people. The Ammonites and Moabites, for example, were said to descend from the incestuous union of Lot and his two daughters. To compound this disreputable past, when the Israelites encountered them on their way through the desert after leaving Egypt, the Ammonites and Moabites flouted the Middle Eastern code of hospitality, and offered them no food or water. Further, as we saw in chapter two, the Moabites hired the prophet Balaam to curse the Israelites. As a result, the laws concerning them state that, "No Ammonite or Moabite shall be admitted into the congregation of the Lord; none of their descendants, even in the tenth generation, shall ever be admitted into the congregation of the Lord."

As in these examples, the prohibitions often regulate who can join the Israelites and who cannot, or how many generations must pass before the offspring of someone who has entered the Israelite community may be considered full members. But if old insults are not forgotten, neither are ties of kinship. The laws specify that "You shall not abhor an Edomite, for he is your kinsman. You shall not abhor an Egyptian, for you were a stranger in his land. Children born to them may be admitted into the congregation of the Lord in the third generation."

Sensitive to a possibly racial interpretation of these prohibitions, some modern commentators argue that they are religious, not racial, in nature, and that the Israelites' special relationship with God posited in the Torah is not to be understood as biological superiority. Indeed, the laws against different ethnic groups reflect social and political hostilities, or fears over the threat of absorption into their pagan neighbors, and are not expressed in racial terms. Even the notion that there is something eternally inimical between some of these peoples and the Israelites is not without contradictions and exceptions. Ruth, whose story we looked at in chapter four, is Judaism's premier convert as well as a Moabite. About Miriam and Aaron's complaint against Moses, "He married a Cushite woman!" which we examined in the previous chapter, the biblical commentator Rashi states that *Cushite* is a figurative term for "beautiful," the numerical value of the letters of the words *Cushite* and *beautiful* being equal. According to another midrash, Miriam's complaint against her sister-in-law was that she was black, and her punishment, being stricken with white scales, constituted divine retribution for bigotry with a vengeance.

Since the biblical era, Jews have lived in nations all over the globe, where their own precarious status was often rationalized in racial terms. In Europe, centuries of anti-Semitism preceded Nazi Germany's attempt to annihilate all Jews, a course justified by a fanatical belief in Jews' genetic inferiority to gentiles, demonstrated, in part, by their supposed close racial kinship to other peoples designated inferior. In *The Jew's Body*, Sander Gilman notes that in European racist ideology, Jews were classified as black. "It was . . . not only the color of the skin that enabled the scientist to see the Jew as Black, but also the associated anatomical signs, such as the shape of the nose. The Jews were quite literally seen as Black."

It was only in the United States in the second half of the twentieth century that Jews' racial status dramatically changed. Jews speak the languages and bear the cultural traits and physical characteristics of the many countries where they have taken up residence. They are Africans, Latinos, Asians, people of the Middle East, and of Europe. But though the first Jews to reach colonial America were Sephardic, or Spanish, the vast majority of American Jews are Ashkenazic, tracing their origins to Eastern and Central Europe. While anti-Semitism still exists, throughout the twentieth century it gradually ceased to be a limitation on Jews' educational, economic, or career success, or on their social integration into the dominant culture. In their introduction to *Insider/Outsider: American Jews and Multiculturalism*, editors David Biale, Michael Galchinsky, and Susannah Heschel write that "American Jews were able to make social and political gains . . . because they were now seen and were willing to be seen as 'white' themselves, as part of a majority whose very self-definition as a majority was based on the exclusion of those termed 'nonwhite.'"

As participants in that majority, Jews are open to the same racist influences and motivations as any other group designated white. At the same time, as a people with a distinct religious, cultural, and historic heritage, they are subject to strong internal pressure, as we've seen, to defend group purity against the diluting effects of outsiders.

Depending upon her ethnicity, a gentile woman searching for a place in a Jewish family or community may be confronted with the fallout from either or both these factors. Marisa's boyfriend told her that to be Filipino was to be something beyond—that is, worse—than a shiksa. He conveyed to her that, nonwhite as well as gentile, she was owed less respect and compassion than even a white gentile girl. The eponymous narrator of Philip Roth's *Portnoy's Complaint* goes a step further, suggesting that a nonwhite woman is hardly a woman at all. "A *shikse* has never been in our house. . . . The cleaning lady is obviously a *shikse*, but she doesn't count because she's black."

In chapter four, Felicia Cruz wondered if her chilly reception in a synagogue was related to her dark skin and Latina heritage. Jane Woo was convinced that she had earned her mother-in-law's disfavor simply by being Chinese. Celia Flemming recalled her in-laws' contempt for the Irish name she gave her daughter. In the previous chapter, Elaine Seldes admitted to a cultural distance between herself and her Chinese daughter-in-law, but felt that the problematic difference between them was not ethnicity but religion. For both the Jews and gentiles in any of these situations, the two factors may be difficult to separate.

What should make it easy to distinguish between issues of race and religion is conversion. As already noted, conversion, an express statement of an individual's intention to practice Judaism and to live her life as a Jew, ought to resolve many of the concerns with which a Jewish family or community greets the arrival of a non-Jewish woman. But some Jews find it difficult to accept the notion that conversion turns a gentile into a Jew. "Oh, it's just a religious thing," a woman who was Jewish by birth once said to Olivia Hamilton, dismissing Olivia's claim to Jewish identity out of hand. Would she have felt confident about making such a statement if Olivia, a stranger to her, wasn't African-American?

Like Olivia, a number of those whose stories we'll explore in this chapter are Jews, women who entered the Jewish people through conversion. Like Olivia, some women find acceptance as a Jew can be color-coded.

Olivia Hamilton

Raised a Methodist, Olivia Hamilton, thirty-six, began to feel dissatisfied with Christianity in her early teens. "I realized I'm not a big fan of trinitarian systems, of which Christianity is one," she says. "I prefer a one-on-one connection with God, and always have."

She got a taste of Judaism while living with a Reform Jewish family in Paris as an exchange student. Back in the States, she began attending services at a synagogue as a senior in college. Beginning life in a new town after graduation, she contacted a rabbi she found by flipping through the pages of a phone book. "I attended services for two months before he would consent to teach me," she recalls. A year later, Olivia converted to Judaism, with the private ritual of immersion in a mikvah followed by a public ceremony at the synagogue the following Shabbat. "I invited everyone I knew—and they showed up."

In the first few years after her conversion, Olivia moved around a bit, eventually settling in the small midwestern city where she lives now, earning a doctorate in French literature and then taking various teaching jobs. She has belonged to a Reform synagogue for nine years. There she attends services regularly for holidays, intermittently for Shabbat, and sings in the choir. On her own, she observes the period from Friday evening to Saturday evening as a day of rest, preferring to date and do recreational activities on Saturday night, after the end of the Sabbath.

Olivia says that she has found a home in Judaism and feels comfortable there. Her biggest problem, she insists, is operating outside Jewish circles, where people assume that she is Christian, and some members of her own family continue to send her Christmas cards. But given Judaism's very communal nature, Olivia's connections to the Jewish community seem tenuous.

"Yes, race has played a role, whether someone said so or not," she admits. "Being African-American, and dark-skinned at that, has not been easy in the Jewish community. Many times I've been mistaken for the help, or someone has asked me what I'm doing someplace. Primarily it's been a case of the double-take, the surprise. My reception in Jewish communities has mostly been positive, but it usually takes time for people to accept me." Olivia's talent for coping with these obviously distressing incidents grows out of her certainty about her Jewish identity, and a striking patience. "I remind myself that I'm Jewish and have just as much of a right to sit at the table in common with other Jews," she says. "Once people realize that I'm just like them in terms of practice, I'm more accepted. Usually seeing me at services a few times or at social events helps. I've come to learn that people need to get to know you to accept you as something they think you are not."

Olivia's experience in the Jewish community hasn't entirely been an ordeal. She says she loves being part of her synagogue's choir, and clearly savors the warm atmosphere at rehearsals. At one point, when she was threatened with eviction from her apartment, congregation members helped her successfully fight back. And when her father died, she found the community very supportive.

Some of Olivia's isolation is what might be experienced by any unpartnered Jew. She is determined to marry a Jewish man, in part because the rabbi she studied with told her that he was reluctant to convert her due to the likelihood that she would marry someone who wasn't Jewish. Olivia thinks it's ironic that the rabbi expected her to marry an African American, while her preference in dating has always been white men. All she has to do now, she says, is find a partner who is Jewish.

"The next step for me in terms of Jewish experiences is being married to a Jew and having a Jewish family. Unlike other religions, Judaism is so family- and group-oriented, it's hard being single. This is something that at twenty-three didn't bother me. At thirty-six, it does."

Will it be harder for Olivia to find a Jewish man to marry than it would be for a white convert? The rabbi who converted her clearly thought so. Rabbi Solomon Rybak, chair of the committee on conversion for the Orthodox Union's Rabbinic Council of America, says that in his own New Jersey congregation, converts of color are entirely welcome, as are nonwhite adopted children. "They find acceptance," Rybak says. "The difficulty is finding marriage partners." Rybak is quick to add that the reason for this difficulty is age, not race, because a convert often enters the community later in life than the relatively early age at which Orthodox Jews pair off. Whether age is really the only obstacle for nonwhite Jews seeking mates in the Orthodox community may be tested when the African-American and Korean children adopted into Rybak's congregation reach maturity. If they have been integrated into the community without stigma, they should be no less desirable as marriage partners than their born-Jewish counterparts.

Conversion for the purpose of marriage is not permitted among the Orthodox officially. In reality, it is well known that prenuptial conversions occur in many, if not most, Orthodox communities. It may be true that in Rybak's congregation, converts of color are embraced, as he says, without hesitation, but it is unlikely that this would be universally true among Orthodox Jews. In a 1995 essay, Mark Sirkin, a psychologist who works with the families of interfaith couples, tells this story from his clinical practice. Saul, a twenty-seven-year-old Orthodox medical student, was planning to marry an Asian woman. Saul's parents, Sam and Minna, had come to Sirkin for help in stopping the marriage.

> As we talked about their objections to the intermarriage, they mentioned in passing that Saul has assured them that his girlfriend would undergo an Orthodox conversion. When I suggested that this must have been quite a relief for them, Sam looked at me wide-eyed and said, "But Doctor, you don't understand, we will never accept this girl, she's not like us, she's not our kind, no conversion can change that." As we discussed the issue further, my fears were confirmed: this was not about religion or halacha [Jewish law]; it was prejudice, pure and simple.
> "Of course my son thinks we're racists," the father added.

How a non-Jewish or converted woman's ethnicity affects her reception in a Jewish milieu is intricately tied up with how alien her background makes her appear to family or congregation members, how bridgeable or unbridgeable they judge the distance between them and her to be. Those who are operating on racist impulses are not likely to be looking for points of contact between themselves and a nonwhite woman, for ways to invite her in. People who see Olivia Hamilton at a worship service and insist on asking whether she is "the help," who wonder what other purpose she could have in their midst, would seem to be operating within a definition of Jewish community that doesn't include a person of African-American descent.

But not all Jews accept such a definition of their communities, or their families. Linda Horovitz, whom we met in the previous chapter, would have welcomed a woman of any race or religion with open arms. For her, the vast differences between herself and her Japanese daughter-in-law work in the relationship's favor, by freeing them from the necessity to pretend to be alike and allowing them to actually get to know each other. Marta Hernandez believes that being Latina actually eased her transition as a gentile into a Jewish family, because her in-laws would not want it to appear that prejudice held them back from welcoming her.

Marta, thirty-eight, described the effects of the matrilineal definition of Judaism on her family in chapter three. She is a Catholic attorney with two young children who lives in Chicago. Her husband, Alex, was raised a Conservative Jew, but Marta describes his parents as secular rather than religious Jews, who are "very plugged in to the Jewish community," and whose friends are almost entirely Jewish. "Jewish identity is very important to them. I agreed to give our son a bris to please them. Otherwise, I would have had him circumcised in the hospital, primarily to ensure that if he chooses Judaism later, the conversion will not be as painful."

Despite the value her in-laws place on Jewish identity, Marta says they have treated her very well, even entering without hesitation into celebrations of Christian holidays with her and their grandchildren. "I'm Latina, and my in-laws are very curious about that. I think that because they are liberals, my minority status may have made them feel more of an obligation to like me. But who can say for sure?"

It's worth noting Marta's uncertainty even in this harmonious family. Though Alex's parents seem to like her, it's easier for her to believe that their affection derives from political correctness than from her own charms.

Whatever their motivations, the fact remains that Alex's parents have welcomed Marta into their family, and since she and Alex have not moved in any wider Jewish circles, this positive experience is all that she has known of the Jewish community. Teresa Ortiz is also a Latina woman who has felt welcome in Jewish settings. But Teresa's involvement with Judaism has been the opposite of Marta's, in that family has played no role at all; religious communities have been everything.

Teresa Ortiz

Born in Cuba fifty-some years ago, Teresa Ortiz grew up Catholic in Boston and Miami. In high school her closest friend was Jewish, and the two girls taught each other about their religions. For Teresa it was the beginning of a lifelong attachment to Judaism, an attachment nurtured and fed by friendship but not by romantic interests. She is a lesbian, and her partner is Christian. Despite having once considered conversion to Judaism, Teresa is also a Christian, and will remain one. In fact, she is a pastor in the United Church of Christ.

"Christianity is rooted in Judaism, specifically in the prophetic tradition in Judaism," says Teresa, explaining why for her, Christianity and Judaism are not at odds. "Jesus was the reluctant founder of Christianity. He didn't want to found a religion, he was just a Jew."

For years Teresa has belonged to a havurah, a group that meets weekly in Miami to celebrate Shabbat on Friday nights. Together with a multicultural array of people, she lights candles, says blessings, and spends "three hours at a table, truly enjoying the sense of the Sabbath, connecting with people, with the sacred. It's been such a blessing, it's been a wonderful thing."

Teresa also worships on occasion in synagogues, feeling particularly comfortable in Reconstructionist congregations. In the anonymity of a religious service, there is nothing about Teresa's looks that makes her stand out in other people's eyes, as Olivia does. When she prays in a synagogue, Teresa does so in Hebrew, wearing the tallit, or Jewish prayer shawl, that she was given by a friend on the occasion of her pastoral ordination. Her Jewish friends, of course, realize that she is Christian, but they accept her presence in Jewish worship. "They already know that I'm a pretty strange Christian," Teresa comments. Among other Jews, Teresa has sometimes been an object of curiosity, but not in the off-putting way that Olivia has. "It's been a 'What are you doing here?' kind of thing. But I've never had a bad experience. I was always respectful, and I think people were tickled that I was interested."

Teresa's career as a pastor has emphasized interfaith work for peace and social justice. She insists that "People who work for justice don't get hung up on theology." Yet she herself locates her Christian dedication to these causes in theology—Jewish theology. "Christianity has the value of working for peace and justice because we are a Jewish religion. It's central to Jesus because it's central to the prophetic tradition."

It's ironic that Olivia, a convert to Judaism, has found the Jewish community slow to offer her a home, while Teresa, who is not looking for a home in Judaism, has felt embraced in Jewish communities. Of course, this distinction may not be incidental to the differences in the ways they have been received. It's easier to welcome an exotic guest into one's home than it is to invite her to permanently move in. The first causes no conflict in Judaism, a tradition that places a high value on welcoming strangers. But for some Jews, the second may require expanding their concept of Jewish community.

There is also the possibility that in the communities they've each encountered, Olivia was perceived as the more alien of the two. This could relate to the simple and obvious fact of her much darker skin, but it could also reflect subtle cultural stereotypes and associations. Regardless of reality, some ethnic groups may appear to have more—or less—in common than others.

As an example of this, Rabbi Nancy Weiner, the clinical director for Pastoral Care Counseling for the (Reform) Hebrew Union College, reports anecdotally that, based on what she hears from rabbis, there is a perception among Jews of greater shared values with Asian than with African-American people. "There's an emphasis on education and family values, values that Jews across the board tend to hold even if they are not affiliated or practicing Judaism. They perceive Asians to hold these values too, much more so than African Americans."

Whether this positive perception of Asians was at work or whether it was simply that luck brought her into contact exclusively with warm, open-minded Jews, Karen Zheng has never encountered barriers to inclusion in the Jewish community. She has felt embraced by the American Jews she's known, despite growing up in an entirely disparate culture on the other side of the world.

Karen Zheng

When Karen Zheng's husband, Jeff, told his parents he was going to marry Karen, they had a reaction unusual even among Jews most distraught by a child's intermarriage: they thought he'd been bewitched.

"His mother sent hysterical telegrams to him to come home immediately, that he was killing his father. She believed he had been bewitched by me or a *bomoh*, a Malaysian witch doctor. She had his cousins and uncles write him urging him to change his mind about this wrong step he was about to take."

Karen, fifty-six, grew up in Malaysia of Chinese ancestry, worshipping "a multitude of gods. We had door gods, household gods, a kitchen god, a sky god, Buddha, the goddess of mercy, and we practiced ancestor worship. We had an altar where my mother offered incense sticks and food, tea, and wine to the gods and the ancestors." Attending a missionary school in her small hometown, Karen learned English—and lost her fluency in Chinese. Her education also led to her conversion to Catholicism as a teenager, a path that was in turn abandoned when she began reading Sartre, Camus, and other existentialist writers as a college student in the late sixties. Then she met Jeff, a Peace Corp volunteer posted in Malaysia. They planned to marry, and Jeff asked Karen to convert to Judaism. So she traded in what she calls the "bleak philosophy" of existentialism in order to raise her children in a life-affirming tradition.

Like the Orthodox couple described above by Mark Sirkin, Jeff's parents weren't immediately appeased by Karen's agreement to an Orthodox conversion. However, they changed their minds as soon as the couple married and traveled from Malaysia to spend a summer with them in Israel, where they had recently moved. They welcomed Karen into the family, and helped her find a woman teacher she could begin studying with for her conversion. When Karen and Jeff moved to the States, Karen completed her conversion with the help of a kindly Orthodox rabbi. They settled in a southern California town and joined a small Conservative synagogue near their home. "The rabbi was cautiously welcoming," Karen recalls. "He asked to see my conversion papers, and later performed a Jewish wedding ceremony for Jeff and me. After that, he accepted me and began urging me to take leadership positions in the community."

At the synagogue, where she has now been a member for some twenty-five years, Karen says she has always felt like one of the family. Describing the congregation as close-knit, Karen says its small size means that anyone willing to lend a hand is greatly appreciated. She has worked on and chaired innumerable committees over the years, at one point serving as synagogue president. To illustrate the congregation's acceptance of her, Karen recalls an incident that took place a few years after she joined. "Someone came to the synagogue asking for 'the Chinese woman.' Everyone kept saying, 'What Chinese woman?' until finally one said, 'Oh, you must mean Karen.' They think of me as Jewish, you see."

At first, Karen admits, she had some trouble thinking of herself as Jewish, and felt particularly inauthentic speaking the prayers in synagogue that asserted her membership in the Jewish family. She says that time has made the crucial difference in her sense of herself as a Jew: years of living a Jewish life and accruing Jewish memories. Becoming a wife, an American, and a

Jew more or less simultaneously necessitated deep internal shifts in her notion of family, her sense of her place in the world, even in her concept of identity itself. Having grown up with a Chinese notion of identity as an outgrowth of a person's position in an extended family and clan, she found herself confronted with the American belief in the uniqueness of the individual—at the same time as becoming a member of the Jewish people, a tradition with a sense of family and clan identity of its own.

An artist, Karen has explored her Chinese and Jewish identities, her Malaysian past and American present, in her work, while also trying to raise three Jewish children with some knowledge of the Chinese aspects of their heritage.

Reflecting on her smooth acceptance into the Jewish community, Karen points to several things that she believes played a role in how she was received: an upbringing that trained her to be very polite and to avoid the conflicts common within all groups, the leadership positions she took on in the synagogue, her wide Jewish learning as a convert, and other people's inclination to credit her with great bravery for leaving her own culture and religion to follow her husband to a new home.

"I also find that people tend to treat you the way you expect to be treated—at least in civilized society—and like [the Jewish sage] Hillel, I generally treat people the way I want to be treated, with honesty, courtesy and integrity. I've been lucky to have received all these qualities back, with the bonus of warm affection. I feel I have been very lucky in my choice of husband and faith, and the people of the Book are very much my people now."

Karen raises knotty questions when she asserts that she was well received in the Jewish community because she herself behaved well, the implication being that those who feel less welcome have themselves to blame. When Marisa's boyfriend refused to take her seriously because she was not only non-Jewish but nonwhite, was it because she wasn't behaving appropriately? When Olivia is met with suspicion while praying in a synagogue, is she responsible for this reaction? Is it possible to celebrate Karen's heartening story without blaming a woman of color who has had more difficult experiences?

Rather than some particular bad behavior on her part, it's likely that in the eyes of those who reject her, a woman like Marisa or Olivia looks like an intruder, trying to slip into a slice of "civilized society" where she simply doesn't belong. In some Jewish settings, her race may be enough to brand a woman a gate-crasher; in others, it may be her class background.

Demographer Egon Mayer characterizes the way some gentile women are received into the Jewish family this way: "Who is this interloper who's stealing our best and brightest?" But Mayer doesn't think this reaction is common to intermarriage situations across the board. Rather, he says, "I think that's a stereotype that occurs when the woman is not as socially desirable. It could be class."

In chapter two, Mary Rosenbaum recalled her in-laws' penchant for referring to her as "the shiksa," particularly when she happened to be washing dishes. She and her husband, Ned, both grew up in Chicago suburbs, and both families were comparably middle class. "But mine had made it into the middle class, his had seen better days." Because of her working-class Italian immigrant background, Mary says, her in-laws "assumed I'd know where to get a servant."

According to the results of the 2000–2001 National Jewish Population Survey, while 19 percent of American Jews are defined as low-income, earning $25,000 or less annually, the median income among American Jews is $50,000, as compared with $42,000 for non-Jews. Membership in synagogues and participation in Jewish day schools, summer camps, retreat centers and other Jewish institutions carry very high fees, and thus often disproportionately reflect the wealthiest segment of the Jewish population. A non-Jew who does not fit this economic profile may find herself doubly alienated in a Jewish setting, in the eyes of those who receive her, if not her own.

But just as economic class sets barriers between people, it also serves as a great unifier. The most striking instance of class insensitivity I came across in my conversations with members of the Jewish community involved a woman who was herself a convert to Judaism.

Nancy Brookes, a single law professor in her midfifties, converted to Judaism a few years ago after a decades-long spiritual search. Almost immediately after her conversion, she got involved in helping the rabbi at her Chicago Conservative synagogue run the Introduction to Judaism program that she herself had been through. She teaches some of the classes and also takes part in the rigorous screening of potential candidates. Nancy is very proud of the high standards for inclusion that she helps to maintain. "We don't allow people into the program unless they agree to live an observant life," Nancy explains. "Once we had a beautician who *said* she had to work on Saturdays. We talked about it, because we wouldn't want to deny someone their livelihood." Nancy laughs. The notion that someone might actually *have* to work on Saturday, the day work is prohibited in Jewish law, is clearly absurd to her, and was reflected in the decision she and her colleagues reached. They offered the woman the names of other synagogues and showed her the door.

Nancy and her colleagues were unable, perhaps unwilling, to comprehend that the woman did not have the economic ability to control the conditions of her employment, having been trained in a profession in which Saturday is the most important working day of the week. To Nancy, such a limitation called into question the sincerity of the woman's interest in Judaism. In her eyes the story illustrates the superior nature of her synagogue's program: it doesn't merely welcome potential Jews, it keeps the wrong sort—in this case, the working-class sort—out. One can only hope that the woman in Nancy's story found a warmer welcome elsewhere in the Jewish world.

While Mary Rosenbaum's reminiscences of her in-laws demonstrate their class perceptions of her, they also reflect an ethnic chauvinism. Her Italian immigrant background was not simply a mark of Mary's difference from her in-laws but of her relative inferiority in their eyes. Given her experiences, perhaps it's not surprising that Mary insists, "There's still the ethnic exclusion. Even when the woman converts, she'll never really be Jewish."

Many converts would flatly disagree with this assertion, and are living lives that refute it. But anyone who takes part in the Jewish community experiences the ethnic as well as religious component to Jewish identity. And among some Jews, ethnic pride carries with it the sort of attitude that Mary encountered.

In the film *Keeping the Faith,* discussed in chapter two, there is a scene in which the young rabbi, forced to reveal his clandestine relationship with a non-Jewish woman to some of his congregants, identifies her simply as "Anna." The suspicious congregants press for more, then react with predictable horror at Anna's Irish surname. Monica Cassia, who we met in chapter four, has had similar encounters in which a warm welcome curdled at the mention of her Italian name. I've the same experience many times myself. It's a phenomenon I identify as the Limp Handshake, in which the admission of a wrong ethnic name has the power to turn a firm handclasp to cold jelly. Often the initially welcoming community member darts his or her eyes back and forth between my face ("You look Jewish!") and the Magen David, or Jewish star, around my neck while recoiling from the name that calls the other evidence into question. Of course, the dismay may simply be over a name that is perceived by some as non-Jewish (others, as already noted, recognize my surname as possibly Sephardic). But I've both experienced and heard too many stories of overt ethnic bigotry not to consider the possibility that an all-American WASP surname would not evoke the same reaction.

But while a white gentile or converted woman may find herself sidelined in the Jewish community by her particular ethnicity, she is unlikely to be taken for "the help" as Olivia Hamilton was, or to be asked repeatedly to explain her presence in a Jewish setting. Discussing the Limp Handshake with an African-American convert placed my own experiences in perspective. "You can use another name," she pointed out. "I can't change my face."

Anecdotal evidence suggests that African-American gentiles and converts may face the toughest odds to finding acceptance in the American Jewish community. Certainly the stories of their experiences there tend to be among the most painful.

Discussing relationships that are both interfaith and interracial in her book *Black, Jewish and Interracial,* Karen Gibel Azoulay asks, "What essential difference should it make whether the non-Jewish partner is white or Black? And yet in the anecdotal material available, it clearly has made a difference for people with this [African-American] background."

It certainly made a difference to the people described by Rebecca Walker in *Black, White, and Jewish: Autobiography of a Shifting Self,* her memoir of growing up in the 1970s and 1980s in a family divided by race, pulled between a black mother and a paternal Jewish family that could not accept her. Describing a visit from her father's mother, she writes, "Daddy seems happy Grandma came to see us, but Mama seems nervous, angry. I think this is because Grandma doesn't look at Mama. When she talks to Mama, she looks at me." Walker calls up fond memories of occasions spent with her father's extended family. But these memories are seen through the lens of her mother's absence. That there was no place for her mother at the family table inevitably calls into question her own right to be there as well. "I pull back and feel . . . as if I am in the family through some kind of affirmative-action plan and don't entirely belong." The memoir culminates in Walker's decision to drop her father's Jewish surname, Leventhal, in favor of her mother's. "When I change my name I do so because I do not feel an affinity with whiteness, with what Jewishness has become, and I do feel an affinity with blackness, with an experience of living in the world with non-white skin."

As already noted, the historical irony here is that "Jewishness" and "non-white skin" would appear to be so much at odds. This is a notion inevitable in the United States, yet easily exploded by a stroll through the streets of most Israeli cities. In modern Israel, Jewish skin comes in every shade and "Jewish ethnicity" encompasses cultures from every corner of the earth. It includes the large, and largely struggling, community of Ethiopian Jews who trace their descent to the most important black woman of biblical Judaism.

The Queen of Sheba

According to I Kings, the Queen of Sheba, having heard the tales of King Solomon's wealth and wisdom, comes to see—and test—the legend for herself. Arriving in Solomon's court with "a very large retinue, with camels bearing spices, a great quantity of gold, and precious stones," she tries Solomon's wisdom with a series of difficult questions. In the end, satisfied with what she has seen and heard, she tells Solomon that he surpasses his illustrious reputation. "Praised be the Lord your God, who delighted in you and set you on the throne of Israel. It is because of the Lord's everlasting love for Israel that He made you king to administer justice and righteousness." With that, the queen and king exchange opulent gifts, and the queen and her attendants return home.

The episode is just a footnote in Solomon's long and eventful reign. But postbiblical writers, Jewish and otherwise, have always been fascinated by the enigmatic encounter, and in particular by the mysterious queen some believe was a historical monarch.

In Yemen and Ethiopia, where her legend is considered a

memory and not a myth, she is called Balqis or Bilqis; in Islam she is alternately known as Belkis or Makeda. Because she praises the God of Israel, there are those who interpret her words as acceptance of the Jewish religion—that is, as conversion. According to some versions of the story, Balqis had a son with Solomon, Menelik I, before returning to her own people. When Menelik reached young manhood, Balqis sent him to Jerusalem to learn from his father. Menelik came back bringing Israelite men who married Ethiopian women, helping to initiate his nation's mass conversion to Judaism. He also brought the Tablets of the Law given to him by Solomon. A church in Axum, in northern Ethiopia, is said to contain these tablets.

Jewish tradition also includes other, less favorable views of the queen. As already noted, the literature on she-demon Lilith claims the Queen of Sheba as one of her guises. The Zohar portrays her as a demon or witch, and commentator Rabbi Moses Cordovero credits her with spreading diphtheria. Commentator Rashi agrees that Solomon and Balqis had a son together, but identifies this son as Nebuchadnezzar, the Babylonian who destroyed the First Temple in Jerusalem, the seat of the Jewish religion. Since Nebuchadnezzar lived in the fifth century B.C.E., and Balqis's visit to Solomon is dated at about 960 B.C.E., he could not in fact have been her son.

Though there are competing explanations for the Jewish community of Ethiopia, the people themselves believe they are the descendants of Balqis and Menelik. Throughout centuries of persecution and desperate poverty, the community harbored a dream of life in Israel. Today almost all Ethiopian Jews have relocated to Israel, including some fourteen thousand who were flown there in 1991 by the Israeli government in a famous rescue mission known as Operation Solomon. Despite an extremely difficult cultural and economic adjustment, many of the Israeli Jews of Ethiopia still believe that they have made it to the Promised Land.

Among Jews of European descent, there are those who have been slow to accept the Ethiopian branch of the Jewish family, perhaps finding it difficult to feel kinship with a people whose history and appearance are so different from their own. But these days, the Ethiopians provide some American Jews with a way of making sense of their community's increasingly multicultural aspect.

"Are you from Ethiopia?" That's a question Amy Weiss hears often, especially when she volunteers to lead Shabbat services in nursing homes for elderly Jews. "No," Amy tells them. "I'm from Brooklyn." Amy used to find the question off-putting, but she's come to see it as a sign of progress. Her eighty-something interrogators recognize that she is clearly a Jew, and clearly of African descent. They're just trying to find an explanation for how those two things go together.

Amy Weiss

As she tells the senior citizens, Amy, forty-nine, grew up in Brooklyn, New York, in a poor African-American family of seven children that she describes as "powerfully Catholic." Amy, a professor of health studies and education, attended Catholic schools through high school, but after a year at an Upstate New York college was no longer practicing Catholicism. In an effort to redefine herself, she began exploring Buddhism and transferred to a college in New York City. It was in a physics class there that she met Eric. They studied together, and he asked her out on a date. It wasn't long before they were living together.

Eric, Amy says, "was not very religiously Jewish," primarily expressing his Judaism by participating in holiday celebrations. His parents had been born in Germany and Vienna, and had escaped Europe during the Nazi era. They belonged to a synagogue in the tony New York suburban town where they lived,

and observed Jewish holidays. They also continued a family tradition of celebrating Christmas Eve in Viennese style.

Eric brought Amy home to meet his parents the first time
for a Passover seder. As Amy recalls, they greeted her politely,
then turned away to discuss their feelings. "They might get married!" Eric's father moaned. His wife reassured him. "No, don't
worry, these days kids live together and don't get married." After that evening, Eric's parents asked that he not bring Amy
home with him again.

"I'll never forget when we told his parents we were getting
married," Amy says. "They literally couldn't speak. I was black
and I wasn't Jewish. As far as they were concerned, they had a
double whammy."

After they were married, Amy says, her in-laws were forced
to accept her, and for the first High Holy Days after their wedding, she and Eric accompanied his parents to their synagogue
on Rosh Hashanah. The synagogue was densely packed with
worshippers, and it was only with difficulty that the four managed to find places together. But as soon as they were seated, a
space began to open up around them. The other congregants
were changing seats, moving away from the family that now included a young black woman. "I always call that episode the
parting of the sea," says Amy. "My parents-in-law were red.
They said, 'We've known these people for thirty years, they're
our friends.' Eric told them, 'Maybe they're not really your
friends.'"

In the early years of their marriage, Amy and Eric lived in a
Jewish neighborhood in Brooklyn. Amy felt the absence of spirituality in their home, but for Eric, nothing was missing. When
their daughter was born, Amy told him that it was time to commit themselves to a religion. Eric's only contribution to the discussion was to insist that there be no Catholicism is his home.

Every day, on her way to and from the subway, Amy would
pass a Reform synagogue with a sign that read ALL WELCOME
hanging on its door. One day, she decided to find out if all really

were welcome. She walked in and was told to come back for Shabbat services. She went home and told Eric that they were going to synagogue.

Amy was not just the first dark-skinned congregant the community had had, she was also the first gentile, and her presence occasioned much discussion of what constituted appropriate participation for a non-Jew. The rabbi tried to resolve the concerns by saying that though there were some things Amy couldn't do, there were many ways that she could be involved. His handling of the situation made Amy felt accepted in the synagogue. So it came as a surprise when she told the rabbi that she wanted to convert and he put her off. She asked a second time, and was again brushed aside. At this point, Amy didn't know about the custom, practiced by some rabbis, of refusing a potential convert three times, the theory being that only the truly devoted proselyte will persist despite discouragement. Nevertheless, Amy was not easily turned away. She confronted the rabbi a third time. "I said, 'I'm really serious about this, you can't put me off, I want to convert.' He turned on me. 'Why do you want to be Jewish? Don't you know Jews are hated the world over?' I said, 'Look at this face, don't you think I know what hate is?' It brought him up short." The rabbi had been acting on automatic pilot, not actually thinking about the woman before him. Amy converted with him soon after.

"That synagogue was a very positive experience, it was a very good door-opener," Amy notes. "But if they hadn't been nice, I would have found another way in."

Eric's career took the family to several different East Coast cities over the next dozen or so years, and in each place Amy joined the nearest Reform synagogue and enrolled her daughter in the Sunday school. Since Eric wanted to attend services only occasionally, Amy learned to drive so that she could get herself and her daughter there on a regular basis. But frequent attendance at services didn't lead to a warm welcome for Amy in any of these congregations. She recalls being constantly asked,

"Why are you Jewish?" "What are you doing here?" At three consecutive synagogues, she was invited to give a talk to the congregation explaining her Jewish identity. The first two times she agreed, and submitted to being grilled by suspicious congregants about her positions on issues such as Israel and black anti-Semitism.

About the latter, Amy told her audiences that she had known hatred and wasn't interested in hating others, even when it was hard not to. She recalled a childhood in which a Louisiana man once trained a gun on her because she had put her foot on his lawn while turning a corner, and in which she was told that she couldn't be a cheerleader for her Catholic high school in New York because "we can't color our uniforms." As adults, she and Eric had been barred from living in neighborhoods where African Americans were not allowed.

When her third congregation asked her to speak, Amy decided that she'd had enough of explaining herself to people motivated by curiosity, not genuine interest in getting to know her. She refused. She remained a member of this Maryland synagogue for ten years. During that time she and her family were never once invited to attend a bar or bat mitzvah, which at this congregation, unlike most, were by invitation only. When she tried to sit in on one of her daughter's religious school classes, she was told, "Mrs. Weiss, you really have to leave, you're making the children nervous."

During these years, Amy gave birth to a second child, a boy. Someone at her synagogue arranged for an Orthodox mohel to come to her house on the eighth day after the baby's birth to perform the ritual circumcision. The house was full of guests, mostly Amy's relatives. When the rabbi arrived, he took one look at Amy and asked if she was the baby's mother. She told him that she was. He barked at her that he would perform the circumcision for the baby's sake, and, literally pushing her aside, demanded to see her husband.

The amazing thing about these experiences is that none of

them convinced Amy to stop searching for a home in the Jewish community. Five years ago, the family moved again, this time to a small city in the Pacific Northwest. One Friday after they were settled, Amy took her children to a Shabbat service at a Reconstructionist synagogue. The evening was to change her life as a Jew.

"When we arrived, everyone was very friendly, greeting us. Afterward I told the kids that maybe we should go back and see if it was real."

Amy's initial impression of a warm and welcoming congregation was not an illusion. She put her children in the synagogue's school, and started her daughter on bat mitzvah preparations. When she told the children's teacher that she wanted to learn more about Judaism herself, the woman opened a Torah on the spot and began to teach her.

"The doors opened," Amy says. "I took adult education classes and served on the steering committee. I chant from the Torah, I lead services, I teach in the Shabbat school and have b'nai mitzvah students myself. My children are growing up in the synagogue and having a wonderful experience." Even Eric is studying Hebrew again, for the first time since he prepared for his own bar mitzvah forty years ago. And when Amy leads services on Friday nights, Eric sometimes accompanies her singing on his guitar. Amy's contributions to her synagogue have been publicly recognized, at an awards ceremony honoring outstanding women from all the congregations in her city. "Once the door was opened I was ready, I just rushed on in," Amy says.

Despite carrying the scars of her early experiences, Amy says she now understands many things about the Jewish community that explain, if not excuse, the icy way she was once received. Prejudice, she says, "is different in the Jewish community because of anti-Semitism. I didn't have the collective experiences of people who were born Jewish. I couldn't talk about slavery the same way they talked about Europe." Her hard-won insights have given her an appreciation for how difficult it is for many Jews to accept outsiders into the community, whatever their ethnicity or the shade of their skin. But not being born to a Jewish heritage doesn't temper the claim she lays to it now.

"I never think of myself as a convert," Amy declares unequivocally. "I don't think I ever wasn't Jewish. I grew up in Brooklyn and was surrounded by Judaism. Catholicism never fit. I read Chaim Potok's first book, *The Chosen* [about Orthodox Jews in Brooklyn], at fifteen and thought, 'This is great, they challenge, they question.' My journey led upward from there."

Can a gentile or converted woman of color find a home in Judaism? Amy's story would seem to offer a qualified yes. Her experiences encompass some of the best and worst a non-Jewish or converted woman might encounter in the Jewish community. Finding herself in the wrong Jewish community too many times, she happened upon the right one by chance, the one where the Jew she wanted to be could finally flower. She herself believes that some of the unpleasant incidents of her earlier years were not based on race but were simply what any non-Jewish woman marrying into a Jewish family or trying to find acceptance in a synagogue might encounter, provided she was identified as gentile. Because of the shade of her skin, Amy points out, it isn't possible for her to blend into the Jewish crowd. Yet the most blatant rejections Amy received do seem to be racially motivated. The scene she describes at her in-laws' synagogue on Rosh Hashanah, with large numbers of congregants refusing to sit in her proximity, is difficult to imagine with a white gentile woman at its center, even if such a woman were widely identified as not Jewish. And the reaction the Orthodox mohel who performed her son's circumcision had upon seeing Amy's face could not have been religious. The man had to know that Amy was Jewish, because his movement affiliation, if not his personal beliefs, would have prevented him from carrying out the ceremony for the child of a non-Jewish woman; he wouldn't say that he was doing it "for the baby" because the baby, in his eyes, would be a gentile.

These incidents point up a curious fact that one bumps up against time and again in a myriad of ways in the Jewish community, and in conversations with born Jews, converts, and gentiles. Even among the majority of Jews, who accept that there is more than one correct way to *be* Jewish, it would seem that there persists the belief that there is only one way to *look* Jewish.

"You can see I don't look Jewish," I've heard from a number of women, describing their difficulty finding acceptance as converts. Pointing to their pale skin, light hair, and blue eyes, these women explain that they are "too white" for the Jewish community, that their pedigree is constantly questioned by born Jews. "You can see that I don't look Jewish," another woman tells me, this time Jewish by birth. Pointing to her pale skin, light hair, and blue eyes, she is tracking the reasons for the sense of estrangement she has always had from the Jewish community. "Look at this face," Amy Weiss says. "I don't look Jewish."

What does Jewish look like?

In American Sign Language "Jewish" is delineated by a sweeping gesture downward from the chin: a beard. In other words, a Jew is a man, an idea perfectly in accord with traditional Jewish notions of who "counts," literally and figuratively, in everything from a prayer quorum to the leadership of a family or community. If a Jew is a man, then all Jewish women, born or converted, would seem to be starting on a level playing field where Jewish looks are concerned.

Though American Jews of Ashkenazi descent and anti-Semites everywhere might think otherwise, there isn't one way to look Jewish, and there hasn't been for much of Jewish history. The increasing multiculturalism in American Judaism is nothing new in the Jewish world. When women like Karen Zheng and Amy Weiss marry into the Jewish family and raise Jewish children, they are doing what women have done for several thousand years, helping to nurture the Jewish people with their own unique contribution to the collective Jewish cultural and genetic mix.

What is new is the leadership roles some of these women are taking on in their synagogues today. Women like Karen and Amy feel secure enough in their religious identities, as well as sufficiently welcomed by other Jews, to make real contributions within their families and congregations. In past decades, a convert might well have had to bury her past in order to be well integrated into a Jewish milieu. But even in a situation in which no one knew that she had been born a gentile, she would not have served as a synagogue president, as Karen has done, or led services, like Amy, for the simple reason that women did not do these things.

The women we will meet next have assumed positions of leadership and prominence in the wider Jewish world. Trailblazers, charting a territory fairly new to all Jewish women and utterly unprecedented for women converts, they are women going "beyond shiksa" in ways that, even a generation ago, no one could have imagined.

7

Women of Valor: Converts as Jewish Leaders

*Give her a share in the fruit of her hands, and let her works
praise her in the city gates.*

—*PROVERBS 31:31*

ALONGSIDE DIRE warnings against the fatal attractions of gentile women, and cautionary tales of the evils waiting to befall the
Jewish man who succumbs to them, the Torah offers non-Jewish
heroines playing dramatic roles in the unfolding narrative of
Jewish peoplehood. Biblical women such as Tamar, Zipporah,
Rahab, Ruth, Yael, and others demonstrate their loyalty to the
Israelites and their God with bold and risky acts. They also suggest that Judaism once envisioned richer and more varied parts
for its adopted daughters than what is usually supposed.

In our own time, converts are helping to change the face of
American Judaism. Though exact numbers are impossible to
come by, it is estimated that some ten thousand to fifteen thousand converts* are entering the American Jewish community

---

*These figures were provided by Lawrence Epstein, author of many books about conversion,
who writes in a personal communication, "No one is keeping careful records and even Jewish
population surveys, by focussing on intermarrieds, miss many people converting outside of re-

each year, most of them women. What's more, in conversations with rabbis, educators, and other Jewish leaders, the anecdotal evidence strongly suggests that those converts who assume positions of responsibility, whether in their own communities or the larger Jewish world, overwhelmingly tend to be women.

"Most of the converts and potential converts I see are women," notes a New York rabbi who specializes in outreach to interfaith couples. "If five to ten percent at a given time are men, that would be a lot."

"The women, but not the men, converts tend to become active afterward and take on leadership roles," adds the teacher of an introduction to Judaism course in Chicago. "The men come to services but don't otherwise get involved. The women are all working full-time or are full-time students, so it's not like they don't have anything else to do."

Indeed, women have more to do than ever before. Yet significant numbers of women converts are choosing to devote time and energy to their Jewish communities, serving on and chairing committees at synagogues and Jewish schools, teaching in Sunday school and adult education programs, chanting from the Torah, acting as lay leaders at religious services and as presidents of their congregations. Still other women, by assuming professional leadership positions, are redefining the very notion of the convert as someone whose role is to disappear into the fabric of Jewish life. In my search for women converts who are Jewish leaders, the number and variety of stories I encountered was impressive. There are rabbis and rabbinical students, women working toward masters or doctorates in Jewish studies and education. There is the woman serving on the board of a national religious organization, the Korean native who is a Jewish cantor, the United States military major in training to be a lay Jewish chaplain, and many others.

What enables a woman to go from outlander to Jewish

lationships with Jews." Epstein reports that the Conversion to Judaism home page (www.convert.org) gets about three thousand visitors each week.

230

leader? Is such a woman seamlessly integrated into the Jewish community? Or, regardless of what she may accomplish, will she retain a distinct identity as a convert forever? A question that has been raised about converts, particularly women converts, throughout Jewish history, is the extent to which conversion *essentially* changes a gentile into a Jew. In other words, how deep does conversion go? Just like the subject of gentile women, this is an issue on which many in the Jewish community have had something to say.

Once a Shiksa, Always a Shiksa?

According to Jack J. Cohen, Avraham Isaac Kook, the first Ashkenazi chief rabbi of modern Israel, "held to the view that only in exceptional cases could it be assumed that a non-Jewish female could want seriously to be a Jewess." Contemporary Israeli society is a milieu in which it is still notoriously difficult to find acceptance as a convert. Unconsciously reflecting this reality, the progressive newspaper *Ha'Aretz* described a Russian émigré couple in a 2002 article this way: "He is Jewish; she is a convert." In other words, whatever a convert is, she is not a Jew.

Closer to home, Jewish popular culture provides a barometer of social attitudes toward converts. The protagonist of Mordecai Richler's 1980 novel, *Joshua Then and Now*, tells a WASP girlfriend who offers to convert to Judaism, "You can learn to play tennis, but you can't learn to be a Jew."

In his graphic novel *Maus: A Survivor's Tale, Volume II: And Here My Troubles Began*, published in 1986, Art Spiegelman grapples with the question of whether a convert is fish or fowl—or reptile or rodent. Chronicling the process of creating the book's images within the story itself, he devotes a handful of panels to his dilemma over whether to portray his wife, Françoise, as a mouse, like himself and all other Jews in the book, or as a frog.

"A mouse, of course!" Françoise protests.

231

"But you're French!"

"If you're a mouse, I ought to be a mouse too. I converted, didn't I?"

Though Spiegelman's alter ego resolves the issue by deciding to have Françoise metamorphose from frog to mouse in the course of the narrative, Françoise immediately throws doubt on the validity of the transformation by admitting that she only converted to please her father-in-law.

Once a frog, always a frog? Expressing the same point of view in bluntly cruder terms, an old Jewish joke quips, "What's the difference between a virgin and a shiksa? The shiksa remains a shiksa."

The sense of an impermeable barrier between Jewish and non-Jewish is deeply felt by many Jews, and it would be misleading to suggest that disdain for women's conversions is strictly the stuff of men's writing and passé sexist humor. Anxiety and confusion about the women who join the Jewish community through conversion can be found in Jewish feminist works as well. In *A Breath of Life: Feminism in the American Jewish Community*, Sylvia Barack-Fishman writes,

> Within outmarriages gentile men married to Jewish women are far less likely than are gentile women married to Jewish men to convert to Judaism. Women still seem more willing to change and adapt in order to please their men. The vast majority of conversionary marriages involve Jewish men married to women who were not born Jewish but now consider themselves to be Jews. Non-Jewish men who are married to Jewish women, on the other hand, often express the feelings that conversion will alter their essential being, an idea they find unpalatable.

The passage packs several interesting attitudes. First, women's conversions to Judaism are dismissed as nothing more than their conditioned desire to please men. Second, women who convert are not Jews, but rather persons who "consider themselves to be Jews." Finally, according to Barack-Fishman, intermarried men believe that conversion entails a deep transformation of self that they shy away from. Are the men Barack-Fishman describes misguided in believing that conversion will rock them to the core? In Barack-Fishman's terms, it would seem that, unlike their all-too-pliable sisters, these men have a healthy sense of self. But they are scared off by groundless fears: conversion wouldn't change who and what they are, only what they might "consider themselves."

My own conviction is that Barack-Fishman's men are right to feel daunted. Conversion is a profound experience of transformation, one that is embarked upon without knowing where—perhaps who—one will end up. No one could attest to this better than Dale Epstein, who took her first steps on a Jewish path solely to facilitate the transmission of her husband's heritage to their children, and ended up traveling much further than she ever intended to go.

Dale Epstein

"The conversion was about my children being Jewish," says Dale Epstein. "It was not my journey. We both wanted the children to be Jewish."

Dale, fifty-four, grew up a Methodist in a New York City suburb. She attended church and Sunday school, but religion wasn't much practiced in her home. In high school, she decided that she no longer believed in God, and read Bertrand Russell's "Why I Am Not a Christian" so that she would have her arguments ready if anyone asked her why. "I probably would have just stayed that way, but once I married someone Jewish, things changed."

Though Dale's husband identified as Jewish, he was not observant, and if his parents weren't pleased by his marriage to a gentile, it was also far from the first intermarriage in the family. Conversion was suggested, but at the time of her wedding in 1970, Dale found the notion that someone could *become* Jewish preposterous. Five years later, she hadn't changed her mind. But she was preparing to become a parent, and by this point she understood that by converting she could help her husband pass on an important legacy. She underwent what she describes as a "minimal Reform conversion," with little preparation and without any of the rituals prescribed by Jewish law.

"When someone first told me what mikvah [ritual immersion] was, I was incredulous, I thought it was so archaic," Dale recalls. Nevertheless, three years later, in anticipation of the birth of her second child, Dale went to the mikvah. She took her first child with her, and both were converted according to Jewish law. Despite going through these motions, Dale didn't feel that she was spiritually engaged. It was when she and her family joined a new synagogue that her connection to Judaism began to deepen.

"The synagogue had dual Conservative/Reconstructionist affiliation, it was very intellectually open but traditional in observance. The congregation valued learning very highly. I started taking courses when my third child was a toddler, first history, then philosophy, then Hebrew. At the same time I was very active in the synagogue. The synagogue was small and eager for people. I had dropped out of a Ph.D. program and become a full-time mom, so I was eager to find an outlet." Suddenly, Dale found herself dazzled by the "many possibilities for understanding the sacred in Jewish life," fascinated by Jewish culture and intensely drawn to her Jewish community. "I had found a very embracing community where I fit. I was very lucky. If I hadn't found that community—I don't know what would have happened."

What did happen was that Dale began to feel Jewish as never before. Like Karen Zheng in the previous chapter, and a number of other converts I've spoken with, Dale mentions the importance of the accumulation of Jewish memories in her developing sense of herself as a Jew. By creating a Jewish home and being active in her community, what she increasingly saw when she looked back at herself was a Jewish life. "You have to 'do' Jewish, and then you begin to feel connected," Dale says. "Finally that connection is internalized. Once you develop that internalized sense of yourself as a Jew, you can take it anywhere."

Dale took her Jewish identity all the way to the Jewish Theological Seminary, where she was ordained as a Conservative rabbi in 1995. Today, no longer married and with her children all grown to young adulthood, she works for a Jewish organization in New York, where she teaches classes for adults, does program planning and counseling, and increasingly, has become a resource for potential converts. She says people come to her from all over the country, and even outside it, because it is difficult "to find someone who isn't scary" to talk to about conversion. Dale believes that it has become easier to convert to Judaism than it once was, that more Jews value and respect people who want to be Jewish. At the same time, she thinks "the community still has a long way to go in reconciling with and being open to interfaith couples, in accepting that in an open society there will be relationships between Jews and non-Jews. We have to keep the Jewish person connected and bring the non-Jewish person as close as that person wants to be. We need to show people the beauty and glory of Judaism and let them relate to it as best they can."

Dale observes that converts still go through many off-putting experiences in the Jewish community, and still face barriers to acceptance. "Converts are often a kind of Rorschach test for Jews," she comments. "Jews meeting converts react from where they are in relation to their [own] Judaism. You know, not everybody loves the fact that they were born Jewish, and here the convert has become something that they aren't sure they want to be. Then there's the tribal piece. For a lot of people it's a violation of some boundary. Converts get a lot of that."

The surest way to silence unkind remarks about converts, Dale jokes, is becoming a rabbi: ordination trumps all overt put-downs. People may still think negative things, but they won't dare to say them.

Based on her own experience, Dale always advises the people she counsels to find a Jewish community that feels right to them. She also tells converts that they can make a real contribution to the Jewish community. "You may not be the most Jewishly knowledgeable, but you won't be the least knowledgeable, by virtue of having studied for conversion."

Dale has come a long way from her early days as a convert, when she would marvel to find herself the mother of Jewish children, and when, like a recovering alcoholic, she would introduce herself by saying, " 'Hello, my name is Dale and I'm a convert.' I always needed to say it as a cover for my felt inadequacy." She no longer routinely identifies herself as a convert, except in her work with interfaith couples and potential converts. When she does reveal her background in these situations, she says, she models for others "a real live person who has actually converted." She also stuns the people she is counseling.

Dale, who believes that she is one of at least five women converts to be ordained in Conservative Judaism, acknowledges that by reaching out to interfaith couples and potential converts, "I'm doing work that not everyone in the Conservative movement feels is of primary concern," and that she walks a fine line to maintain her credibility and not marginalize herself within her movement. But it's a line she feels she has to walk. "I think it's very important to be out there as a Conservative rabbi on these issues."

Dale's story is a striking illustration of the power of community in shaping Jewish identity. Even after her conversion, Dale didn't believe that she could—much less had—become a Jew. Then she happened upon a pocket of the Jewish world where the Judaism practiced was so dynamic and engaging, where she fit so well and felt so accepted, that she knew she was home. In this nurturing milieu she developed a secure Jewish identity that, as she says, she could take anywhere. Making a leap beyond the niche she had found, she is now a respected representative of the very community she once stood outside, responsible for helping other marginal Jews and would-be converts find their way into the fold.

That others have a much harder time finding their way is something Dale is keenly aware of. Among the stumbling blocks encountered by others who look for acceptance in the Jewish community, she mentions converts whose future in-laws insist that marriage to a converted woman "can't work," and the position of her own movement, which places little value on her efforts to counteract the alienating experiences so many intermarried couples and converts encounter in the Jewish world. Given the Conservative movement's particular emphasis on intermarriage as the archvillain behind the American Jewish community's shrinking numbers, a reluctance to reach out to potential converts among the intermarried would seem to be a self-defeating position. But according to Gary Tobin, president of the Institute for Jewish and Community Research in San Francisco, and author of *Opening the Gates: How Proactive Conversion Can Revitalize the Jewish Community*, much Jewish opposition to conversion is actually unconscious.

"The Jewish community is not very open to converts, but they think they are," says Tobin. "They throw up all these barriers because they don't really want them." Tobin points to the Conservative movement's claim that the Jewish community has become too accepting of intermarriage, and that this has led to a decline in the conversion of intermarrying gentiles. "It's a lie! It's because the spouses don't care enough. One of the barriers is the husbands themselves—they married shiksas and they want them to stay that way. When the husbands want their wives to convert, that's the situation in which conversion is most likely to occur."

Even so, Tobin believes that in the Jewish community at large, converts are rejected on an equal-opportunity basis, with men no more likely to be warmly welcomed than women. "We resist them because we don't want strangers, we're very elite. A lot of Jews believe in bloodlines, you're either chosen or you're not. Of course," he adds, "that's historical and sociological nonsense. Jews have always intermarried, *always.* Just ask [the patriarchs] Abraham, Isaac, and Jacob, to start. There's a very complicated psychology at work in denying this."

There is also a complicated psychology—and a complicated history—at work behind Judaism's evolving stance toward conversion and converts from the Jewish people's beginnings right up until the present. Let's take a brief look at conversion to Judaism over time.

Lepers and Children of God

The Torah takes for granted that converts will be present within the Israelite community. In Vayikra, or Leviticus, God admonishes the Israelites, "When a proselyte dwells among you in your land, do not taunt him. The proselyte who dwells with you shall be like a native among you, and you shall love him like yourself, for you were aliens in the land of Egypt." The fact that the Torah assumes people need to be instructed not to taunt proselytes certainly suggests that not everyone greeted newcomers with open arms.

When it comes to attitudes toward conversion, Judaism is rich in contradiction. At one end of the spectrum stands the Talmudic statement that converts are as hard for the Jewish people as leprosy. At the other is the story told about the medieval scholar Moses Maimonides. When asked by a convert named Obadiah whether he should pray the words "our God and God of our ancestors," having been told by some Jews that he shouldn't, Maimonides reassured him: "If we trace our descent from Abraham, Isaac, and Jacob, your descent is from him by whose word the world was created."

In *Conversion to Judaism: From the Biblical Period to the Present*, Joseph Rosenbloom argues that as far back as the biblical era, conversion to Judaism served as a means of assimilating conquered groups as well as providing a way for individuals to join the Israelite community.

> During and after the exile, when it appeared that there would no longer be a Jewish state, conversion continued with the old motivation but with a new aspect as well. Not only would it serve to bring born gentiles into the Jewish group, but it would help Judaism to survive by compensating for the dramatic losses suffered through the destruction of the state and later while in exile. So strong was this drive that the exilic literature was filled with statements indicating the universality of Judaism.

It is generally believed that circumcision was the only conversion ritual known during the biblical period, and that it was the postbiblical rabbis who introduced immersion in a ritual bath, creating a formal rite of conversion for both sexes. Beyond that innovation, the rabbis instituted many laws and commentaries concerning converts and conversion. True to their inclinations in all matters, the rabbis' effect on conversion was to complicate what appears to have been fairly straightforward previously.

According to Gary Porton's *The Stranger Within Your Gates: Converts and Conversion in Rabbinic Literature,* in the eyes of rabbinic Judaism the convert undergoes a change of status, but that change is something short of a complete transformation from gentile to Jew. In postbiblical days, he writes, converts were expected to sever all ties with the past, but were not fully embraced by the Jewish community. They were not accorded the same rights, status, and obligations as those born Jewish, and their participation in ritual and family transactions, such as marriages and inheritance, was limited. According to some views, they were not even permitted to claim the God of the Israelites as their own.

Distinguishing between converts and born Jews, the rabbis were particularly concerned with female converts.

> While on the one hand claiming that one should not remind converts of their gentile background, Mishnah [a compilation of Jewish law] also posits many regulations which mandate that converts be recognizable, for some purposes, throughout their lives. Especially with regard to women, the fact that they were converts would be important throughout their lives.

As already noted in chapter two, females who entered the Jewish people after the age of three years and one day were assumed by Jewish law to be sexually experienced. In the ancient Middle East, a woman's virginity was calculated in hard cash. Among the Israelites, the female who converted after this age wasn't much of a commodity. Whether she was four or fourteen, the bride price she commanded was strictly bargain-basement. And if she was "seduced"—i.e., raped?—in the Jewish community, the man involved wasn't subject to a fine. Porton notes that women converts tend to be classified along with other groups whose legitimacy was considered suspect, particularly female ex-slaves. Both, he says, "are examples of persons who have undergone a radical change of status . . . the sexual purity of a female slave was questionable in the same way that the sexual purity of a female gentile was a matter of doubt. . . ."

The stance toward converts evolved slowly in rabbinic thought, and in Midrash, which are later writings, an attitude of greater inclusion begins to appear. "But," reports Porton, "they are still considered a subclass, particularly women, in regard to their sexual status and who they can marry."

For all their emphasis on keeping women converts in their place, the rabbis weren't above exerting pressure on certain women who showed an inconvenient reluctance to convert. The rabbis put a spin all their own on a biblical passage related to women entering the Jewish community against their will in Dvarim, Deuteronomy.

Along with setting standards for coping with commonplace situations from burial rites to the treatment of animals, Dvarim lays out the ground rules for Israelite men regarding the beautiful captured women of their defeated enemies. The law states simply that a man who wants such a woman for himself is to allow her one month to lament her father and mother, and then he is free to take her as his wife. In the event that he changes his mind about her after that, he is required to release her. So much for the biblical text; later Talmudic writings flesh out the minimal language of the law by specifying that the woman's mourning period is not just for her parents but for the faith of her people as well. If, after having her, the Israelite wants to keep her, and she is willing to accept Judaism, she is converted. If she refuses to convert, she is to be given twelve months to change her mind. A woman who clings to idolatry after that period is to be put to death.

Modern women who convert to Judaism and also marry Jewish men are often startled by the nonchalance with which the sincerity of their Judaism—"Were you forced into it?" "Did you do it for him?"—is called into doubt even in casual conversation. Under a rabbinic law like this one, such questions would have unique meaning.

For most of Jewish history, the disposal of female prisoners of war has not been much at issue, and converts have arrived at Judaism's doors on their own powers, not in chains. If those doors haven't always been wide open, Jewish attitudes toward converts has been almost irrelevant in light of the way the Christian and Islamic societies in which Jews lived viewed conversion to Judaism. Joseph Rosenbloom notes, "The Millennium and more following the establishment of Christianity as the religion of the Roman Empire, and the rise and success of Islam, was a period when Jews were generally embattled." From this period until the French Revolution, Jews lived under conditions of virulent anti-Semitism laced with mass expulsions from their home countries. Jewish communities turned in on themselves in an effort to survive.

"The attitude of Christianity toward conversion to Judaism," Rosenbloom writes, "may be easily and concisely summarized: it was prohibited." Indeed, in many times and places it was punishable by death. Given this reality, it may be supposed that for thousands of years converts to Judaism would have been few and far between. However, Rosenbloom insists that this was not so. During the Middle Ages, for example, he reports that there are records of "a considerable group of converts, primarily from the clergy and upper classes."

What is not surprising is that Jews became distinctly skittish about allowing gentiles to join the fold, an attitude Jewish immigrants brought with them to the New World. According to an unpublished dissertation, "Conversion to Judaism in America 1760–1897," by Dana Evan Kaplan, would-be converts were strongly discouraged, often rejected outright, in early America. As already noted, when a woman did manage to convert, she and her husband were likely to be barred from synagogue membership, except in some cases where the man's social position in his community was especially high. Even when such couples were allowed to join, the converted woman might later be refused burial in a Jewish cemetery.

As Kaplan's research into the early Jewish press demonstrates, anxiety over women's conversions was rampant. For example, in the *Jewish Messenger* of February 17, 1865, Rabbi Bernard Illowy writes: "[W]e here are . . . convinced that it is not God, but the 'altar of God' to which these proselytes are coming. To find or please a husband whom they love, the daughters of the Gentiles join our religion. . . . [I]t is not the power of truth but the sharp arrows of cupid. . . ." The following month, the same newspaper adds this from one Samuel Myer Isaacs: "[T]hese conversions are merely nominal; they have done serious mischief to our cause."

Throughout the twentieth century, Jewish communities continued to hold converts at arms' length. Rabbi David Kirshenbaum, whose diatribes we've sampled previously, railed against converts in his 1958 *Mixed Marriage and the Jewish Future*. In Kirshenbaum's view, no matter how much converts seem to adapt to new ideas and traditions, the transformation is never more than skin deep. "This is why our sages declared, 'Most proselytes return to their origin for the most trivial reasons and their behavior seduces the Jews.' "

Kirshenbaum was not a lone voice against conversion. Joseph Rosenbloom reports that at a symposium held in 1956 to examine the question "Should Jews Missionize Christians and Muslims" some rabbis argued that "ready acceptance of proselytes would disturb the integrity of the Jewish religious way of life." Though not all those present agreed with this point of view, the overall stance toward converts was not enthusiastic. Rosenbloom also quotes from a study conducted more than twenty years later that found that half of converts in the early 1980s "felt that Jews were reluctant to recognize converts as full members of the Jewish community, and this discrimination burdened converts with a tremendous sense of disappointment."

That sense of disappointment is not entirely a thing of the past. We've already seen that while some gentile women are now warmly received into the Jewish community, others are still met with suspicion and dislike. When Nan Fink Gefen describes her first experiences in a synagogue it sounds more like she wandered onto a battlefield than into a religious community. Treating Nan to a campaign of shunning, threats, and hate mail, synagogue members thought that they would send her packing from the Jewish world.

Nan Fink Gefen *

In her book *Stranger in the Midst: A Memoir of Spiritual Discovery*, Nan Fink Gefen writes of converts that "Many of us make ourselves invisible, like the salt religious Jews sprinkle on challah on Shabbat." But invisibility wasn't really an option while Nan was working toward conversion and beginning her life as a Jew. In the mid-1980s Nan was in her forties, a psychotherapist no longer in practice, the ex-wife of a Protestant minister, and the mother of three recently grown children. Having long felt a spiritual attraction to Judaism, Nan was looking for the right rabbi to guide the process of her conversion. Meanwhile, she and her partner, Michael Lerner, were working together to create a new Jewish magazine, *Tikkun*. Both alone and with Michael, she was making frequent trips to Israel, a land to which she felt a deep connection. Back home in the Berkeley Hills of California, she reveled in creating a richly Jewish domestic life with Michael and his teenaged son.

In many ways this was an exciting time for Nan, but it was also a time of stress and confusion, thanks, in great part, to her experiences in synagogue. Along with Michael, Nan attended a small Orthodox shul near their home in Berkeley. For Nan, this institution can only be described as the synagogue from hell.

Following traditional norms, the congregation consigned women to separate seating behind a mechitzah. While Michael evidently relished a warm sense of community in the main part of the building, behind the mechitzah Nan suffered the women's

---

*In this chapter, Nan Fink Gefen and Rachel Cowan, both public figures, are identified by their real names.

icy hostility. At home, she received an anonymous letter telling her she didn't belong at the shul. When another congregant finally spoke to her after services one Saturday, it was to tell her that she wasn't welcome and that everyone wanted her to leave. Nan also suffered through a number of disheartening experiences in her search for a rabbi to convert with. When she did begin studying with a Conservative rabbi, the man received threatening phone calls in the middle of the night, warning him to stop working with Nan. Repeatedly, Nan tried to communicate with her attackers at the shul, to no avail. When she approached the congregation's young rabbi for help, he told her that it was up to her to make peace with the other congregants, and refused to get involved.

Speculating about these experiences, Nan writes in her memoir, "The problem . . . likely had to do with my connection to Michael. He had recently broken off a relationship with a woman highly regarded in the congregation, and the sympathy of the people was with her. I was the interloper, the seductive *shiksa*, the non-Jewish stranger who had come in and stolen a Jewish heart."

Today she adds that "the Jewish world is quite hard on converts and it's a struggle not to feel rejected."

Fed up with her status as local pariah, Nan stopped going to the synagogue. But the congregation didn't succeed in turning her off to Judaism. She had two conversions, one Conservative, the other Orthodox, and she and Michael were married. Together they devoted themselves to getting *Tikkun* off the ground, Michael as spokesperson, the name and face associated with the magazine, Nan for the most part backstage, the quiet, but not silent, partner. Today Nan says she feels she gets more than enough credit for the work she did to bring the magazine to life.

"Michael and I balanced each other," she recalls. "He as the promoter and visioner, me as covisioner and the one to make it happen, and neither one of us could have done this alone. I certainly couldn't, because I was just new in the Jewish world. With all its politics and complicated history, it was a bewildering place to land, and I really had to fast-track learning the lay of the land through those early years."

In 1990, five years after the first issue appeared, and three years after marrying Michael, Nan was burnt out, ready to leave that fast track, and her marriage, behind. Parting from Michael, Nan also knew that she didn't want to continue the strictly observant religious life they had led. For the first time, she would have to find her own way as a Jew. "Born Jews most often assume I converted because of Michael, although that certainly wasn't my major reason. When we split, people assumed I'd stop being Jewish, and were surprised that I didn't. There's a certain amount of approval in the Jewish world for 'converting so that the marriage is Jewish.' The idea is that's what a woman should do. I see this as chauvinistic and sexist."

Nan didn't stop being Jewish as a result of her divorce. She stayed involved in the Jewish community by serving on the boards of progressive nonprofit organizations where she felt quite comfortable as a convert. At the same time she was writing her memoir and beginning to study Jewish mysticism. She began teaching classes on spiritual practice, and got involved with a new center for Jewish meditation called Chochmat HaLev. In 1995 she became codirector of the center. "I spend my time teaching, leading meditation and prayer services, administering, counseling, organizing," Nan explains. "We now have almost eighty students in our three-year Jewish meditation teachers' training programs, and that's a lot of folks to supervise." As an outgrowth of this work, Nan wrote another book, *Discovering Jewish Meditation*, published in 1999.

Now keeping to her own daily practice of prayer and meditation, Nan doesn't belong to a congregation. She is married to Rabbi Jonathan Omer-Man, and describes their friends as mostly secular Jews.

These days, Nan assumes that it is well-known that she is a convert to Judaism, but it isn't something she usually brings up herself. Still, she wonders whether it affects the dynamic between herself and her students who were born Jewish. "I notice that when I talk with born-Jewish students about their lifetime experiences, they're culturally different from mine. I sometimes feel that creates a difference," Nan notes. "Also, I sometimes feel, 'How can I be teaching this material when I wasn't born Jewish?' Even though I'm Jewish through and through, and even though I've worked in the Jewish world for the last seventeen years, I have moments of disconnect, asking myself, 'How did I get here?'"

Occasional doubts, moments of bafflement—these are par for the course for any convert, indeed, for anyone who has radically altered her identity and way of life. But Nan has done something more than transform herself. By becoming a prominent teacher of Jewish mysticism, a field that has been the exclusive domain of a small, select group of Jewish men, she has become part of the transformation of Judaism itself. It takes a certain amount of daring for a woman convert to assume such a role, but Nan brushes off the suggestion that she is doing anything special.

"There are so many wonderful converts making great contributions today, a lot of them women," she points out. "I don't particularly see myself as a trailblazer, but I know I'm a role model for women, both born Jews and converts. I love to mentor other women. The struggles I've had as a convert are shared to some degree by all Jewish women. It's hard to find a voice that feels authentic and to be seen by Jewish men as entitled."

Having struggled to find that voice, Nan is especially sensitive to her students' struggles, and to their need to feel welcomed by the Jewish world. In this way, her experience of entering Judaism as an outsider has become a source of strength in her work. "I'll always be a convert, but it's not my foremost identity. I'm a Jew and a woman, and incidentally, a convert. It's not a bad thing, and I'm glad I've had such a full, rich life."

How does Nan account for her journey from gentile outcast

to Jewish leader? Despite its problems, she says she loves the Jewish community, and is deeply committed to giving it all she can. Then too, she is stubborn. "I won't let anyone tell me I'm not good enough to do what I feel called to do. If people don't approve, that's their problem, not mine."

That sort of determination, and perhaps a thick skin as well, would seem to be a necessary part of many converts' arsenals— and not only because of what they may encounter within the Jewish community. In her memoir, Nan touches on an issue usually given short shrift in the literature about conversion. In addition to an uncertain reception among the people they are attempting to join, many converts must also grapple with gentile families who can neither understand nor give their blessings to a daughter's new Jewish identity.

As we've seen, postbiblical Jewish law expected converts to make a clean break with the past, while settling for something less than full acceptance in the Jewish community. Even without that sort of break, a child's conversion can come as a major blow to the family with no choice but to accept it. While some parents react with interest and enthusiasm, for others the transition represents a painful loss, a radical separation between their child and themselves, their values, and way of life. They may experience the conversion as a rejection of their beliefs, and may be saddened that their own traditions will not be passed on to their grandchildren. Intentionally or not, they may communicate that a daughter has betrayed her people and her heritage.

In Nan's case, her parents and other relatives were not able to support her decision to become a Jew. Her children were less disapproving but just as baffled, and she felt that it put a wedge between them and her. For Beverly Jackson, thirty-seven, conversion to Judaism caused serious strife between herself and her non-Jewish husband, and ultimately contributed to the breakup of their marriage. Tricia Woodward, forty-five, who converted over twenty years ago, says the feeling of having hurt her family still runs deep. Though they keep a kosher kitchen at home, when she and her husband and children visit her parents, she puts her mother's feelings ahead of dietary laws. "We eat pork at my mother's house when it's served to us," she says. "I don't want to reject my family any further than I already have."

Pointing to this kind of emotional conflict, Rabbi Steven Mason, the Connecticut therapist who counsels intermarried couples, believes conversion can be hard on the people who choose it. "I'm opposed to pushing conversion," he explains, "because of the destruction of family ties, altering to a great extent the psychosocial identity of the convert." In the case of intermarriage, Mason says, "I'm satisfied if the person is willing to be a fellow traveler."

Of course, women who have decided to commit their own lives to a Jewish path will not be satisfied with fellow-traveling. For them, family conflicts become yet another of the challenges of remaking themselves as Jews—and yet another sign of the strength of their dedication.

The Torah offers a striking example of a convert's dedication in the figure of Rahab, a character who embraces Judaism and the Jewish people through a dramatic and risky betrayal of her own community. But in abandoning her country, Rahab safeguards her parents and siblings. When she runs away to join the Israelites, this biblical heroine takes her family with her.

Rahab

The Book of Joshua relates an incident in which the eponymous prophet sends two spies to stake out Jericho, a city-state on the Israelites' to-be-conquered list. The spies lodge in the house of a prostitute named Rahab. When the king of Jericho hears that Israelite spies have entered his domain, he sends his men to capture them. Rahab tells the king's men that the spies left the city just before the gates closed at nightfall, and urges them to hurry after the Israelites and overtake them.

In fact, Rahab has recognized the spies the moment they appeared at her door and has planned ahead, hiding them under stalks of flax on her roof. After convincing the king's soldiers to chase after shadows outside the gates of the city, with an equally cool head, she confronts the spies. She tells them that she knows God has decreed that her country is to be theirs, and that "all the inhabitants of the land are quaking before you. For we have heard how the Lord dried up the waters of the Sea of Reeds for you when you left Egypt," and about other Israelite victories as well. For Rahab, these events are proof that "the Lord your God is the only God in heaven above and on earth below." Her statement conveys the sense that she has been following the Israelites' progress closely, and has reached her own conclusions.

After explaining to the spies when the king's men will return, and what they must do to escape, Rahab makes them pledge that when they take Jericho, she and her parents, her brothers and sisters, and their families will be safe. When the spies pledge themselves to Rahab and the lives of all who dwell in her house, they refer to "the oath which you have made us take." The power here is all in Rahab's hands. Later, when the Israelites burn Jericho to the ground, "Only Rahab the harlot and her father's family were spared by Joshua, along with all that belonged to her, and she dwelt among the Israelites—as is still the case."

Rahab takes a bold and unusual step in acting as head of her family, deciding all their fate apparently on her own authority alone. What her family make of her actions we can only guess at. The Torah doesn't mention whether they remain with the Israelites or move on, but presumably they are happy to find themselves alive and well after the destruction of Jericho.

Rahab puts herself and her family at grave risk by choosing to protect the interests of the Israelite army against those of her own king, and for her act of bravery she wins a place in the small pantheon of Jewish heroines. But Rahab is more than daring. A woman of cunning, self-assurance, and strength of will, she is a biblical protagonist in the style of Jacob and David. Insightful and intelligent, she reads the lay of her land far more keenly than the Israelite spies who blunder into Jericho believing they won't be noticed.

Not surprisingly, these are not the qualities that captured the attention of the large number of rabbinical commentators who had something to say about Rahab. Their primary interest lay in Rahab's apparent profession of faith in Judaism. Supported by the information that she remained with the Israelites, the rabbis decided that Rahab converted to Judaism, and that she married Joshua, the Israelite's military and political leader. Further, they designated many priests and prophets, including the female prophet Huldah, as Rahab's descendants.

Discussing the commentaries on Rahab in her book *Midrashic Women*, Judith Baskin notes that some use her story as proof of the greatness of God's mercy and forgiveness: even a prostitute could be redeemed and accepted into the Israelite community. In the rabbis' hands, Baskin argues, Rahab is domesticated, becoming a vehicle by which "midrashic tradition demonstrated how otherness could be vitiated, foreign origins superseded, threatening sexuality defused, and disturbing female independence undercut."

We've seen innumerable examples of the anxieties raised by female sexuality—symbolized by the gentile woman—in biblical and rabbinic Judaism. A prostitute, Rahab inevitably calls up the specter of women's autonomous sexuality. The rabbis' recognition that Rahab can become a Jewish woman, and be integrated into the highest reaches of Israelite society, represents a considerable departure from their beliefs about other non-Jewish figures from Lilith to Jezebel. It is also an echo of the historical fact that the Jewish people has always survived with the help of the gentile women in its midst. But though they could make Rahab Jewish, the rabbis couldn't supersede the limits of their notion of Jewish womanhood. In their minds, the best outcome for any woman was marriage and motherhood, so to Rahab, whom they wished to reward, they gave a prominent husband and an illustrious line of descendants. The rabbinic imagination stopped far short of being able to envision Rahab an honored member of the Israelite community, happily operating in the same profession she had in Jericho, or living out some other independent life.

Yet the amazing woman who plays her scene in the Book of Joshua survives the offstage tales spun around her, her act and her voice remain undiminished by rabbinical ruminations. Rahab presents a quintessential image of convert as witness. In the Israelites' triumphant progress through the desert she sees the work of their God, and makes the leap to monotheism, declaring this God "the only God in heaven above and on earth below." That rabbinic lore made her the ancestor not only of celebrated men but also of the prophet Huldah—another unusual woman in the Jewish story—suggests that even the rabbis realized they couldn't entirely blanket the glow of Rahab's heroism.

What does it take for a woman to encounter the Jewish world as a complete novice and end up negotiating herself into a position of power? "Chutzpah," says Marilyn Bloom. Among her assets, that's a quality that Rahab exhibits in abundance, and that her other descendants—the converted women leaders of today—wouldn't get very far without.

Marilyn Bloom

When Marilyn Bloom was growing up in the 1950s, the spiritual life, if not the grass, always looked a little greener on the other side of the fence. In the postwar Seattle suburb where her family lived, everyone was white, unethnic, "vanilla," says Marilyn. But at least the other kids came home from Sunday school with verses and prayers to learn. Adverse to religious doctrine, Marilyn's parents sent her to Unitarian Sunday school, where secular humanism and appreciation for nature were preached, and euphemisms were used for God. "I wanted more than that," recalls Marilyn. "I felt dumb and deprived because we weren't being given anything to learn. I had a craving for God, thoughts and questions about God, and it wasn't okay in my family. Also, I loved holidays and wanted them to have meaning. I felt impoverished in ritual and meaning."

Marilyn married right out of college and the couple moved to Washington, D.C., where both entered graduate school. There, she and her husband, who was also a nonpracticing Christian, found that all their friends were Jewish. It was Marilyn's first exposure to Jewish people, Jewish humor, Jewish secular culture, and she loved it all. A fellow student invited them to a Passover seder and Marilyn was stunned. "I thought, 'Oh, they teach their children at the table, this is wonderful.' I thought this was a great group to belong to, but I didn't realize yet that there was a way in."

In her midtwenties, Marilyn divorced. She dated Jewish men for a while, but ended up remarrying another nonreligious man of Christian background, and becoming a stepmother to his two sons. She was working in corporate sales, and had taken to begging Jewish co-workers to invite her home for Jewish holidays. She taught her stepsons about the holidays, and recalls that the only gift they ever gave her was a Hanukkiah, a Hanukkah candelabra, that one of them had made from the branch of a tree.

When the marriage ended, Marilyn went through a long bout of ill health during which she was unable to work, but had lots of time for introspection. "I realized that I wanted to find a spiritual community, a community that was about all of life. I wanted to make a connection to something old, to a wisdom tradition." She considered Christianity, but knew it wasn't right for her. "You had to make a leap of faith to be Christian, and I couldn't do it. I couldn't get behind the idea that we needed to be saved from anything. I looked at New Age religions, but they had no history, and were very focused on the self."

Marilyn asked some Jewish neighbors if they would take her with them to High Holy Day services at their synagogue. The service, for the eve of Yom Kippur, spoke to her as nothing else ever had. She noticed two things that night that were key to enabling her to enter into the unfamiliar worship, things she continues to this day to feel are important to making services accessible to newcomers. The prayer books provided transliteration from the Hebrew, so that non-Hebrew readers could participate fully, and there was lots of singing.

From early childhood, Marilyn had been involved in music, playing piano and guitar, singing in choirs, writing her own songs. But just as she had not known where to go with her spiritual yearnings, "the question was what to do with my music. I never felt like an entertainer. Again, I felt a need for meaning." For Marilyn, Judaism became the way to give that meaning to both her spiritual and musical inclinations. That fall she began attending a Reconstructionist synagogue where she found "lots of opportunities for lay leadership." By March, she was leading the singing at services, and in June she went to the mikvah for her formal conversion.

"I always felt very welcome in that first congregation," she says. "The surprise was not always feeling welcome in other places, feeling inspected. I had experiences of being singled out as 'not like us.'" Because she was always leading music, Marilyn says that, with her blond, blue-eyed looks and then un-Jewish surname, she was highly visible. "People would come up after services and ask questions. 'You're not from here, are you? You're not Jewish, are you?' I found it very offensive and hurtful for a long time." Even a close friend was fond of telling Marilyn, "'There's really two kinds of Jews, there's those of us who grew up Jewish and then there's people like you.' He thought it was a bad thing to have grown up Jewish, and that I didn't have the baggage that he had. He would say, 'You can tell you're a convert because you're so enthusiastic.'"

In fact, Marilyn was enthusiastic. Even her feelings of inadequacy as a neophyte took the form of urging her on in her quest for Jewish learning. "I always felt that everybody else knew more than me because they grew up Jewish. I learned more and more, and then I knew more than the people I was trying to catch up with."

Within two years of her conversion, Marilyn was working as a cantor, a leader of Jewish ritual music, in a variety of venues. She took over as spiritual leader of a small congregation and entered a program for official cantatorial certification. In addition to leading Shabbat and holiday services, she brings healing services to nursing homes and works in hospices with the dying. As the leader of a congregation, Marilyn has many of the responsibilities and privileges usually reserved for rabbis. The law recognizes her authority to conduct wedding ceremonies, and because her cantatorial certification is through the Reform movement, she is permitted to officiate at interfaith weddings. Most rabbis can't or won't conduct interfaith weddings, so Marilyn is called upon to do quite a few. Conservative certification, which would eliminate this aspect of her work, is something she has decided against. "I think it's a mitzvah [good deed or commandment]," she says of doing interfaith weddings. Marilyn explains to the couples she works with that the traditional Jewish wedding ceremony doesn't apply in an interfaith union. But the adapted service she uses retains a "Jewish flavor" and includes traditional blessings. "When couples who would like a rabbi to help them with an interfaith ceremony get turned down they get very, very hurt, they take it personally even though it isn't meant personally. We need to keep a door open." With this controversial stance, Marilyn seems to echo Dale Epstein's sentiments about outreach to intermarried couples. Although Dale, a Conservative rabbi, would never perform an interfaith wedding ceremony, she too is concerned with making a place for the intermarried within the Jewish community. As spiritual leaders, both women have taken on the responsibility for keeping an open door—and an open mind—to disaffected or minimally engaged Jews and their non-Jewish partners.

Marilyn herself is also remarried, to a man from a secular Jewish background. "When his mother heard that I kept kosher, she said, 'Oh, she's Orthodox, she's too Jewish!' His first wife wasn't Jewish and he had never dated Jewish women. I think he was pretty thrilled to find someone who was Jewish and didn't look Jewish." Her husband has remained secular despite twelve years of marriage to a religious leader. "He doesn't like to come to services, and he still forgets about kashrut and brings Parmesan cheese to the table with a meat meal. He did appreciate that I gave his daughter a Jewish home, that meant something to him." Still, not being able to share a spiritual life with her husband, Marilyn says, "is kind of sad for me."

In other respects, she feels well ensconced in her Jewish community as a well-known cantor and congregational leader. "I'm now just a Jew, not a convert, though I've gotten less shy about mentioning it when I'm working with interfaith couples because it helps people. I see myself as a role model not for converts but for continuing learning, adult learning. I really like building community with people, helping Jews connect with each other, their heritage and God, through music and learning."

Having worked over many years to make a Jewish place for herself in the Washington, D.C., area, Marilyn decided not to seek cantatorial jobs elsewhere when she completed her training. "I didn't want to start over with my Scandinavian face," she comments.

But the reactions she got in her early days as a convert, and still sometimes encounters when she leads services and sings in new venues, don't rankle as they once did. Like Dale Epstein, Marilyn says she understands now that born Jews respond to converts from the deepest reaches of their own identity conflicts.

"Sometimes older Jews, particularly people without much joy in Jewish life, are amazed that someone would be drawn to it. They're interested in me as a way of shedding light on their own experience." Marilyn finds it particularly poignant that most of her interrogators have been older Jewish women. "Their only connection is tribal," she comments. "They don't have Jewish learning, and they've experienced the Holocaust, the negative social consequences of being Jewish in this country. They identify as Jewish because they were born that way, so how could I be Jewish? They don't want their own Jewish identity negated. Also, because it wasn't safe to be Jewish, they've spent their whole lives sorting out who they can trust. When they meet me, I don't test out as Jewish. They have to be sure their testing is still working."

Just as the rabbis coped with Rahab by trying to absorb her into existing parameters of Jewish womanhood, converts have traditionally been admitted to Jewish communities—when they have been admitted—with the expectation that they will blend into the crowd. It may be difficult for some Jews to accept a newcomer who arrives brimming with so much zeal for Judaism and Jewish life that she instead becomes a leader, even an innovator, in her community.

As Marilyn points out, a person who has experienced Jewish identity as a source of pain or conflict is likely to be baffled or angered by such a stance. For Jewish women, relegated to ritual nonexistence within traditional Judaism, this may be especially true. As we saw in Nan Fink Gefen's story, most Orthodox synagogues consign women to a small balcony or other cordoned-off space within the sanctuary. Women are not permitted to read from the Torah or lead services, and in some Orthodox communities, it is held that women's voices should not be heard singing or praying. Key prayers in the Jewish service can only be said when a minyan, a quorum of ten adult Jews, is present. In Orthodoxy, a boy becomes a fully functioning adult Jew on his thirteenth birthday; a woman never does. Women's legal status is highly circumscribed in Orthodox communities. Bat mitzvah is rare among Orthodox girls, and when it does occur, an Orthodox bat mitzvah is a watered-down version of the ritual for boys, necessarily stripped of its original meaning: the occasion marks the first time a Jew is called to the Torah and Orthodoxy maintains that women are never so called. It isn't hard to imagine that a woman brought up with this version of Judaism might find it hard to accept a female leader who had none of these indignities in her personal or ancestral past, who, as a Jew, had more or less been born yesterday.

Similarly, some marriages are also strained when a convert's enthusiasm for Judaism outstrips her Jewish-born partner's. Marilyn reflects on the spiritual discontinuity that divides her from her husband. Her situation and her sadness over it are not uncommon. In Marilyn's case, because her religious identity and career as a Jewish leader were already established before her marriage, her husband's uninterest hasn't stunted her growth as a Jew. Women who convert in the context of marriage may hesitate to assert a fledgling Jewish identity in the face of a partner's indifference or active opposition.

Tricia Woodward describes herself as far more interested in Jewish involvement than her husband or their four children. "I want to be a little more observant, my husband a little less. I want to go to synagogue every Saturday, he doesn't. I should be a little more independent and go, but it's hard when I have five people against me."

Rabbi Nancy Weiner, clinical director of Pastoral Care Counseling for the Reform movement's Hebrew Union College, says she thinks it would be ideal if born Jews were asked to meet the same standards of education and reflection, and to engage in Jewish practice at the same level that is expected of converts. "If there's a marriage involved, few rabbis feel they have the right to ask the same questions of the Jewish partner as they ask of the potential convert. From what I've seen, the person who is converting often finds it frustrating because they want to be actively part of the Jewish community in a way that their partner isn't interested in. The partner wasn't making a commitment to being more Jewish by marrying someone who is converting."

It would be a mistake to suggest that a convert's enthusiasm for Jewish life always outclasses that of a Jewish-born husband. In some relationships, a woman's conversion is inspired by her partner's passion for his heritage. In others, the fact that even the Jewish partner approaches Judaism as an absolute beginner can actually work in a couple's favor. Daring to take spiritual baby steps side by side, a gentile and a disaffected Jew—Rabbi Harold Schulweis's aptly named "interfaithless" couple—may actually wind up spurring each other on, supporting each other on separate but intertwined paths. That's what happened for Paul and Rachel Cowan.

Rachel Cowan

In his anti-intermarriage primer, *It All Begins with a Date,* Alan Silverstein backs his assertions about the pitfalls of interfaith unions with quotations from Paul and Rachel Cowan's *Mixed Blessings,* a book drawn from the Cowans' work with interfaith couples. What Silverstein doesn't mention is that the Cowans themselves were a very happy Jewish-gentile couple who could have been poster children *for* intermarriage. Not only did Rachel choose to convert to Judaism fifteen years into their marriage, she also became the very first woman convert, probably in the history of Judaism, to be ordained as a rabbi.

How does it feel to be the first woman convert to become a rabbi? Rachel is blasé about it. "It's not something that I think about."

A descendent of Mayflower pilgrims, Rachel was raised by nonreligious, socialist parents. Reminiscent of Marilyn Bloom's parents, Cowan's opted for Unitarianism by default when the family moved to Wellesley, Massachusetts. "It wasn't acceptable not to belong to a church, so they chose the Unitarian church as least objectionable," Rachel explains.

In 1965, Rachel married Paul Cowan. Like Rachel, Paul was

a recent college graduate, and like her, he had been raised in an entirely secular—in his case, Jewish—household. Paul's family didn't mind in the least that Rachel wasn't Jewish, and their Jewish friends were open and welcoming. Only two really uncomfortable memories of being a gentile woman married to a Jewish man stand out from the early years of their marriage. "When we went to Israel on our honeymoon, for the first time I heard things like that I was completing Hitler's work," Rachel recalls. Then when they arrived back in New York, Paul, a journalist, wrote a series of articles on poor Jews living on the Lower East Side. "I found myself in a different Jewish milieu, and got the shiksa comments, which I, to this day, really don't like."

Rachel and Paul's Upper West Side neighborhood, populated by secular Jews and dotted with a handful of dying synagogues, might have been a million miles away from this milieu. But both Paul and Rachel were interested in exploring Judaism. Paul's upbringing had been so devoid of religious education that, coming to Judaism as young adults, and as the young parents of a daughter and son, he and Rachel were almost starting on level ground.

"I think Paul and I were on parallel tracks," says Rachel. "He was looking into what being Jewish meant to him in terms of a sense of identity. I thought the holidays were very meaningful, and good for the family. I was interested in Jewish history, so I pursued that." They joined a havurah, a group that celebrated holidays together and educated their children Jewishly. Rachel was very comfortable there. "I didn't think of converting because I didn't believe in God. I was part of the community, I shared in the culture. I couldn't change my genes. But after a while it became something that I was intensely interested in."

The decision to convert, Rachel says, grew out of her studying, and her realization that on the spectrum between absolute atheism and unswerving belief, there are many shades of gray. At first she told no one about her decision, not even Paul. "I talked with all these rabbis first. When I told Paul he was surprised. He was pleased, but he didn't realize how pleased until after."

Rachel's conversion was not received quite so enthusiastically by her Jewish friends. People wondered why she wanted to convert, assuring her that they loved her the way she was. "It made them uncomfortable in some ways, probably because they weren't religious for one thing, and here was someone becoming religious. I think a lot of people have a problem with whether you can really convert to being Jewish." Rachel adds a key point, relevant to the way many converts are received in the Jewish world. To a secular Jew, she notes, Jewish identity is derived from history, ethnicity, family heritage—all things conversion doesn't confer. "To this day, people can't understand it."

Having worked as a community organizer, Rachel found herself involved in a project to revitalize one of the fading synagogues in her neighborhood. Soon she was single-handedly running the synagogue, which had no rabbi. She loved the work, and the decision to go to rabbinical school seemed like a natural progression. Though she preferred Conservative liturgy, the Conservative Jewish Theological Seminary had only just started admitting women in 1983, and Rachel says she knew "no one was asking feminist questions there." She thought the Reform Hebrew Union College would provide a more congenial atmosphere, and she was right. She entered HUC in 1984, at the age of forty-two, four years after her conversion.

Even before deciding to go to rabbinical school, Rachel had begun traveling around the country with Paul, exploring the subject of interfaith relationships with congregants in hundreds of synagogues. They offered talks and workshops jointly for five years, before Paul became ill with leukemia. He died in 1988, and Rachel continued their work on her own.

"When we spoke to congregations, I would tell them the funny thing was I grew up never knowing that I was a non-Jew. To me the world wasn't defined by Jews and non-Jews. No one grows up thinking of themselves as a non-Jew, it's a meaningless category. When I said this, I would blow people's minds. It would open up the discussion in a whole variety of congregations and families. Every time I would speak, four or five converts would come up after and say, 'Oh, that's my story.' So many people told me they'd had negative experiences, and I felt I had to speak for them because they didn't feel they could speak about it. It pissed me off and I felt empowered to talk about it."

Particularly at Conservative synagogues, Rachel found that people had no idea how to begin a dialogue about interfaith relationships and conversion. Converts, she would tell them, don't enter Jewish communities because they want to dilute or destroy them but out of a love of God and Torah. "It's painful the way you talk about us," she would say. "Painful and alienating."

Rachel became director of Jewish Life Programs for the Nathan Cummings Institute when it was founded in 1989, a position from which she makes recommendations to the board regarding organizations to fund. Thanks to this position, the *Forward* newspaper placed Rachel fourth on its list of the fifty most influential Jews in America in its 2000 roundup, "Forward Fifty."

But in contrast to Dale Epstein's experience that rabbinic ordination silences negative asides about converts, at least in the rabbi's hearing, Rachel says such remarks never end. "You always run into people who say, 'Gee, you don't look Jewish.' I do a lot of weddings and I'll hear people say, 'That's the rabbi? She's a shiksa!' It truly doesn't get to me. I just see it as a stupid, ignorant attitude."

Asked whether she considers herself a convert or a Jew, Rachel answers, "Both. I think of myself as a Jew who made aliyah [ascent] from being a lapsed WASP. I'm a Jew with a particular perspective. I'm always aware that I have a different background from other Jews I know. I bring it up a lot, it's something that I talk about very often. Mostly I get recognition, and the people who don't consider me Jewish I don't care about. Some Jews are from wherever—I'm from here."

Success stories like the Cowans' don't change the fact that Jewish tradition holds clear taboos against intermarriage, and has tended to view conversion in the context of marriage as something short of true conversion. Rabbi Solomon Rybak, chair of the Orthodox Union's committee on conversion, demonstrates this attitude when he explains that in Orthodoxy, "Generally conversion for marriage doesn't happen. Generally when someone in that situation wants to convert they don't come to the Orthodox, because the Orthodox have meaningful norms and standards." In fact there may be other reasons why a woman thinking of conversion in the context of a relationship with a Jewish man may not seek out an Orthodox rabbi—not least among them, Orthodoxy's strong antipathy to such conversions. According to *Conversion to Judaism in Jewish Law*, edited by Walter Jacob and Moshe Zemer, "There is . . . considerable Orthodox objection to converting to Judaism any non-Jewish woman who has lived with a Jewish man in marriage or common-law marriage or civil marriage. . . ."

Even among the more liberal and welcoming Jewish movements, it's not uncommon to encounter the expectation that the conversion of a woman romantically involved with a Jew won't outlast the relationship. Along with many other converts, Dale Epstein, Nan Fink Gefen, and Rachel Cowan are living lives that belie this expectation. Each found her way into Judaism partly as a result of a relationship with a Jewish man, but for none was Jewish identity dependent on the relationship. Nan and Dale's survived divorce, Rachel's the tragic early death of her husband.

According to Dru Greenwood, who began teaching introduction to Judaism classes in 1981 and is now the director of outreach for the Reform movement, by being relatively accepting of intermarriage and of the children of Jewish men and gentile women, Reform Judaism encourages people to convert only if they really want to. "People take conversion seriously," Greenwood says. "It's not forced, it's not pressured. They do it because they choose Judaism, because they want to be Jewish." She adds that by reaching out to potential converts, Jews have reclaimed the ancient mitzvah of welcoming the stranger into the community. "It's a very strong thread in Judaism," she explains. "It wasn't made up in the twentieth century in response to high intermarriage, though it certainly has been recovered because of that. It's ironic that outreach is seen as growing out of assimilation. Actually, it allows people to assimilate *into* Judaism."

What allowed Dale, Nan, Marilyn, and Rachel to assimilate so well into Judaism that they could move into leadership roles? All found encouragement at crucial stages of their journeys—but that encouragement varied greatly from one woman to the next. For Marilyn, Rachel, and especially Dale, welcoming communities played an important role in bringing them into the fold. But the opposite was true for Nan, whose Jewish muscles toughened fighting off a congregation that didn't mind flouting Jewish law when it came to its treatment of strangers. Dale, like a number of other women I have spoken with, found a particularly congenial environment in a small congregation that needed every active member it could get. But Nan's congregation was also small. Though Nan and Rachel were able to share growing Jewish lives with partners, Marilyn's conversion occurred before she had ever met her Jewish husband. In their initial investigations into Judaism and the Jewish world, Dale and Rachel were urged on by their sense of the importance of raising Jewish children. But Marilyn doesn't have children, and Nan's were grown when she embarked on her Jewish journey.

These women came to Judaism in many ways. Marilyn, a spiritual seeker, would probably have become a Jew years earlier if she had realized that such a thing was possible. Dale, by contrast, became a Jew in name long before she became one in spirit, and slowly grew to fit her new identity. For all these women, Judaism wove together the disparate threads of their lives, fulfilling spiritual longings they may not have even known they had, providing an arena in which deep intellectual probing was not only permitted but prized, offering a community in which to live and do the meaningful work to which they could bring their passions and their talents. They are all the better for finding Judaism, and Judaism is the better for finding them.

How deep does conversion go? For these women, it seems safe to say, deeper than any of them imagined, and deeper all the time. For some, the very word "convert" has ceased to have relevance. For others, it is an aspect of their Jewish identities that they embrace. For Rachel, having been born a gentile is just one of the places a committed Jew can come from. This is a profoundly liberating perspective, not only for converts but for those Jews who grow up with little or no Jewish experience and education and come to Judaism as adults with a sense of inadequacy they find hard to shake. Whether born or made, Jews tend to agonize over the validity and depth of their Jewish identities. Having once been there themselves, women like Dale, Nan, Marilyn, and Rachel are now bridges to the Jewish world for people of all backgrounds. Asked whether they consider themselves trailblazers, these four women modestly demurred. In fact, as part of the first generation of women converts to assume spiritual leadership in Judaism, that is precisely what they are. Their lives offer inspiration to other converts, both female and male, and other women, born Jewish and not, to recognize the potential for finding a home within Judaism, and for taking an active stance in making that home the place they would like it to be.

In the months leading up to my own conversion, I heard few stories of contemporary women converts. The Jewish women I admired, and still admire, were those daring to step outside the cameo roles the Judaism they had been born into had assigned them, to write themselves speaking parts in a drama that had presumed their silence for roughly four thousand years. Still, I had a need to see my own situation—the situation of an outsider—reflected in the tradition I was preparing to make my own. I began to follow the weekly cycle of Torah readings. I read very personally, as someone about to become a Jew and a Jewish parent. Though only half conscious of it, I was searching for clues about how and where a convert might enter the Jewish story. In this state of mind, I glimpsed a remarkable dynamic at work in the book of Shemot, Exodus, in the family of Moses and

Zipporah. Through marriage to a Jew struggling with his own identity, Zipporah enters the volatile, evolving community of Exodus and, once there, takes an aggressive stance within a family out of balance with its people and its God. To this day, when I ponder the mystery of conversion, it is Zipporah who rises up in my mind, an enigma, an inspiration, and a challenge.

Envisioning Zipporah

In Moses the Torah presents the quintessential slave-prince of assimilation, a man who knows himself to be a Jew though he was not raised among his people and doesn't live among them, a man in whom strangers see an Egyptian, not a Jew. As commentators have noted, Moses possesses a keen and indiscriminate sense of justice that brings him to the defence of Jews and gentiles alike. But when God calls upon him to assume the leadership of his people, Moses demurs, and God is angered.

What follows is an obscure, almost dreamlike scene in which we have our sole image of Moses' Midianite wife, Zipporah, who appears as briefly as if in the flare of a match flame. With his family, Moses leaves Midian to return to Egypt:

> At a night encampment on the way, the Lord encountered him and sought to kill him. So Zipporah took a flint and cut off her son's foreskin, and touched his legs with it, saying, "You are truly a bridegroom of blood to me!" And when He let him alone, she added, "A bridegroom of blood because of the circumcision."

In this highly cryptic confrontation, Moses is revealed as having so tenuous an ethnic identity that he has not even fulfilled a Jewish father's responsibility to perform brit milah on his son. Though commentators have noted that it may have been customary for circumcision to coincide with a boy's adolescence or mar-

riage—stages the son in question presumably hasn't reached—
that doesn't explain why Zipporah's act instantly appeases God's
anger.

Seeing her husband under attack by his God, Zipporah
reaches an immediate (and evidently correct) conclusion about
its cause, and acts upon that conclusion without hesitation. By
her dramatic gesture, she brings her son into God's covenant
with Israel and saves her husband's life as well, with a blood pact
that narrows the gap between him and the Jewish people. Most
unusual among biblical women, Zipporah even gets the last
word here. Having given her husband back to his God and his
people, she seamlessly asserts his identity in relation to herself,
in a kind of symbolic naming of him that concludes the scene:
"You are truly a bridegroom of blood to me!"

It is one of the mysteries of this evocative passage that we
have no way of knowing what has prepared Zipporah for this moment. Ethnic and religious differences have probably not been at
issue between Moses and Zipporah. For the whole of their marriage they have lived in her world, Midian, a world Moses has not
been eager to leave. Zipporah has had no opportunity to imagine
a place for herself in a Jewish milieu. At the same time, no one
has told her that her marriage represents the annihilation of the
Jewish people. In a very real sense the Jewish people does not yet
exist and will not come into being until her husband's return to
Egypt. And it is Zipporah who ensures that return.

Perhaps today, too, Jews are laboring to emerge into a new
stage of peoplehood, awaiting the return of every daughter and
son. At a time when concerns over continuity prevail, it is important to recognize that, like Zipporah, one of the things many
converts have to offer Judaism is their families. As we've seen,
some converts are the partners of disaffected or minimally engaged Jews. Some bear responsibility for raising the next generation of American Jews. In Judaism, a convert is called a *ger*, a
"resident alien." A resident alien is unlikely to engender the kind
of rock-solid Jewish identity twenty-first-century Judaism needs.

Embedded in the story of Moses' return to Egypt is the story of a woman leaving her family, her childhood home, to join a new people. Perhaps it is Zipporah's rookie status, her perspective as an absolute outsider that accounts for her acute discernment. Perhaps it is the innocence she brings to what may well be her first Jewish act that allows for her amazing courage. But by the certainty with which she takes the covenant into her own hands, she places herself at its very center.

In our time, we are beginning to see converts take a bold Jewish lead of their own within relationships, families, and in the Jewish people. By doing so, they are playing a historical role in creating the Judaism of the future. At the same time, they are transforming the nature of conversion, of Jewish identity itself. Does a convert have the responsibility—and the right—to enter into a partner's spiritual grapplings, to impart a child's Jewish identity, to take over the leadership of a community? Like so much in Judaism, these questions call up contradictions. The convert who is called a resident alien is also said to be a person who has come under the wings of the Shekhinah, the female aspect of God. The Shekhinah doesn't rent out rooms for the night. For one who is granted a home beneath those wings, there is a tremendous obligation to serve Judaism, to give something back. For one who has known that shelter, the idea of qualified belonging can have no meaning at all. If the terms of a convert's personal relationships, her membership in *am Yisrael*, the Jewish people, don't support such activism as Zipporah's, they must be renegotiated. It is time to stop selling each other and Judaism short.

By itself, ritual immersion doesn't create a Jew. It's only a watery passage to the Jewish path on the other side. As contemporary converts walk that path now, I imagine this fleeting vision of Zipporah appearing at every turn, beckoning. Envisioning Zipporah as a convert's model, her singular act becomes an intimidating, and exhilarating, challenge.

Afterword

LIVING IN Israel while at work on this project, I had a certain experience twice. Asked by two separate women for the names of non-Jewish heroines in the Torah, I started to provide a list, only to have each react with surprise at two of the names. As it happened, both these women had named daughters Tamar and Yael, and neither had been aware that their daughters had biblical namesakes who were not Jewish.

These twin episodes are emblematic of the gentile woman's place in Jewish history. So much and so long a part of the Jewish family, she hasn't so much challenged the stereotypes about her as lived quietly side by side with them. Sometimes those around her haven't even realized that she was there.

An Orthodox rabbi I once spoke with expressed the view that all or most converts to Judaism, if they dug deep enough, would find evidence of Jewish ancestors. It can now be said that all or most Jews, if they dug deep enough, would find evidence of gentile ancestors. The gentile woman is an inseparable part of the Jewish people, not only in the flesh, but in the bloodlines of Jews the world over. That she has always been a significant presence is a half-told story, written between the lines of Jewish texts going back to the Torah, and in Jewish DNA itself. The results of genetic research released during the writing of this book reveal with startling clarity that Jewish communities have taken root and thrived in far-flung lands throughout all of Jewish history with the help of the non-Jewish women local to these places. The desire for Jewish ancestors—for a past that seems to lend a kind of legitimacy to the conversion, that says "I have been here before"—is common to many converts to Judaism. Some can trace their lineage to Jewish forebears, some cannot. But all can find a Jewish past in the stories of their biblical precursors, and in the genetic evidence as well. For gentile women and women converts, entering the Jewish community is like déjà vu all over again.

The very fact that gentile women are so intimately connected to the Jewish family may help to explain the absence of any serious consideration of their history or their present role in Jewish communities. Despite generations of shiksa slurs and cultural caricatures, there has been silence in place of these women's voices and stories, a sense that it's been too risky for them to make themselves heard. It may also seem too risky for Jews to speak openly about them. Even those who are not hostile to the presence of gentile women in their midst may hesitate to rock an uneasy boat by grappling with stubborn, still-potent prejudices festering in the Jewish community.

It is the silence that allows these attitudes to fester. Few, if any, prejudices evaporate without soul-searching and open discussion, and the stereotypes of gentile women are not exceptions. The Jewish families I've encountered who have most successfully incorporated a non-Jewish daughter are often those who were able to discuss their fears and concerns most openly.

A strong stance against intermarriage has been central to the Jewish community for generations. These days, the explanation most often given for this stance is that interfaith couples are unlikely to create Jewish homes and to raise Jewish children, with the result that intermarriage robs the Jewish people of its future. If the primary objection to intermarriage is its impact on Jewish continuity, then it stands to reason that there should be a warm welcome extended to every non-Jewish woman who enters a Jewish milieu with a desire to explore or participate with her Jewish partner, or to raise her children Jewishly. Yet as we have seen, such women are often summarily rejected. We need to recognize that those individuals and institutions who convey antipathy to the woman who comes looking to connect herself or her children to the Jewish community are not acting in the best interests of Jewish continuity. Rather than vilifying those women whose families are lost to Judaism, we would do well to celebrate the many women who refuse to give up on the Jewish community despite discouragement. We would also do well to consider the role played—or not played—by the Jewish partners in disaffected families.

The fear is sometimes voiced in the Jewish world that including gentile family members, even welcoming converts, entails watering down all that makes Judaism richly and complexly distinctive. But dilution of Judaism's unique mission in the world is not a necessary price of inclusiveness. Judaism has incorporated newcomers since the beginning of Jewish time. Along with the commandment to welcome the stranger, Jewish law once had a spectrum of classifications to designate foreign-born members of the community from those who lived among the Jews as distinctly other to those we now call converts, with different ritual roles for each. A paradox of Jewish identity is that while it may appear fixed and impermeable, it has always been porous.

In our own time too, being part of the Jewish community and being Jewish are not always the same thing. Some gentile women and some Jewish demographers express frustration that the partners of Jews who take on a Jewish life and help to raise their children as Jews without converting themselves are not considered Jewish by synagogues or survey takers. It is essential to recognize these women's contributions to the Jewish people—Judaism is unlikely to survive without them. At the same time, Judaism contains meaningful rites for conversion. Those who choose not to undergo these rites are not Jews, and to say otherwise renders the profound transition of conversion meaningless. Yet they can be embraced as valued members of the community of which they are so much a part.

One of the converts who shared her story noted that her struggles to make a place for herself in the Jewish world are to a great extent the struggles of all Jewish women. Judaism has been slow to champion its daughters, born and adopted: if convert and Jew are two disparate things in the traditional male-centered Jewish psyche, woman and Jew would also seem to be discordant entities. Though born-Jewish, gentile, and converted women have historically been cast as oppositional competitors for Jewish men, in different ways all have been marginalized in Judaism.

Not surprisingly, converted women owe much of their progress in the Jewish world to their born-Jewish sisters. Claiming Judaism for Jewish women, feminists have shown converted women the way in: to active membership in the community, to leadership and learning, to being fully present at the moments of ritual that powerfully affirm our past, present, and Jewish future.

Thanks to Jewish feminists, families can now observe the arrival of daughters with ceremonies that welcome them into the covenant, their coming-of-age with rituals that mark their transition to the responsibilities and entitlement of Jewish adulthood. In prayer, we invoke the God of the matriarchs along with the God of the patriarchs, affirming the participation of all Jews in the covenant. Thanks to the examples of Jewish feminists, I am able to envision my own ways to remember all our mothers. On Friday nights I offer my son the traditional blessing of wishing him the prosperous fate of Menassah and Ephraim, the sons of Joseph and his non-Jewish wife, Asenath. When I bless my daughter, I find that tradition tells only two-thirds of the story, so I add the missing pieces myself. I wish for her to flourish like

matriarchs Sarah, Rebekah, Rachel, and Leah, and I also speak
the names of Bilhah and Zilpah, acknowledging the other two
non-Jewish mothers of the twelve tribes of Israel.

I spent my childhood in an immigrant neighborhood of Eastern
European Jews, surrounded by Ashkenazi customs and accents,
the sights, smells, and sounds of an ethnic culture that to me, as
to many, has always meant *real* Judaism. For years I disdained
the notion that conversion could turn a gentile into a Jew, even
after I longed to believe such transformation possible. Because
of this, I am sympathetic to Jews who are challenged by the
notion of a multicultural Jewish family, populated by faces of
every shade, names from all corners of the globe, and histories
of every variety. For me, seeing has meant believing. Just as I
was once privileged to grow up in a now-vanishing pocket of
the Jewish world, I am privileged to be present at the birth
of twenty-first-century Judaism. I have entered the lives and
homes of Jewish women who are leading their Jewish families
and communities, assuring the future by helping to create a rich
Jewish present—many of them doing these things with a confidence and strength that would convince the uninitiated that
they'd been born to it.

Having begun with one anecdote from Israel, I'll end with
another. One Shabbat, I stayed with two poets and their families
in a remote and starkly beautiful hilltop community a few miles
south of Lebanon. While there, I was taken on a tour of the land
and brought to the mouth of an underground cave. Now a pool
of natural, flowing water, the cave was a burial place that dated
from the time of Joshua—and thus from the time of Rahab as
well. The poet who took me to see the pool explained that when
her community was founded some twenty-five years before, two
of the women, wishing to observe the rites of niddah, needed a
ritual bath that they could visit in the course of their monthly
cycles. They arranged to have a rabbi come and consecrate the

site as a mikvah, and it is for this purpose that it is used today. My hostess, who had been born to and lives a secular Jewish life herself, was very proud of her friends' contribution to the community, and of their spiritual commitment.

Intensely moved by the life-and-death aura that emanated from the pool, I did not think about a fact that would occur to me much later: the two observant women, whom I had met, both happened to be converts. Immigrants to Israel and to Judaism as well, these women had uncovered an ancient tomb and engaged the process of Jewish law to reclaim it for the purposes of life. Dipping my hand into its icy water, listening to the echoes of the songs we sang reverberate against its stones, it was easy to imagine the cave as a portal through Jewish history. It was easy, too, to believe my hostess's description of immersion in its depths.

"When you emerge from this mikvah," she said, "you feel reborn."

Bibliography

Azoulay, Karen Gibel. *Black, Jewish and Interracial: It's Not the Color of Your Skin, but the Race of Your Kin: & Other Myths of Identity.* Durham: Duke University Press, 1997.

Barack-Fishman, Sylvia. *A Breath of Life: Feminism in the American Jewish Community.* New York: The Free Press, 1993.

Bartlett, Barbara. *The Shiksa.* New York: William Morrow, 1987.

Baskin, Judith R. *Midrashic Women: Formations of the Feminine in Rabbinic Literature.* Hanover, New Hampshire: Brandeis Univ. Press, University of NE Press, 2002.

Becker, Avihai, "Because They Can." *Ha'Aretz.* March 15, 2002.

Belzberg, Wendy. "Ask Wendy." *Forward.* December 22, 2000.

Berger, Maurice. "The Mouse That Never Roars: Jewish Masculinity on American Television." *Too Jewish?: Challenging Traditional Identities.* Norman L. Kleeblatt, ed. New York: The Jewish Museum; New Jersey: Rutgers University Press, 1996.

Berman, Louis A. *Jews and Intermarriage: A Study in Personality and Culture.* New York: T. Yoseloff, 1968.

Biale, David. *Eros and the Jews: From Biblical Israel to Contemporary America.* New York: Basic Books, 1992.

Biale, David, Michael Galchinsky, and Susannah Heschel, eds.

Insider/Outsider: American Jews and Multiculturalism. Berkeley: University of California Press, 1998.

Case, Adam. "Visiting Israel—A Land I Feel a Strong Bond With, But Where I Am Not Considered a Jew." Interfaith-Family.com.

Clapp, Nicholas. *Sheba: Through the Desert in Search of the Legendary Queen.* New York: Houghton Mifflin, 2001.

Cohen, Jack J. "A Reasonable Future." *Judaism* 133 (1985).

Cohen, Randy. "The Ethicist." *The New York Times.* October 14, 2001.

Cohen, Shaye J. D. *The Beginnings of Jewishness: Boundaries, Varieties, Uncertainties.* Berkeley: University of California Press, 1999.

Cowan, Paul and Rachel Cowan. *Mixed Blessings: Marriage Between Jews and Christians.* New York: Doubleday, 1987.

Dye, Kerry Douglas. "Keeping the Faith." Leisuresuit.com. April 17, 2000.

Eden, Ami. "Conservative Body Extends Hand to the Intermarried." *Forward.* September 28, 2001.

Fink, Nan. *Stranger in the Midst: A Memoir of Spiritual Discovery.* New York: Basic Books, 1997.

Finkielkraut, Alain. *The Imaginary Jew.* Kevin O'Neill and David Suchoff, trans. Lincoln, Neb. and London: University of Nebraska Press, 1994.

"Forward Fifty." *Forward.* December 29, 2000.

Friedman, Edwin H. "The Myth of the Shiksa." *Ethnicity and Family Therapy.* Monica McGoldrick, John Pearce, and Joseph Giordano, eds. New York: Guilford Press, 1982.

Genesis Rabbah: The Judaic Commentary to the Book of Genesis, Vol. 3. Jacob Neusner, trans. Atlanta: Scholars Press, 1985.

Gilman, Sander L. *The Jew's Body.* New York and London: Routledge, 1991.

Ginzberg, Louis. *The Legends of the Jews.* "Moses in the Wilderness," Vol. 3. Paul Radin, trans. Philadelphia: Jewish Publication Society, 1911.

Goldenberg, Robert. "Halakhah and History." *Judaism* 133 (1985).

Gordis, Robert. *Love and Sex: A Modern Jewish Approach.* New York: Farrar, Straus & Giroux, 1978.

Gordis, Robert. "Patrilineal Descent—A Solution or a Problem?" *Judaism* 133 (1985).

Greenberg, Blu and Linda Tarry. *King Solomon and the Queen of Sheba.* New York: Pitspopany, 1997.

Hauptman, Judith. "Patrilineal Descent—An Examination of the Issue." *Judaism* 133 (1985).

Hyman, Paula. "The Jewish Family: Looking for a Usable Past." *On Being a Jewish Feminist: A Reader.* Susannah Heschel, ed. New York: Schocken Books, 1983.

Hyman, Paula E. "The Modern Jewish Family: Image and Reality." *The Jewish Family: Metaphor and Memory.* David Kraemer, ed. New York, Oxford: Oxford University Press, 1989.

Jacob, Walter and Moshe Zemer, eds. *Conversion to Judaism in Jewish Law: Essays and Responsa.* Tel Aviv and Pittsburgh: Freehof Institute of Progressive Halakhah, 1994.

Jaher, Frederic Cople. "The Quest for the Ultimate Shiksa." *American Quarterly* 35 (1983).

Kaplan, Dana Evan. "Conversion to Judaism in America 1760–1897." Dissertation. Tel Aviv: Tel Aviv University, 1994.

Kirshenbaum, David. *Mixed Marriage and the Jewish Future.* New York: Bloch Publishing, 1958.

Lewisohn, Ludwig. *The Island Within.* Philadelphia: Jewish Publication Society, 1928, reprinted 1968.

Manewith, Toby. "There Goes Another One: A Single Jewish Woman Laments the Loss of an Eligible Jewish Bachelor." *Washington Jewish Week.* May 2, 2002.

Mayer, Egon. "The Coming Reformation in American Jewish Identity." *Imagining the Jewish Future: Essays and Responses.* David A. Teutsch, ed. Albany, New York: State University of New York Press, 1992.

McClain, Ellen Jaffe. *Embracing the Stranger: Intermarriage and the Future of the American Jewish Community*. New York: Basic Books, 1995.

Mirvis, Tova. *The Ladies Auxiliary*. New York: Norton, 1999.

Patai, Raphael. *The Hebrew Goddess*. New York: Ktav Publishing House, 1967.

Petsonk, Judy and Jim Remsen. *The Intermarriage Handbook: A Guide for Jews and Christians*. New York: William Morrow, 1988.

Pogrebin, Letty Cottin. *Deborah, Golda and Me: Being Jewish and Female in America*. New York: Crown, 1991.

Porton, Gary G. *The Stranger Within Your Gates: Converts and Conversion in Rabbinic Literature*. Chicago: University of Chicago Press, 1994.

Prell, Riv-Ellen. *Fighting to Become Americans: Jews, Gender, and the Anxiety of Assimilation*. Boston: Beacon Press, 1999.

Prell, Riv-Ellen. "Why Jewish Princesses Don't Sweat." *People of the Body: Jews and Judaism from an Embodied Perspective*. Howard Eilberg-Schwartz, ed. New York: New York State University Press, 1992.

Resnick, Mike and Lawrence Schimel. "The Shiksa." *Ancient Enchantresses*. Kathleen M. Massie-French, Martin Greenberg, and Richard Gilliam, eds. New York: Daw Books, 1995.

Rosenberg, Shelley Kapnek. *Adoption and the Jewish Family: Contemporary Perspectives*. Philadelphia: Jewish Publication Society, 1998.

Rosenbloom, Joseph R. *Conversion to Judaism: From the Biblical Period to the Present*. Cincinnati: Hebrew Union College Press, 1978.

Rosmarin, Trude Weiss. "Matriliny—A Survival of Polygamy." *Judaism* 133 (1985).

Roth, Joel. "An Halakhic Perspective on an Historical Foundation." *Judaism* 133 (1985).

Roth, Philip. *American Pastoral.* Boston: Houghton Mifflin, 1997.

Roth, Philip. *The Counterlife.* New York: Farrar, Straus & Giroux, 1986.

Roth, Philip. *Portnoy's Complaint.* New York: Random House, 1967.

Schindler, Alexander. "Facing the Realities of Intermarriage." *Judaism* 133 (1985).

Schneider, Susan Weidman. *Intermarriage: The Challenge of Living with Differences Between Christians and Jews.* New York: Free Press, 1989.

Schulweis, Harold M. "The Mitzvah to Encourage the Convert." www.vbs.org/rabbi/hshulw/mitzvah.

Sigal, Phillip. "Halakhic Perspectives on the Matrilineal-Patrilineal Principles." *Judaism* 133 (1985).

Silverstein, Alan. *It All Begins with a Date: Jewish Concerns About Intermarriage.* Northvale, N.J.: Jason Aronson, 1995.

Sirkin, Mark I. "Clinical Issues in Intermarriage: A Family Systems Approach." *Crisis and Continuity: The Jewish Family in the 21st Century.* Norman Linzer, Irving N. Levitz, David J. Schnall, eds. Hoboken, N.J.: Ktav Publishing, 1995.

Spiegelman, Art. *Maus: A Survivor's Tale, Vol. II, And Here My Troubles Began.* New York: Pantheon Books, 1986.

Staub, Jacob J. "A Reconstructionist View on Patrilineal Descent." *Judaism* 133 (1985).

Wade, Nicholas. "In DNA, New Clues to Jewish Roots." *The New York Times.* May 14, 2002.

Walker, Rebecca. *Black, White and Jewish: Autobiography of a Shifting Self.* New York: Riverhead Books, 2001.

Wurzburger, Walter S. "Patrilineal Descent and the Jewish Identity Crisis." *Judaism* 133 (1985).